FREEDOM

Arunaraje Patil is a writer, editor, award-winning film-maker and producer. Her critically acclaimed feature films include *Shaque, Gehrayee, Situm, Rihaee, Bhairavi, Keh Do Na* and *Tum*?, with many of them having strong women-centric themes.

Arunaraje has served on many juries including that of the National Film Awards. She has also been a Landmark Forum Leader and has led transformational programmes for more than 10,000 people. This is her first book.

FREEDOM

my story

ARUNARAJE
PATIL

FOREWORD BY SHYAM BENEGAL

HarperCollins *Publishers* India

First published in India in 2017 by
HarperCollins *Publishers* India

Building 10, Tower A, 4th Floor, DLF Cyber II,
Gurugram Haryana - 122002, India
www.harpercollins.co.in

P-ISBN: 978-93-5264-138-3
E-ISBN: 978-93-5264-139-0

2 4 6 8 10 9 7 5 3 1

Typeset in 11.5/14.8 Adobe Garamond
By Saanvi Graphics, Noida

Printed and bound at
MicroPrints India, New Delhi

To my mother, who nurtured in me a love for art, music, movies and unconditional love;

To my father, who inculcated in me values, a love for people and a commitment to empower them;

To my daughter, Gaagi, who taught me courage and compassion and how to live life in the face of adversities

CONTENTS

FOREWORD

Autobiographies sometimes tend to be like confessionals. At other times they can seem like self-congratulatory essays listing the author's achievements in a variety of fields through a lifetime. They can be self-conscious, egotistical, self-justifying and often written with a belief that one's life is of interest to other people. Yet it goes without saying that life experiences of each human being has worth even if these experiences are common to others as they often are. A good autobiography is one that is unselfconscious and written with little regard to the kind of profile that would emerge of oneself.

Every life has something in it that is important since each experience is unique and the way human beings react to them are singular and never alike. An autobiography is successful when it evokes not just empathy but transcends individual experiences to make them universal, helping us value life in all its diversity.

Arunaraje Patil's autobiography *Freedom: My Story* is a book that does not merely recount her own life but deals with traumas that could easily have been debilitating. It is a story of self discovery. Of finding the inner strength and self worth that have helped her overcome terrible tragedies of loss and circumstance.

An uplifting story of life and hope.

Shyam Benegal
April 2017

PREFACE

Being born before Independence to a freedom fighter father, instilled in me a strong sense of freedom and self-reliance. Though I did not know it then, my understanding of freedom began to get better as I grew up, as did my perception of the country in its new form, as one united India.

There were old traditions to be broken, new spaces to be negotiated as I went along, often bungling my way through – learning, however, to live a life alongside people I didn't know most of the time but who I was willing to discover, to know.

Girls from supposedly 'good' families did not enter films at the time unless they came from modern-thinking homes or were already a part of that system. Since my family could qualify as neither, being a first-class student at high school, I went on to study medicine though my heart was in films all along. Though the subjects were anatomy and physiology, I studied life instead, preparing myself to get into films through FTII.

I thought, you don't make a film because it is a good idea or you think it will make some money. I was inspired by a breed of film-makers who made films based on their experiences of life – past or present, what mattered to them, what called out to them, or what expressed them just like any other artiste. And that for me is cinema, a medium of self-expression – like a painting.

Except that it is expensive and a collaborative effort by many diverse talents and needs an audience. And each person, technician or actor, brings their creativity to the central idea or theme that is determined by the director. The director who is understood to be the 'captain of the ship' steers the ship along with the entire cast and crew and creates the narrative. It is this story that ultimately helps the audience understand the film. It is always the director's perspective that makes the film.

There are other kinds of film-makers too, who believe that the film they make is a vehicle to make money. Obviously, if that is the intention, you would need to have a huge audience, which means often catering to the lowest common denominator, given that in India we have a very wide spectrum of people; uneducated, rural, poor, city folk, educated, rich, belonging to diverse regions. These film-makers believe their job is to entertain every kind of person, which means there is bound to be a clash of tastes, values, as also the contexts on which diverse people base their lives. So these films remained superficial at one level, afraid to offend any community or audience type and often ended up being mindless entertainment.

Like all kinds of art and entertainment, there is an audience for every kind of film. Movies get categorized according to audiences: niche or semi-niche, or mainstream or mass.

Bollywood, which has operated mostly on formulae, has changed its plots and characters over time – new audience tastes with widespread media exposure have created new whiz kids and destroyed old veterans who did not reinvent themselves. The technological changes that came snuffed out old studios, equipment and even master technicians as business became global.

The more 'cinematic' films are a reflection of their makers – their philosophy, their concerns, even their confusions. If you notice, most of the Bollywood films, driven by the formula of song, dance, comedy, action, romance, sex, etc., tell you little about what the film-maker is thinking or feeling – their views on life, society, commitments, their questions. Though I am glad to say that all this is beginning to change with the advent of the 'indie' (independent) film.

Whether it was Mehboob Khan in *Mother India* or Guru Dutt or Bimal Roy they all had something to say – blatant or hidden. You experienced the life and emotions of the characters. Later on, it was Satyajit Ray and Shyam Benegal who made films that you would want to keep in your library like a good book. So often it was a simple love story reflecting the times or circumstances of families, situations, cultural trends, or even country. There were more commercial film-makers too took up subjects that had a soul, if I may say, like B.R. Chopra, and the early films of V. Shantaram or Raj Kapoor.

For me it is not possible to separate my life and my personal experiences from the films I make. It doesn't mean that all my films are biographical. I am interested in life, people, relationships and sometimes disturbing issues in society and that's the kind of films I made. However, I chose to make 'middle cinema' or 'middle-of-the-road cinema' as I wanted an audience for my films. I have also seen how I have felt alienated from my own self when I made a film to meet the demands of the producer or the market and diluted it to a degree that robbed it of its soul.

Such compromises don't work for me and I decided long back that I would rather not make a film if there is no artistic freedom. That explains why I made fewer films than I could have. The other reason was that I was working in a male-dominated, sexist industry and did not want to compromise myself as a woman.

The lack of artistic freedom is also probably why most of the directors from FTII found it hard to create their films in the commercial atmosphere of Bollywood. Though the technicians from FTII got absorbed into the industry even before they had received their diplomas, there were only a handful of directors who found their feet in Bollywood. Stories can be told in various ways, and it is not the plot or even characters but how a writer or director views it that is central.

As a woman film-maker I found myself going against the trend in the male-dominated industry, against the backdrop of where young women found themselves in the 1960s and '70s, facing whatever was available in India for them as a future, which wasn't very much. So my struggles have been both professional and personal.

After my first feature film, *Shaque* was released, Sai Paranjype who had been doing theatre and TV released her first film *Sparsh* (1980). Then there was Aparna Sen who did her first feature film, *36 Chowringhee Lane*, in 1981. And still for years there were just a handful of us. And we held our ground for over so many years and made films that we were proud of. Aparna continues to do that and I admire her immensely.

I have been teaching since the 1970s and most of my girl students veered away from features preferring to work on ads, documentaries and television simply because of the way the industry operated in those days and also it was likely to be a long haul. Today there are women directors in every kind of film and that for me is satisfying. Thankfully it's not just women film-makers but girls from almost all strata of society who have become vocal and carving out their own space in an unequal society.

In spite of heavy commercial demands and catering to the lowest common denominators some actors not just survived but honed their craft over time. People like Naseeruddin Shah, Om Puri, Smita Patil and Shabana Azmi not just survived Bollywood but attained stardom and continue to contribute to meaningful cinema. Then there were composers, singers and musicians who kept the spirit and the art alive. Asha Bhosle for one, is someone who again I admire for taking life by the horns and continuing to survive with great gusto all kinds of challenges, never letting it affect her singing, never giving up.

For me, the journey has been not just fascinating but one that is really rich with insights about people's behaviour, the change in values over the years and the hypocrisy of the make-believe world of films. I wonder, sometimes, whether people here in the film world – creative, crazy, hungry for fame and name or unlimited wealth, are living in the real world or acting out their life like characters from a movie! The tragedy is that their struggles were real, as were their agonies and ecstasies as many had to compromise on their art, their self-esteem or their personal life in the face of business and box-office interests. And I learnt compassion as I watched their struggles over the last so many years.

Looking back I have been fortunate to have had access to a range of people from the film industry, from the stars to the spot boys, and from the highly creative and intellectual to the pseudos and vendors of flesh. In the end, everyone wanted a piece of 'the cake'. But no matter how much they got, it was never enough!

My journey has been a long one – also a very eventful one. There has been no dull moment in my life. I have been a learner all along. My parents gave me the immense wealth of education and independent thought. And I was fortunate also to have access to a world of transformation through the Landmark Forum and through the teachings of Werner Erhard.

Whether faced with success or failure, I could remain grounded and work to better myself and make a difference in the world through my conversations, lectures, workshops, or my films which gave me an unimaginable power to communicate my thoughts and feelings to the world – sometimes to question, sometimes to provoke, sometimes to guide and, sometimes, simply to share.

1
LIBERATION

Rihaee – Freedom – Liberation! At some point of time in my life, I realized that if I have freedom, I have everything. Anything would be possible for me. I had to first liberate myself from the narratives and conversations of the past, from who I knew myself to be, from the image that I had trapped myself in, and rediscover myself. This is true even now as each day unfolds and allows me to create myself anew and find hidden strengths and new possibilities.

My first big expression of that freedom was my film *Rihaee*.

Thirty years ago, in 1987, Vadnagar, Gujarat where I shot most of the film, looked like the back of beyond. It was a dusty village with a big lake that remained dry for most of the year. After searching for three weeks, driving cross-country through difficult terrain all over Kutch and parts of Gujarat with my art director Meera Lakhia and her actor-husband Snehal Lakhia, I finally zeroed in on this village, the same village that became famous as Narendra Modi's native place when he was elected prime minister.

It seemed just like the village of carpenters I was looking for – houses with carved columns and pillars, finely etched intricate beams, doorways decorated with little brass discs. My film was set in the Gujarat–Rajasthan border and with its small lake, fields, camel carts and dusty tracks, it was just perfect.

Shooting a film in that village was not an easy matter. We were scheduled to be there for a month, but there were no hotels or guest houses. The nearest town, Visnagar, was twelve miles away but even that did not have any hotel. I had stars in my film who were used to the best that Bollywood could offer, all their whims and fancies fulfilled promptly by their producers, and I was now confronted with the dilemma of how to make them comfortable. The nearest airport, Ahmedabad, was 1.5 to 2 hours away and commuting every day was out of the question. The actors had to be housed on location. I was told by many that it was good that the location was far away from an airport because the stars could not abandon the shoot and run away from the sets, like they were known to do in the '80s.

Personally, I did not think anyone on my sets would do that, but one could never be sure. All I had was a good script and my commitment, which perhaps had everyone in the film bringing forth their own commitment and cooperation. Eventually, we found houses for the actors and technicians to live in – surprisingly large, empty houses belonging to diamond merchants and transporters.

It was not just a crazy but also difficult time for me and that too is an understatement. To give a little background, I had been part of the Aruna–Vikas duo and now I was making a film on my own. I had limited resources, including a loan of 10 lakh rupees from the National Film Development Corporation (NFDC). It had taken me a lot to get to this stage. While the shooting was on, I was going through my divorce with Vikas. To add to my woes, the house I was going to move into after the divorce was not just being renovated but almost getting rebuilt because it was a dilapidated old structure. But all this was extraneous in a way, given what I was dealing with on the shoot.

Rihaee means liberation and it actually liberated me. For a woman who had just lost her nine-year-old child to cancer and had been asked for a divorce by her husband within twenty-four hours after that, things couldn't have been worse. In fact, it had seemed like the end of the road for me.

But I am getting ahead with my story and need to cut back to 1982 where it all started.

Vikas and I were shooting our film *Situm* with Smita Patil and Naseeruddin Shah in Pune. My daughter Gaagi was with us, doing a role in the film, when she developed terrible pain in her legs. We got the check-ups done and the diagnosis was bone cancer. After a couple of chemotherapy sessions, we took her to Memorial Sloan Kettering Cancer Center in New York and came back with a clean chit. Well almost. Six months later, the cancer returned with a vengeance. During the year of Gaagi's illness, my husband had become involved with my friend, someone I had supported emotionally when her marriage had broken up.

Almost a year from the date of Gaagi's diagnosis, one Saturday afternoon, Gaagi breathed her last as I sat next to her, holding her hand. A full breath, half breath, a quarter breath and then no breath at all. All of her there one moment, and suddenly no more of her.

I had not slept that past year as I was looking after Gaagi round the clock. Somebody gave me a Calmpose the night Gaagi passed away and I drifted into a world of nothingness, where I could feel no joy or sorrow.

The next morning, I think it was around 7, when my husband woke me up and told me he wanted a divorce. I thought it was a bad dream and tried to shrug it off as a nightmare. But Vikas shook me awake and calmly told me that he couldn't stay with me any longer. At that time, the line between real and unreal became a complete blur. It was too bizarre. It couldn't be. How could I lose my daughter, my husband and my friend, all in one go – just like that? They couldn't do that to me, I thought. But it was really happening. I was devastated. Yet, at the same time, the biggest concern for me was my second child, my son Hith, who was two years younger than Gaagi.

I went on to battle severe depression, the desire to end it all. The desperation to do away with my life and a failed attempt was followed by visits to my psychiatrist friend – and I learnt better to deal with what life had thrown at me. As a mother I wanted to bring up my little son to be a healthy and happy individual but it was an extremely difficult task.

I didn't know how to go on with my life from then onwards. I said 'no' to the divorce but my confidence was totally shattered. What would I do with my life, how would I bring up my son? Would I be able to work? Would I even get work?

My husband and I had been the Aruna–Vikas duo, a film-making team who wrote, directed and edited films together, and now...? I was not sure if as a woman I would get work on my own steam. Besides, my husband was very popular with his easy-going manner and good humour while I was the more serious one. Who would give work to a woman in a male-dominated film industry? I knew there were many who acknowledged my talent, but did people really care for how committed or technically qualified I was? Would they invest their time, money and talent in my ideas and creativity? I was unsure about the next step.

However, clarity began to emerge slowly. My mother, who was affluent and lived in Bangalore (now Bengaluru), asked me to come live with her. She promised to take care of me and my son. The idea did not appeal to me. On its heels came another offer that most would find hard to refuse.

My father had been a freedom fighter from Dharwar district in north Karnataka. He was part of the Morarji Desai ministry in the old Bombay State, which then had parts of Karnataka, Maharashtra, Gujarat and Telengana as they exist now. With the formation of the new states, we moved to Bangalore in 1956 when north Karnataka became one with the old Mysore State. From 1958 to 1962, my father was a minister in the Karnataka government.

He was a staunch Gandhian and a member of the old Congress party. Being an idealist and seeing the state of politics in the party and country, with high levels of corruption already seeping in, he left the corridors of power around 1963–64 and settled in a small village Hanumanmatti and founded a girls' school and college in the adjacent town of Ranebennur. My mother, on the other hand, was still active in politics.

It was 1984. Rajiv Gandhi, after his mother's assassination, had arrived on the horizon as a fresh young leader full of promise. I was asked to contest the elections, riding on my father's goodwill and my mother's influence, and was promised that I would win hands down. It was the Rajiv Gandhi wave and my father's constituency in north Karnataka was waiting for me, I was told. All they wanted was a signature and they would handle the rest. I could not get myself to agree to such a proposal. I felt that I could not ask for votes without working at the grass-roots level for at least two years. I refused the offer.

My heart lay in film-making. Somehow I had to pick up the threads and start working again. I had a son to raise and it was not his fault that our lives had fallen apart.

I was considering where to begin with respect to my career, when I got an offer to make an ad film. I had no company and no staff. I put together my company almost overnight. I took an A4 sheet of paper and a marker and created a production company using the names of my two children – the one who had left us and the other who was very much with us – Gaahimedia: 'Gaa' from Gaagi and 'Hi' from Hith. The next morning I submitted the budget on my new letterhead and got the film.

I made films for Tata Tea, Tata Salt and innumerable others but my heart was elsewhere. I desperately wanted to make feature films again. I began working on scripts. The first script that I submitted to National Film Development Corporation of India (NFDC) did not go through; the second made it. And that is how the seeds of *Rihaee* were sown.

I had stuck to my guns regarding the divorce because I truly believed that it would not be good for my son and also for Vikas's parents whom I had come to take care of. I thought the family had suffered enough. But Vikas was hell-bent on the divorce and moved out of the house to a paying guest accommodation nearby just to create separation and grounds for divorce. That completely upset the equation between my parents-in-law and me. They had been sympathetic so far but Vikas's decision to move out did not go down too well with them. They couldn't have their only child not living in his own house. After that I became the unwanted outsider and stayed in that house on sufferance.

Those years of my personal grief and suffering allowed me to open my heart out to people. I was not just a woman evolving but a film-maker trying to make sense of the world – of people and their emotions and even their choices. A lot of women in that period and later too found the freedom to share with me their sufferings and their stories threw a new light on life. As I empathized with them, my courage to face life grew.

Coming back to *Rihaee*, I was confronted with a new set of problems. My bosom friend, Smita Patil, who was to act in the film, was pregnant. We decided to shoot after her delivery and made plans of how we would take care of her child on location. Smita was keen to also assist me in the film because she wanted to be a director too.

For me, a woman's pregnancy is a special time, when she needs to be pampered silly. I still rate the experience of giving birth to a child an all-time high. Those moments when you see your newborn – a life you have created and nurtured over nine months – give you a fulfilment which is unparalleled. Every day, building up to that moment when the child is delivered, one needs to be loved and cherished so you can bring the child into a happy environment.

But for Smita, those times were especially difficult. We shared the same birthday, 17 October, and were like soulmates. Fate had brought us together and we were like two sides of the same coin, our circumstances were so uncannily similar. She was the other woman in Raj Babbar's life and I was the forsaken woman, a wife abandoned by my husband for another woman. We were playing completely opposite roles but both of us were suffering.

In fact, Smita's mother, Maa, who was like my mother, often said that she could not understand how I could be so close to Smita and tolerate her after what she had done to another woman's marriage. It wasn't Smita's fault, as I saw it. She had tried not to get involved with Raj but sometimes life just takes over, you get overwhelmed and are swept away. You end up having no say in the matter. And that is what being human means, I suppose.

Smita's pregnancy, unfortunately, was not a happy one. There were differences between Raj and her but she was caught in a bind. I was with her a lot of the time and she was miserable. After Prateik was born, I think, she almost wished her life away – it was too painful. Within a few days of the delivery, she came down with a severe infection and passed away. I was once again at the mercy of fate and began to slide into depression. Maa was worried for me. She said, 'You have lost Gaagi all over again. What's to become of you?' At that time, my only worry was my son.

I knew I had to bounce back but I could not think of making *Rihaee* without Smita. In fact, I had written the script with her in mind. My friends urged me not to throw away the opportunity of making *Rihaee*. Besides, the loan from NFDC, if not used, would lapse.

At that time, five actresses were in the running for the protagonist's role. One of them, an actor par excellence, came over one day with two dozen red roses, almost fell into my arms and declared, 'Aruna, I am doing your film.' Though I am one of those nice people who can't say no (a quality that I abhor), strangely enough at that time, I had the presence of mind to quickly retort, 'No, X, you are not.' After that I felt so embarrassed and awkward, I settled her down and tried to appease her in many ways, to make up for my bluntness. Thankfully, she took it in her stride but I don't know whether she really forgave me. There were three other actors but I could not somehow visualize them in that role or perhaps it was their image that stopped me. I wanted to steer clear of all this and find someone else.

Suraj Sanim, the dialogue writer of *Rihaee* and a good friend, insisted that Hema Malini would be a good choice. Why would she want to do this film, I asked him. She was a top star and the 'dream girl' of millions. After some persuasion I decided to give it a shot, bracing myself for a 'no'. Surprisingly, she said 'yes' and her reaction to the subject was very refreshing. In many ways she was right for the film but it would not be the film I had initially planned to make with Smita.

Naseer was already in the film but was supposed to play the role of the husband. I asked him to play the role of Mansukh instead, the other man, which he did with so much aplomb. In fact, people still remember his character – the outrageous behaviour, the flamboyant clothes, the audacious dialogues and the rakish persona even after thirty years. I spoke to Vinod Khanna who had just returned from his stint with Osho in Oregon, about doing the husband's role. He agreed and the film was on.

Human beings are unimaginably resilient, but the problem is that they don't think so. I was one such example, discovering my ability to cope powerfully with life. In spite of everything that had gone wrong in my life, I could still stand up and face the world freely. I was free to think and do what I needed to or wanted to.

The logistics for the film were somehow taken care of but there were many things that I had no idea about. The theme of the film itself had been challenging – the repressed sexuality of women. I discovered many things at the ground level where it was not conceptual anymore, as real-life drama unfolded before me. But to get the effect, it would be necessary to know the theme of the film in greater detail.

Men from villages go to the city to work – women are left alone. They look after the old, nurse the young, till the fields, take care of the cattle and at the end of the day they are alone and very, very lonesome. The men in the cities live in shanties, in overcrowded rooms in distant suburbs or slums occupied solely by male workers like them. They work hard all day and the only outlet or entertainment for them is a Hindi movie loaded with song-dance-sentiment or the red-light area at night. They send money home and go back once a year or once in two years. In such a scenario, when a woman gives in to her needs or feelings, all hell breaks loose.

In the film, Mansukh, a widowed carpenter, returns to the village from Dubai, having made some money that he is looking to invest in land. The love-sex-companionship-starved women in the village try to woo him for themselves or for their daughters as a good marriage alliance. Mansukh quite happily sleeps around, resulting in two of the women, Sukhi being one of them, getting pregnant. Sukhi decides to abort the child, afraid of the havoc it would wreak when her husband would return, while the protagonist, Taku, chooses to keep the child against all advice. When the husbands return, Taku tells her husband Amar about the child she is carrying. He loves her and being the reasonable man he is, tells her to abort the child, agreeing to overlook and forgive her trespass – her adultery.

But Taku fights to keep the child even when the case goes to the panchayat. She argues that just because she had erred and had been unfaithful, the child should not be done away with. The panchayat

decides to ostracize Taku from the village and community. The women of the village, who so far had abandoned Taku, stand up for her. They say, 'If she goes, we all go too,' knowing that they have all been vulnerable and possibly in a similar situation at one time or another. They take it head-on and expose the double standards of men and society. The meeting breaks up and in the end it is left for Amar and Taku to resolve the issue/impasse and he accepts her with her child.

Normally when a film unit is on an outdoor shoot, the men in the unit scout around to figure out what is available where – for example, cigarettes, liquor and sex. As far as liquor was concerned, I had made sure that everyone was informed that Gujarat was a 'dry' state. You could not buy liquor or drink in public unless you had a licence. And if people went against the law, they would be liable to be arrested. And if they still wanted to do it, it would have to be clandestine and they would have to do it at their own risk and I did not want to even know about it. Of course, it was a risk for me too as every unit member was important to me and I had to, on the quiet, make sure that they did not get into trouble.

But trouble came from unexpected quarters. About eight to ten days into the shoot, a female actor came to me. She began to complain that there were no interesting men available. Most of the actors in the film on location were women and sure, there was a dearth of male actors in the village simply because the script demanded that. I did not know how to respond to that. She continued, 'Your cameraman is benign – he doesn't look at us women except through the camera.' I knew my cameraman well. S.R. Krishnamurthy was one of those decent individuals who would not make a pass at a woman or take advantage of them. 'And your assistants – you keep them so busy – they are working all the time ... There's no time for a chit-chat even.'

This was not a joke, she was very serious and I did not have a solution. Over the next few days, others too expressed how lonesome they were in that godforsaken village, as they called it, and how they

were missing male company. I thought – what did they want me to do? Surely, it was their own lookout. I could not help them out except listen to their rants. I questioned myself, is it so difficult for them to be without a man for ten days? If that is so, how would we last a month? How would they last the whole schedule without men? And it only served to make my conviction that what the women suffered in the film could not be more true, strong. It made me think – being creative artists they could express their feelings and needs but what about the average women who were denied their sexuality altogether by the male-dominated patriarchal society.

I don't know what arrangements the men had made for their sexual gratification during the shoot, but we had another incident involving one of my male actors. He had apparently been hitting on the village girls. One night a whole bunch of villagers armed with sticks came to beat up the actor. They stood outside the house and demanded that he be brought out. The actor in question was a regular drinker and had fallen asleep somewhere and thankfully could not be found. After a whole lot of threats and a heated exchange of words, the villagers had to go away from the scene, disappointed. Next day, I had to confront the actor and tell him that if he did not behave we would not be able to protect him; we would have to send him back and it could even cost him his role.

The shoot was full of challenges and off-screen dramas too. One of my stars would always be late for the shoot and in spite of being outdoors, we would not get the soft morning light. When my requests went unheeded, I went to my actor and said, 'I am packing up the shooting. We are going back to Bombay (now Mumbai). I am not getting what I really want. We are missing the morning light every day. People will say, "Oh! Aruna could not do it." It's fine, whatever money I owe people for the film, I'll make some ad films and pay them off but I will not compromise.'

Result: She ended up persuading me not to pack up and that she would be on time. After that incident she was the first one to reach

the sets, before any other actor. Another actor had an issue which was actually just a trivial matter but the shooting got disrupted one day because of it. I used the same lines about going back and what I got was a promise to respect his commitment to the film and let other issues be, which could be resolved with dialogue. The issue was resolved in about thirty seconds. What I gathered from the incident was that people react to things on the basis of how things occur for them. Sometimes we lose sight of reality and do not look at things objectively.

A huge problem we had to face during that month was the public. Almost every day we would have a crowd of 50,000 or more people coming to Vadnagar or Visnagar to catch a glimpse of Hema Malini, the dream girl. They came in droves – hanging from overfilled trucks, tempos, riding on top of buses, taxi-cabs and so on. It was unimaginable for people in that area to think that a major star like her could be in their village or district. It turned out to be a 'jatra' or mela. We had a hard time managing the crowds. I would be hoarse, begging them with folded hands to let us shoot.

At least thrice we had a situation where the police could not manage the crowds and resorted to using lathis on people who tried to break through the cordon. Each time I had to pack up the shoot and send the actors home to safety. The situation turned ugly once. The crowds were surging through and as the cops used the lathis on them, they picked up stones and started throwing them at us. I rushed the actors off in their vehicles with great difficulty. My unit tried to persuade me to leave too but I could not. So what if I was a woman, I was the captain of the ship and I stayed. Which led to both of us – Mohan Agashe, who had also stayed back, and me – getting injured. It wasn't very serious, though, and we were back at work the very next day. The film took blood, sweat and tears in its making.

Both my artists and technicians were very cooperative during the shoot in spite of such hiccups. Hema Malini used to worry for me as I would be very demanding on myself and not stopping to rest. When

shooting in the hot scorching sun, every so often, she would send me a glass of juice with her maid or send her 'boy' with an umbrella to shield me from the sun. Harish Patel, on the other hand, would forcibly sit me down and give me a head massage by rubbing coconut oil on my scalp once in ten days.

Francois Truffaut, the French film director, says in his film *Day for Night* (1973) that every director, when he begins a film, sets out to make a masterpiece. Halfway through, it is a great achievement for him to just complete it. For me, it took every iota of strength, courage and determination and God knows what else to complete the film. In fact, when the film was complete, I had a breakdown and had to be hospitalized.

Towards the end of the film, I ran out of money. I had managed to borrow money, get an advance from an overseas distributor, and put in some of my own besides the ten-lakh loan from NFDC. I had also got a lot of credit and goodwill from people but I did not have money for the first print. It was during the dubbing of *Rihaee*, that Vinod, finding me preoccupied, literally cornered me into telling him what the problem was. When he found out what was bothering me, he stepped out of the studio, went to his car and got me thirty thousand rupees. This was exactly what I needed for the first print. When I made a fuss about taking it, he thrust it in my hands and said, 'Don't worry, payable when able.'

He had been extremely cooperative even during the shoot. Since I could not afford a special make-up man or attendant for him and knowing I worked on a small budget, he came to Vadnagar alone. He got off the flight at Ahmedabad, carrying his own bag, and lived with us in the same house where my cameraman, my assistant and I were staying. Even when he was not required, he would be with us on location, every so often lying on a 'khatiya' in what was supposed to be his house in the film.

I completed the film but my ordeal was not yet over. The film I was making did not obviously fit into the typical Hindi film mould.

Vinod Khanna, the hero of my film, who was playing a Rajasthani carpenter, wore a dhoti and sported a moustache. My overseas distributor literally hounded me to show Vinod Khanna wearing trousers at least in one scene. In fact, he wanted me to shoot a dream sequence where Vinod and Hema wore urban modern clothes and sang a song. I was stubborn and did not give in. Such a compromise was beyond comprehension. After the film was released, there were so many women who loved the way Vinod looked – they found him sexy in that get-up and drooled over him.

The problem with the film was that people did not know how to categorize it. For the commercial industry it was an art film and for the art film crowd it was a commercial film. An art film, in those days, was recognized by the commercial film industry as one if it had certain values. When parallel cinema came into existence in the '70s, some excellent films had been made but by the late '80s, it too had developed a formula of its own. What characterized those films were elements like slow-paced storytelling, non-acting, meaning just being the character or being present, be wooden or boring with no histrionics, underlit photography, shooting on live locations, sometimes the absence of a plot, no songs, no dances, no hero-heroine-villain-vamp characters, no romance, no fight scenes or comedy, all of which were the staple of commercial films. People joked that if you fell asleep while watching a film, it was the hallmark of a good art film.

Having been associated with art cinema and having contributed to that movement, I knew that I was making no art film but the commercial industry had no idea what those films were and their real impact on cinema as an expression of an art form. Art cannot exist in a formula or stereotype – it is about expression and needs to grow, develop and go beyond old boundaries and paradigms. One thing the commercial industry grudgingly acknowledged was that they had good technical values but they did not see the point of those films which had no connection with box-office returns.

So here I was with a film that did not belong. Around that time a new word was coined and *Rihaee* fitted perfectly into something called 'Middle' cinema.

The next challenge for me was the Central Board of Film Certification (CBFC) or what was called the censor board. Everyone had scared me saying the censors would have a field day, chopping off parts of my film, given the theme. The content was repressed sexuality of women and there were love scenes but there was nothing in the film that men and women did not normally do together. In any case, just to be on the safe side, I had kept the love scenes extra long in my edit so that when the censors were done with the chopping, there would still be something left. As we waited with bated breath for the axe to fall and mutilate my film, I got a call from the CBFC officer that they wanted to meet me. Having had literally harmless, non-controversial bits of my earlier films hacked off, I expected the worst and walked into the office with great trepidation, ready to argue my case.

The officer was a lady but that didn't mean anything because I had dealt with righteous, holier-than-thou ladies who were highly moralistic. As I sat down ready for battle, the officer looked at me and said, 'Congratulations – I loved your film. It is so rare that we get to see a film like this.' As she showered me with compliments I was dumbstruck, not believing anything I was hearing. She said that they didn't want to cut anything – not even a frame but would I take an 'A' certificate, which meant adult viewing only. Relief washed over me that there were to be no cuts but an 'A' would restrict the business, I had been told. I asked her if we could make it 'UA' but she said the content would be too controversial and it would be safer for me to go with the 'A' certificate.

I had thought making a film and getting it censored was the hard part. But in those days the most frustrating part was selling the film. We had a lot of trial shows – private screenings of my film for distributors. Everyone said they enjoyed it but would not buy it.

It was bold according to them all but … In fact, it shook the male chauvinists so much that even on the awards panels, there were jury members who could not digest it. The reaction from the women was just the opposite. They loved the film.

I was told that most of the distribution deals were done in four- or five-star hotels when the outstation distributors would be visiting. There would be whisky followed by food and women. Obviously I was a misfit since I would meet them in an office or the lobby of a hotel. The brokers and agents too began to get frustrated. Some distributors complained, 'We can't do business with a woman.' I just could not get that. For me it was very simple. If I quoted 'X' and you quoted 'Y', we could surely find a number between 'X' and 'Y' and close the deal. But it was not to be. Finally, I had to get a friend, a male, to talk business with them and clinch the deals.

That is how we finally did manage to sell the film. We had a premiere at Nehru Centre and raised money for the Smita Patil Foundation which had been formed by then. The premiere was followed by a party and I made sure that I fulfilled all my monetary commitments to my actors and technicians that night. I was surprised, however, to find that some people were shocked to receive the balance payment – it seemed that balance payments on release were not honoured most of the time in the industry.

My press conference was yet another battle, given the content of my film. Though my husband and I had been well written about for our earlier films and were quite the darlings of the press, I had not forgotten my first encounter with them before the release of *Shaque*, my first film. A journalist had asked me then, 'Do you expect us to believe that Vinod Khanna, the star, listened to a chit of a girl like you?' I had been quick to retort, 'Ask Vinod Khanna!'

Sure enough, as expected, a journalist stood up during the press conference of *Rihaee* and asked me, 'What do you want? Are you asking for sleeping rights?' I smiled wryly and replied, 'Who can give anyone sleeping rights? People sleep with who they want when they want!' Another shot up and said, 'You are spoiling our women. Our women are not like that.' I looked at him, thought for a moment, and replied, 'Tell me something, when you have an affair or want to sleep with someone, do you go to the red-light area or find someone in your own social circle?' In response, he looked a bit shamefaced. I looked at them and said, 'People are always having affairs, in every class of society, so what's new?' Sure, what was new was my approach and the exposé of the double standards of society and that must have hurt some.

With my honesty, my straight speak and the film itself, I got good reviews. The first week grossed 98 to 100 per cent all over India. Thankfully, no morchas or sloganeering happened in front of my house as I was led to believe. The film did well abroad too and received a standing ovation at the Creteil International Women's Film Festival in Paris.

There were some weird things, however. Women in Lucknow and Bhopal were not allowed to go to the theatre to see *Rihaee*. A lot of the women saw it on video – I was told it was really hot on the video circuit and people had to book in advance for it. Everywhere I went, the film was appreciated and women said I was their voice. A new Arunaraje was getting created in the consciousness of the people.

I was curious, however, that if men were patronizing my film in the theatres, how were they reacting to it. I started going to the theatre and watching the film with the audience, especially the climax where the women rebel against the men.

I watched the film in Delhi, in a theatre in Connaught Place, where the film was released. Male chauvinism is rampant in north India and I was surprised at the reaction. In the film, during the climax, the women of the village challenge the men and expose their double standards. And every time a dialogue attacking the men was spoken by a woman there were loud claps and cheering.

I looked around to see if it was real but as the climax built up so did the applause.

On giving it serious thought, trying to analyse and understand the phenomenon, I realized that human beings have the tendency to fight for the underdog. And in the film women were the underdogs. So, in reality, people in the theatre watching my film were not just men but human beings who cheered the underdogs. And in the darkness of the theatre they were faceless, voiceless, almost identity-less as males. Unfortunately, the impact of cinema is not transformational and does not last. New thoughts, new perspectives do open up people's minds and give them some exposure but the system is so strong that it does not take people time at all to slip back into the older mould or given culture.

After *Rihaee*, I slipped almost imperceptibly into the role of a women's activist, talking to groups of men and women in India and abroad, taking up women's issues and causes. I featured on many talk shows too on television as a strong voice for women.

Given what we are dealing with today, I feel with whatever efforts we, and I mean as a society, have made over the years, we have not been able to make much difference in the way men think about women. To know that, all we need to do is read the newspaper or switch on the television to see the headlines and breaking news – endless stories about women being raped, abused, exploited and even done away with. Having said that, regarding women at least, I think we have gained a lot of ground. Women have got a voice – they have learnt to speak up. Twenty years ago, rape was something shameful, something to hide at all costs. Today girls and women talk about it, demanding justice, not willing to accept the domination of men that is a threat to their fundamental right of freedom.

So *Rihaee* was one drop in that mighty ocean – my single effort to share my beliefs and demand a fair order in society with a large number of people. When it comes to new stories and ideas, Bollywood has been quite bankrupt. Barring a few, most producers, directors and now studios, keep hashing and rehashing the same old stories, investing in blockbuster remakes and sequels. It is not surprising, therefore, that I got a lot of offers to remake *Rihaee*. But I kept turning them down over the years. Even now people are approaching me for the rights to make it or have it made. *Rihaee* was a product of that time – according to me, it cannot be remade.

2
MAGNIFICENT OBSESSION

My earliest memories as a child are of flashing lights on a window pane. We lived on Marine Drive in Bombay and I was so fascinated by images of cars moving and lights flashing on the glass panes that I could watch them for hours together. It was perhaps an indication of what would become my magnificent obsession – moving images and cinema.

When I was around seven or eight years old, we moved to a cottage on Foreshore Road. 'Mantralay', the seat of the government, then known as Sachivalaya, was being built right across the road. Living on the ground floor gave me access to the garden where I could daydream for hours together. That helped immensely in nurturing my ability to make up stories and songs that I would recite or act out.

But this did not make any difference when it came to group games. I was always left out by my elder sister Chitra and the neighbouring kids who were of the same age – the Fakihs and the Mohites. I was called kachcha nimbu (raw lemon) and left to my own devices. I could only watch the others having fun, at best.

The highlight of those days was going for movies with my mother. I remember going to Opera House and watching *Jhanak Jhanak Payal Baaje* and many black and white films starring Meena Kumari, Madhubala, Nargis, Dilip Kumar and Ashok Kumar in Roxy, Metro and Liberty cinemas. My mother was often called to judge drama competitions and I went along. I enjoyed watching the plays and, perhaps, the first foundation of my love for theatre was laid at these drama festivals. My parents were invited for government functions and my sister and I accompanied them sometimes. I vividly remember the Chinese premier Chou-en-Lai's visit and seeing President Dr S. Radhakrishnan, who looked so distinguished and elegant. The Manipuri and Bharatanatyam dance programmes we watched that evening made a huge impression on me.

Another memory clearly etched in my mind is Mohammed Rafi singing '*Bapuji ki amar kahani*' at a function we were invited to. My father was a staunch Gandhian and even though India was a free country and Gandhiji was no more, we as a family still spun khadi a few times a week. My parents had charkhas and we kids had taklis or long spindly tops. Having heard of Bapuji's stories from my father, I was moved to tears by Rafi's rendition of the song. Even today, when I hear the song, I am deeply moved. I have been a fan of Rafi and it was a privilege for me that I actually could have him sing a duet with Vani Jairam in *Shaque*.

In 1956, the old Bombay State ceased to exist. The linguistic reorganization meant that the different regions went to Gujarat, Maharashtra and Karnataka, depending on language that was in majority in each region. Since my parents were from north Karnataka, we moved to Bangalore. I was ten years old then and we travelled southwards, bag and baggage, lovebirds and all. I bid goodbye to St. Anne's High School, where I was studying, in Colaba.

In Bangalore, I studied at Sophia High School with my two sisters. Both my brothers were in King George Military School and later in St. Joseph's Boys' High School. My classes got over at

3.30 p.m. but we were frequently pulled out of the last class with a call from my father's secretary that the children needed to be let off early. That was the only way we could catch a matinee show. I am aghast now that we did that and I would not, in fact did not ever, pull my kids out from school no matter what the emergency. My mother was an avid film buff and it was only on account of her interest that we children watched so many movies. My father on the other hand hardly watched any.

The moment we were in the car heading for the theatre, my tension would start. I hated to miss even a single frame of a film, not even a split second. I would sit near the door, behind the driver and begin to chant quietly in my mind 'Om Namah Shivaya', praying, 'Oh God, let the picture not start till we reach!' I did not care about the newsreel or advertisement shorts but I had to be there when the banners came on. In those days they would come on with a lot of fanfare, like they were heralding some major event or some magnum opus drama. I still remember the logos of Mehboob Khan Productions, V. Shantaram Productions, Gemini Studios, AVM Productions and the music that accompanied them and the excitement that ran through my whole being as I waited for the film to begin. I loved the MGM lion and the lights that flashed from the 20th Century Fox logo just before the movie began.

We watched almost all the films that were released in Bangalore in the eighty-odd theatres at that time. Language was no barrier for us. Apart from Hindi films we also saw those in English, Kannada, Tamil and Telugu. The fact that we hardly understood Tamil and Telugu was no deterrent.

Watching so many films also meant having to manage homework. Since I was good in studies, I would end up doing the homework for my siblings or at least helping them get it done.

We had a huge collection of 78 RPM and 45 RPM records and song booklets, which were sold at the theatres in those days. Fed on such a diet of movies, it was almost inevitable that at least one of the children would become a film-maker.

At that time, apart from school studies and sports, I had two other major preoccupations. I could indulge in them because I topped the class and was also in the school basketball and throwball teams. I was also good at discus throw so nobody had any complaints from me as far as school was concerned.

I was a voracious reader. By the time I was thirteen I remember I had already read *The Complete Works of Shakespeare* from cover to cover; though how much I understood it then is anybody's guess. I read almost everything that was called classics of English literature, from Charles Dickens to Jane Austen to H.G. Wells – everything I could lay my hands on, delving into the verses of A.F. Tennyson, J. Keats, W.B. Yeats, later T.S. Eliot, and I don't remember who else. It seems such a long time ago.

The second preoccupation was music, which played a major role during my adolescence by giving rise to romantic fantasies. We had a Marconi radiogram that could stack eight records at a time. I listened to Hindi film songs and lost myself in the melodious renderings. The lyrics in those days, laced with the philosophies of life, were extraordinarily meaningful. Whatever stage of life you were in, you could refer to a song that could guide you, empower you, cheer you up or show you a new path.

I had a transistor of my own, which was a constant companion. As a family we listened to *Binaca Geetmala*. Ameen Sayani was like a family member. I admired our soldiers on the front, listening to the 'Fauji bhaiyon ke liye' programmes and was glad that I could, later as a film-maker, be part of the programme and share my favourite songs with them. My sister and I knew all the songs of those times, word for word, and we loved to sing them. We were experts at antakshari too. In fact, when we went on long road journeys, especially from Bangalore to Mysore, or Ooty, we would sing non-stop until we reached our destination.

Though I watched so many films, I had my favourites: Guru Dutt, Bimal Roy and Alfred Hitchcock. I was fascinated by the way these film-makers told their stories, etched their characters and left you with an experience that you could take home and cherish. When I think back I wonder how it is that I remember scenes from those old movies which inspired me but I do not remember the films I have seen recently.

I was the second of five siblings, the daughter in the middle. For some reason, I had the perception that I somehow did not matter. The first-born was a girl. She was special because she arrived first in our family. The other reason why she got special treatment and extra love, almost as compensation, was because she had been denied having my father around when she was young as he was in the Yeravada jail for three or four years between 1942 and 1946, imprisoned by the British because he was a freedom fighter. The last-born was also a girl – the baby of the family for all of us, to pamper and protect. There were two boys – twins – in between. Though there was no obvious discrimination, they were special because they were boys. So where did that leave me? To make matters worse, I was very dark-skinned. My family did not seem to have a problem with that but the others around – extended family, friends, so-called members of society – worried about me and my future.

I had no unique selling point (USP). But to lay claim to some USP, by default, I used my intelligence, diligence, hard work and imagination and became the pride of the family. At a very young age I could rattle off Sanskrit shlokas and later 'Friends, Romans, Countrymen' from Shakespeare's *Julius Caesar*. In the process of being different and noticed, I also became a tomboy. My grandmother, who was disappointed that the second-born was a girl, was determined to make me a boy and encouraged me to behave like one. Over the years I found myself amongst the boys because of my ability to play cricket and boys' games. I loved horse-riding and flying too. Later, I found that I was the lone woman among the men by virtue of my accomplishments and capabilities. I had many 'first woman' or 'only woman' tags given to me in professional and leadership groups, or even at conferences. I was the first woman technician to come out of FTII, the first woman Landmark Forum Leader in India and the first woman president of Indian Documentary Producers' Association, among other firsts.

I have always loved cricket. I nursed a deep grudge until college because there was no cricket for girls. In college, my diary was full of cricket scores. Even today, I make time to watch cricket matches. I rejoice when any girl breaks the male order to do something women have not done before. I am surprised, looking back, that the sense of gender equality was present in me even as I was growing up and I think the credit goes to my mother for bringing us up in a certain manner.

A favourite haunt of mine was the treetops. Every so often, I would be perched on a tree with my transistor and book while the whole household would go crazy looking for me. I created my own space, my own world filled with stories from all over the world, treetop travelling to different countries packed with adventure. When I was in company, I got used to being invisible and even now sometimes I wonder how I can so easily merge into the background. It was enormously useful for me later in life, because it helped me observe people and situations without drawing attention to myself, without being a threat to anyone.

I was so obsessed with movies at that time that I created a production company, comprising us – four of us – as my elder sister was married by the time. We called it AUSS Productions, the name derived from Aruna, Uma, Satya and Sheel. We played at making films and acted them out. We even had fancy titles written calligraphically.

When it wasn't a film it had to be a play. I used to make up the scenes, write stories and even adapt some classics. The enactment would be some revolutionary Rajput drama, played out with heroic dialogues or we would indulge in sword-fighting as pirates on the high seas on the four-poster bed. I am surprised that the posts did not break though we climbed on them, using them as lookouts.

In those days, almost every 'good' south Indian family taught their children either music or dance or both. My sisters and I learnt north Indian classical vocal music and Bharatanatyam. My mother's love for art fuelled my passion. She was a voracious reader herself. She wrote poetry and loved listening to Pandit Bhimsen Joshi. I don't know how she did that as well as put great food on the table and bring up five children, almost all on her own, as my father was always so busy with working for the people and the country. My grandmother lived with us and she always had her own special 'take' on everything.

There was one significant incident during that time that perhaps shaped my life. Every summer, the family, with the exception of my father, would go to Ooty with friends. That particular year, there was a whole lot of us travelling in two or three cars. On the way we stopped at a forest lodge in the Bandipur forests to take a loo break. I too went to relieve myself and when I came out, to my utter shock, all the cars had gone. It was late and dusk was setting in. From around the lodge, I could see the twinkling, shining eyes of the deer that had wandered close to the lodge. To say I was scared is an understatement. But the overriding emotion was, 'I am alone' and 'I don't belong' followed by 'I have to fend for myself'. It is not surprising that I became very independent and self-reliant as far as possible, not willing to take help but struggle and try to make it on my own. And that has been a drawback in some ways when I look back at my life now. Of course, sometime later, when they discovered that I was missing, there was panic and a car came back to fetch me.

We had three dogs and I loved them utterly and unequivocally. I was also in charge of them and I would wake up at six in the morning and take them for a walk even in the cold, foggy winters of Bangalore those days, when you could hardly see anything a few yards ahead of you. The climate of Bangalore has changed so much that people would find it hard to believe that today. In fact, I even remember hailstones raining down on us at times. After the walk, I would come back, make breakfast for them, feed them and then go to school. When I returned from school, I would take them for a second walk and later give them dinner too. Weekends were for bathing and brushing them. As a young adolescent, I would share with them the 'crushes' I had, considering I did not have any close friends then.

When I finished school, my career choice was very obvious. Though I yearned to be in the movies, it was quite out of the question. Though my mother, who was fond of movies, theatre, dance, music and poetry, was not averse to my being in films, there was no career path or entry point we knew of. So even voicing my desire was out of the question. There was talk of sending me abroad to study medicine at Edinburgh, or to Bombay. I needed to do at least a year of college to get into a medical college and we zeroed in on Sophia College, run by the same order of nuns as the school I was in.

The first year of college, when I was sixteen or seventeen, away from home, was a time for growing up. I was naïve, innocent, trusting and stupid, with no worldly wisdom and no native intelligence either that could help me. I used to be in my own world and, in a sense, another level of education began. I had led such a sheltered life, I could not even go into a shop and buy something. In the early days, when I went shopping, I would forget to collect change or leave behind the stuff I had bought and walk out of the store or sometimes do both.

My mother was from an erstwhile royal family and we were brought up shielded from society. I was never allowed to go to friends' houses. I don't know what their houses looked like or how they lived. It was like being ensconced in a capsule or cocoon. If we wanted to be with friends, the friends were called home. Anything we wanted was provided, even a badminton court in the large compound. When we kids wanted to cycle, cycles were bought for all of us with the condition that we wouldn't go out of the compound. However, we often sneaked out of the back gate and went on the road next to the Golf Course. Thankfully, it was a quiet road and we didn't get into trouble.

So for me, being in Bombay, in that first year of college, was not easy at all. To begin with, it was the first time I was living away from my mother and my home and I was very homesick. I waited eagerly for letters from Mom, Dad and my siblings and responded with long letters, sharing almost everything that was happening with me.

Though I was comfortable with boys, I did not know the intricacies of girl–boy, man–woman relationships. What was most shocking for me was discovering the facts of life. When I heard from the girls about their infatuations, crushes, affairs and 'going all the way', I had no idea what it meant until one of them shared with me what it was. It had nothing to do with the romantic notions I had in my head. I was so disturbed, I lost my sleep. How could that be? It was not like the birds and bees they talked about in school. How come I had missed out on such important information that all the other girls had and I didn't. Did it mean that Dad and Mom did that? And my sister and my brother-in-law? My mind raced through the names of all the couples I knew and I was actually quite aghast at the images that I conjured up.

Lights out in the hostel was at 10 p.m. But who could go to bed at that time? Though I was a junior, my room was one of the meeting places at night for a tuck-in because it was always well-stocked with pickles, jams, bread, biscuits and cartons of chocolates. Sometimes the senior girls met in another room while we juniors tried to sleep early. If you wanted to read you had to do it by torchlight and that too after the nun walking down the corridor had passed by between 10 and 10.15 p.m., checking if the lights were out.

Necessity is the mother of invention. I found another way to read. I would put my table lamp under the bed and read lying flat on my stomach with the book on the floor. It was not the most convenient position but I was beginning to miss reading with so much college work during the day. My reading comprised stuff like Leon Uris's *Exodus*, *Dr Zhivago*, *Fountainhead* and *Atlas Shrugged*. At some point, I added Somerset Maugham and Guy de Maupassant, whose writing I came to absolutely adore.

And then there were these girls with their raging hormones in a women's college who were committed to spreading the good cheer about love and sex. Certain books were passed on from room to room and, one day, one of them gave me *Lady Chatterley's Lover* to read. The book had been banned and its presence in the hostel could have caused the expulsion of the girls involved. I could not stop reading it. I read all through the night until I finished it. Of course, the next day I slept through my classes. I could not believe what I had read but many things began to fall in place gradually – things I had seen and heard over the years. That year, when I went home for the vacations, I got the younger siblings together and shared with them the facts of life because I did not want them to be shocked at the discovery when they grew up.

Right from a young age, I loved dancing. Every now and then, a bunch of boys, my friends' friends, would land up at the college and we would go to Volgas, Bistros, Venice, etc., for jam sessions on a Sunday morning, where a live band would be playing. We would tire ourselves dancing the twist, rock 'n' roll, cha cha cha or some other dance form.

I got a first class in Inter Science, which was like a pre-degree public exam, and secured admission in Grant Medical College. I was relieved that I got in on merit and my parents did not have to pay any capitation fee or pull strings to get me in. In the first year (1st MBBS), we had to study anatomy and physiology. I did very well in physiology but I hated the practical part of anatomy. Dissection was particularly distasteful for me and I could never get used to it. The sight of the cadavers lying on the tables to be cut up by young medical students was not just depressing but appeared to reflect a disrespect for human life.

The dead bodies, most of them unclaimed, were laid on tables in a large hall and groups of six students worked at the tables, in shifts, on various parts of the bodies. Each one had their own dissection kit and once we finished doing the dissection, learning for ourselves how the human body was constructed, we had to pack the part with swathes of cotton soaked in formalin or formaldehyde. Sometimes some students would not pack the part well and the next day the rot would have set in with maggots crawling all over. It is one of the most disgusting sights I have ever seen in my life. The smell of formalin used to be bad enough but the smell of putrefying flesh is something most people cannot even imagine. Ugh!

In Grant Medical College, I got to see the underbelly of life – poverty, disease, suffering, human degradation, perversity and the lowest of the low experiences human beings go through. The college, founded in 1845, was situated in the large 44-acre campus of J.J. Hospital in Byculla, an area of south Bombay, which was overcrowded with a lot of poor population, also close to the red-light area. Being a large government hospital with a forensic department as well, one got to see and hear a lot more than one would normally be exposed to in an educational institution.

I lived in the girls' hostel on the campus and every day we shared with each other the horror stories that we had seen and heard. Outside the gates there were always the poorest of poor beggars with hardly any clothes on them, sometimes very sick persons lying around, smitten by disease, uncared for until they breathed their last on the pavement, after which some of them being unclaimed bodies probably ended up on the dissection table. Sometimes all kinds of disreputable and even dangerous characters would be seen wandering in the campus – drunks, stalkers or even guys who would expose their genitals and masturbate in public. I for one carried a flick-knife at all times to protect myself, unlike my brothers who were more used to guns and pistols since they were living the life of royalty.

Without that exposure and understanding of human beings dealing with such inhuman situations, I could never have become a film-maker, given the protected upbringing I'd had. I discovered compassion and altruism – wanting to make a difference at that early age.

Travelling by air to and from Bangalore, I would invariably run into some film producers or directors and the flight would end with them offering me a movie. One such film was with Shashi Kapoor but truly, though I was tempted, I had no guts to jump off the trodden path since one had heard enough stories of the wicked ways of the film world. It was 1966–67, when I was even offered to be in a book of photographs called *100 Beautiful Indian Faces*. But to be very honest, though I was flattered, I was afraid to go for that photo shoot.

I took part in a lot of extracurricular activities and acted in plays in Hindi, English and Kannada. I thought that if I did graduate and become a doctor, I would study psychiatry and deal with people's minds rather than their bodies. So it was not surprising that for the first time in my life, I flunked in an exam – in anatomy, in the practical as well as viva. I got good marks in physiology but I would have to repeat anatomy. I stayed on with a renewed determination to crack the practicals but I was not happy.

My mother was simply extraordinary. Every now and then she would visit Bombay and take me and my friends out and show us a good time. My friends looked forward to her visits just as much as I did – good food, long rides on Victorias and the company of a fun person who laughed with them and listened to their stories. It was magical riding in those open horse-drawn carriages at night on Marine Drive, the Queen's Necklace as it was called, the entire length glittering with lights.

On one such visit we caught up with an old friend of my mother's, Mrs Indumati Tendulkar. She thought I should be in the movies but my mother and I did not know anyone in the Hindi film industry and were hesitant to jump right in. Mrs Tendulkar suggested that another possibility could be the Film Institute of India in Pune, as FTII was known then, and she knew someone who could tell us more about it as their son was at the institute.

So we went to meet the Desais – Motiram Desai, Sunita Desai and Vasant Desai. They received us warmly and told us that their son Vikas was at the institute, studying direction. Vasant Desai, who was a well-known music director of those times, offered to take us to the institute and one day he did exactly that.

At FTII, Vikas was our guide. We met up with the Principal, Mr Jagat Murari, acting professor Mr Roshan Taneja and a few others but I don't remember them that well. They had given me a script and an hour to prepare for an audition but my heart was somehow not in it. Needless to say, my performance was neither to my satisfaction nor theirs. The interview went off very well though and the examiners found me both intelligent and knowledgeable.

After some time they told me that they thought I would be well suited for a technical course. The argument they presented was that none of the well-known successful actors and actresses had ever been to a film school. And I had already won awards for acting at intercollegiate competitions. So I could really do it if and when I wished to. However, they felt that I would do well taking up a technical course.

When faced with this new proposition I told them that I would like to join direction, if not acting – I could discuss with them the films of Bimal Roy, Guru Dutt or Hitchcock, all of whom I adored.

In those days, 1967 to be exact, the entrance requirement for the direction course was either a BA or BSc degree. And I had done two years and received my 1st year MBBS certificate. This was a public exam but not a degree. They suggested a way out of this dilemma

– a package of editing and direction over four years instead of the five years it would normally take.

I had no clue what editing was and I was not interested. I went back to Bangalore. Vikas kept writing to me that I should join and so did the FTII people. Finally, I condescendingly decided to give it a shot – to do a double diploma.

People were aghast that my mother had shifted me from Grant Medical College to the Film Institute of India. They said, 'Mrs Patil, you are ruining your daughter's brilliant career.' My mother, the dynamic person that she was, replied calmly, 'My daughter is not frivolous. I want her to be happy.'

I joined at the end of the first term with only a month to go before the vacation. A whole new chapter was opening up for me and I had no clue how irrevocably my life was about to change.

3

ALMA MATER AND MARRIAGE

It was at the Film Institute of India, television having been added later, that I met Vikas, the man I believed was my soulmate. Well, for a few years at least, until we grew apart. We thought alike and had the same concerns about film-making, about society, even about the country. And *Perhaps Tomorrow,* our diploma film, which was the final showpiece of what we had learnt at the institute and how we had matured as film-makers, reflected that. We found that young people like us talked a lot about what was needed in society, where we were headed as a country and people. We discussed it to distraction but did nothing about it. The film presented a hope that perhaps the next generation would take action and bring about the positive change that was needed in society.

But I realize now that many things have just got worse compared to what they were back then. People seem to have become more selfish and self-centred and there is no 'we' anymore. Money has become the new 'God'.

In my experience, the feeling of insecurity has reached such monstrous proportions that people are amassing and hoarding huge amounts of money here and abroad, forgetting that it will not buy them any extra breath when they are dying. I can say that because I have seen three people in my life suffering from cancer, struggling for breath on their deathbed. Most of the time the ill-gotten gains or amassed fortunes don't even reach those it is intended for. Cases of putting parents in old homes and usurping their property were unheard of but with the emergence of the nuclear family it has become a reality.

I feel that, overall, the respect for women has gone down. Rape has become a common occurrence and the institution of marriage has become defunct. It might sound slightly exaggerated but for someone born just a year before India got her freedom, we had high hopes about the future and wanted to contribute and build a nation where freedom, and not just tolerance, prevailed. We expected to live in a country of diverse communities with love, togetherness and integrity but it is a pipe dream. Not a day goes by when communal clashes are not reported from somewhere in the country.

Film-making for me was a medium to express myself and reflect on the world around me, engage people in stories that would make them think or give them memories to take home. It was also the most powerful medium of communication. It could make people introspect and discover hidden emotions.

I could make a living out of film-making, even have a good lifestyle, except for the fact that I could never relate to films as just being vehicles to make money, as pure business. Because somehow I had seen that when business considerations came in, the art and expression of cinema went out.

Which is where I found myself disconnected from Bollywood, the film industry of which I was very much a part. I remained on the fringe as it were, trying to balance film-making and business. Someone once said, 'Some people make money to make films while others make films to make money.' I found myself in the former category, needing to make sure I made enough money so that I could survive and also make my next film.

I believe Bollywood is about glamour and big bucks with all the fringe benefits thrown in. It has very little to do with cinema or any kind of 'pure' art. Of course, now it has gained some respectability as 'pop art' but if you scratch deeper you will find it difficult to agree even with that justification because of the level of kitsch. I think India must be the only country where awards are given in two tiers – Best Popular Award and Best Critic's Award – whether it is for the entire film, direction or acting, further delineating the divide between art and commerce. However, there have been some exceptions where a few films were authentic expressions of human life or art, coming out of Bollywood, but they only go to prove the point. I also want to add that there is no dearth of talent in Bollywood in all aspects of film-making but it's mostly box-office driven. It's simply that Bollywood has developed a style of its own which is weak on the storyline and even weaker when it comes to characters.

Bollywood is about entertainment of the obvious kind – song, dance, comedy, action – instant gratification in three hours where the audience is treated to colour and cleavage and opulence and orgasm.

This is not meant to demean the kind of fare Bollywood dishes out. It has its own place in the scheme of things and it has served the teeming Indian millions with entertainment very well. It has made them laugh, cry, sing and dance and forget their worries. It has been inclusive, catering to the lowest common denominator. Also, that's where most of the people in India learnt their national language Hindi from, over the length and breadth of the country. If there's one thing that unites India, it is Bollywood films with no bars of caste, creed, colour, religion or language.

In the '50s and '60s there were still a lot of films that told stories and engaged you with the dilemmas and conflicts of the characters as they evolved. As the audience, you got to go on a journey with them, experiencing their highs and lows. There were very few films that you could call mindless entertainment. As we came into the '70s and '80s, the storylines got weaker and flimsier, the characters got more diluted and extraneous situations led to group songs with catchwords and dances which were mostly aerobics, less dancing, action where the hero could be a superhero beating up eight or more goons effortlessly, comedy which wasn't really funny most of the times.

History tells us that, initially, even before it was called Bollywood, there were a lot of well-educated, talented, intelligent people, artists in their own right, who made films. Later, a lot of fly-by-night people came in wanting to make money. They had no idea about cinema or the art of storytelling, which it predominantly was, and looked at imitating the formula of successful films. They were proposal makers and were actually responsible for a lot of B- and C-grade films and a huge number of incomplete films, which never saw the light of day.

When I came into the industry in 1969, I was shocked to find that many directors stayed away during the shooting of some portions of their films. These portions were done by the experts in those fields. The fight masters elevated to action directors handled the fight sequences. The directors, finding themselves redundant during the shooting of those scenes, chose to remain absent. Many directors would also not attend their song/dance picturizations because the dance master/director was shooting the song. This was also because these scenes, both the fights and dances, were, in a sense, extraneous to the film and the narrative, and the director felt no connection with them. There were other directors, though, who loved to shoot the songs themselves because it gave them the opportunity to carry forward the narrative or depict with depth the character's emotions.

I remember the early Raj Kapoor, Dilip Kumar, Dev Anand films – they had real characters with real problems. They were vulnerable and heroic when they needed to be without bashing anyone up – just people dealing with huge obstacles in their lives and either succumbing to them or overcoming them with grace and dignity. The women were real too – Nargis, Nutan, Meena Kumari, Madhubala were so individualistic. Each one looked different and you could never mistake one for another. When their hearts ached for love, yours did too. Later, the heroines began to look the same, clones with similar hairdos, make-up, figures, clothes.

For me there were two directors who were very special – Guru Dutt and Bimal Roy. Both were extraordinary storytellers who knew the pulse of the audience and could engage you entirely in the journeys of completely believable characters. Even the plots and narratives were credible. The songs in their films carried the story or emotions forward and were never an impediment in the narrative. The music of the earlier films was melodious, the words soul-stirring and philosophical. There were quite a few master craftsmen – writers, directors, music directors, lyricists – for whom film-making was a passion. The other director who I hugely admired was Alfred Hitchcock – a master storyteller who could manipulate the audience so they just followed wherever he chose to take them. This was until I came to the institute and discovered other film-makers.

Our diploma film, *Perhaps Tomorrow*, was Vikas's brainchild and I was happy enough to add to it. At that time and for many years to come, we were completely on the same wavelength. He directed it and I edited it, though later we wrote, directed and edited together. Incidentally, I also acted in *Perhaps Tomorrow*.

The film showed a girl getting ready for a party. She realizes that she needs to use the bathroom one more time and does so. While sitting on the potty, she thinks about the party, and mulls over how everyone wears masks pretending to be what they are not. She questions the existence of God and his design, the abject poverty around her and the hypocrisy in society and such weighty issues. She reflects on her relationship with her boyfriend. She is constipated and gets up realizing that she will be late for the party. She flushes the toilet and the credits start to roll. All the thinking, the introspection, all gone to nought!

The film caused an uproar for all the wrong reasons. People could not get past the fact that a girl was shown in a toilet. We could not understand what the fuss was about because she was never shown lifting up her dress or pulling down her panties. We only had a mid-shot or a mid-close of the girl's face with the handle of the flush behind her in the frame. The film created a furore in Parliament when someone questioned how an Indian girl could be shown in a toilet! We were amused at the ridiculousness of the question – as if Indian girls did not answer the call of nature and use toilets.

As a result the film was literally put away, to be hidden from the eyes of the world. There was one small mercy though. It was shown with a bunch of FTII films at the Films Division theatre. Shyam Benegal was at the screening and he made a special mention of it, appreciating our work. Later, it got sent off to some festival and was appreciated there too. So we were vindicated to some extent.

When I joined the institute, I knew nothing about editing. As it is I had joined about three months late, just a month before the first term was supposed to end. But I was eager to learn. In no time at all, I began to understand what it meant. I did not know how well prepared I was till I actually began cutting film. All my life I had done jigsaw puzzles – to me editing was like putting one giant jigsaw puzzle together except that the pieces were not two-dimensional picture parts but live visuals with their own audio. In no time I had caught up with both the theory and practicals. Having been a voracious reader and someone who loved to tell stories, it was not too difficult to construct a story from the given material. In fact, I got so super efficient that I would finish my edits before the stipulated time and would be free for the rest of the day while the boys in my class would still be at it.

But I was smart enough not to while away my time. I would go and sit in the direction class, where I was very welcome. It often seemed that I was doing two courses simultaneously. I began spending more time with the direction boys, because that was where my interest lay – to become a director.

We did all kinds of editing exercises from old Hindi movies and some south Indian ones too. There were dialogue scenes, song picturizations, dances, action sequences with sword-fighting, fist-fighting and chase scenes. We also had the experience of editing at least three complete short films right up to a final mixed track. These included a dialogue exercise, a documentary and the final diploma film.

The dearth of girls at the institute was a problem because it left the boys starved for female company. The result of the skewed ratio of girls to boys was that every girl had dozens of boys pursuing her. When I joined there were two girls in acting in the second year and two or three girls in the first year and one in the screenplay writing course. Jaya Bhaduri was a year junior to me and often sat with me while I edited and would wind my reels for me. Back then, she was a mischievous, naughty little delightful spirit who brought joy wherever she went.

The boys were always eager to sit next to me in class, sometimes actually pushing each other to grab a seat next to me or escort me. They would vie to walk me home down Prabhat Road, insisting on carrying my books as if my 'delicate' wrists could not take the burden. When I went cycling sometimes, they would join me for long rides. The camera students needed models to shoot and I would be called to pose for them. Some of them were very clever and would entice girls into the dark room on the pretence of showing them how the stills were developed and try to take advantage of them. But, of course, I was too smart to go into a dark room with anyone.

What I did not anticipate, however, was some boy coming and declaring his love for me every second week. Vikas, who was a good friend, kept predicting which boy would come next, rather which wicket would be the next to fall. I would deny that any such thing would happen but Vikas was always right and, sure enough, someone would come along. There were poems being written, sher o shayari recited, songs sung, letters and notes given and sometimes, even tearful pleading. The sad scenes of unrequited love, when I turned them down, sometimes brought tears to my eyes too. Through all of this, neither Vikas nor I thought for a moment that we would fall in love and get married.

A very common scenario in the institute those days was Shatrughan Sinha performing in the canteen. He was in the final year of the acting course or maybe he had just passed out, I don't remember which. But without fail he would start off with the dialogue from *Devdas*, *Kaun kambakht peeta hai*..., with a glass of cutting chai.

The classes I enjoyed the most were those on film appreciation where Professor Satish Bahadur opened our minds into looking at films from a different perspective. He introduced us to the films of Satyajit Ray, whom he was so passionate about. I got to see some work of Ritwik Ghatak but never got to meet him as he had stopped coming to the institute after I joined. However, Mrinal Sen and Subroto Mitra, who was Satyajit Ray's cinematographer, came frequently and inspired us with their thinking and approach to work.

Professor Rao, the head of the editing department, was very inspiring and had solutions to every problem in editing. I learnt to cut music from him. In our documentary exercise we made a film on Bhimsen Joshi and though classical music is not the easiest to cut or mix, I learnt to do that.

Being in a film school, not hemmed in by considerations of the client or business, we could take liberties to experiment with the material we had. Normally when the picture and sound are aligned or in sync, we take it for granted. But when they are not matching and not together, you can't help but notice the two different elements.

Bhimsen Joshi was a very visual performer and it was almost like he would reach for the notes, grab the alaaps, throw them back, seize them once again and so on. There was so much energy in his singing. In one sequence, we deliberately put the song out of sync so attention would be drawn to the visual aspect of his recital.

I think it was before the May vacation, when we found out that there was a secret project about to happen. Vikas being the topper in direction was asked to assist. Though told to keep the matter confidential, he spilt the beans. For the first time, a feature film was going to be made for the acting students in the institute, directed by the acting professor. Of course the students were agitated about being left out. The secretiveness of the project spoke badly for it. Everyone argued that when there was a direction department why was the acting professor and not someone from the department directing. Since no one was ready to answer any questions and the government did not deem it fit to have a dialogue with the students, which was the need of the hour, the first strike at the institute was called. Vikas and I were its prominent players.

I am sorry now that we were part of what became a trend in the years to come: strikes by students. Strikes happen when students have a grievance and it is not even heard, let alone be addressed by the authorities. In every strike the students are blamed for disruption of schedules which results in wastage of a lot of time, money and resources, but the Information and Broadcasting Ministry has invariably and almost always refused to take any responsibility for it. The government, regardless of which party runs it, does not understand that the students who come to the institute are not undergrads or children and may have pertinent issues that could be resolved with dialogue.

With no dialogue between the authorities and students, the strike in 1968 continued. The authorities tried their best to mislead us but the student body stood firm. Finally the secretary of the ministry, I think it was Ashok Mitra, flew down to meet us. By now the students had firmed up their stand even more. They demanded that all films at the institute should be made by students only, involving all the departments, so that everybody benefited.

The secretary asked us, 'How can a feature film be made by a body of fifty or sixty-odd students?' We said in unison that we could and we would do it! He gave in to our demand and the students were assigned their first feature film.

It was going to be a first-of-its-kind experiment in the world, with about nine directors, twelve cameramen, about twelve editors and nine or ten sound recordists. Roles had to be created for all the acting students and it was a tall order. The head/deputy head of the direction department was supervising the project and Vikas and I were supposed to be present throughout the film to ensure there was a general continuity and also continuity of the film's style. This meant that it was our job to make sure that the film flowed seamlessly, the actors remained true to the characters they were playing and there were no jerks or jumps in storytelling.

The search for the subject began. On Vikas's suggestion, a Marathi short story 'Kuchambana', by well-known author V.P. Kale was chosen. The script was written, the scenes were divided between the students, with each one assigned a segment – a bunch of scenes – to shoot. Thus the film went on the floor.

It was called *Piya Ka Ghar*. The story was set in Bombay, in a typical Maharashtrian chawl. We recruited Vikas's father to help us, and he managed to get us a chawl that suited our need perfectly. The film was about the paucity of space in Bombay where many couples share a room and lack private space.

In the film, three couples – one set of parents and their two young married sons and their wives – lived in a single room with just a sari spread like a curtain separating them at night. All private talk had to be in whispers and during their moments of physical intimacy, they had to make sure they were not heard by the other couples. They also had to ensure they did not fling their arms and legs around. When the kids came, the situation got worse. It was all about constrained living.

Those days Vikas had a huge bungalow on Peddar Road, opposite the Films Division building; and the large guest room was turned into a dorm where quite a few students stayed during the shooting of the film that went on for two to three weeks.

One of the scenes was to be shot on Chowpatty beach. It showed the young couple in the film sitting on the sand and talking like young couples in love do, despite being in such a crowded place. The scene highlighted the desperation of the couple seeking privacy even in a crowd because there was none to be had at home where they shared a room with two other couples.

Our own situation while shooting was as bad. We had to shoot without getting noticed, or crowds would gather and disrupt our work. The sight of a film camera or crew could bring normal life to a standstill and people would crowd around to see the shooting.

We knew the beach would be crowded in the evenings. Many ideas were floated on how we could avoid being noticed. Finally we agreed on one. We had two carts with boxes on them, the sides of which had cigarettes displayed on little shelves. The front had an opening for the camera and the cameraman sat inside the box. The back was covered but could be opened. The students dressed themselves up like cigarette sellers and pushed the carts on to the beach.

We had also finalized a sign language with the actors for 'Get ready', 'Action' and 'Cut'. The boy and the girl, according to the plan, I think, picked up some 'bhel' and sat on the beach, on the sand, close to each other. But the carts were unmanageable, it was too crowded and the entire setting was a recipe for disaster. So Vikas and I got A.K. Bir, who was also a student with us at that time, to take the camera in his hand and follow us.

We got the actors to enact the whole scene three to four times and shot from various angles to capture the scene with different magnifications so we had our long, mid and close shots. We walked through the crowd with the handheld camera and got the ambience in the process. The day of the shooting or the day before, I don't remember which, the director of that segment, M.O. Devassy, had an accident. So Vikas and I had to manage the Chowpatty shoot.

Another highlight of being in the institute was the daily screenings organized by P.K. Nair. He built up the archives and students were always welcome to watch the films with him. The exposure we got to good cinema from all over the world was phenomenal, and I doubt if it was matched anywhere in the world. We found new icons to admire – Vittorio DeSica, Ingmar Bergman, Jean-Luc Goddard, François Truffaut, Alain Resnais, Federico Fellini, Akira Kurosawa, Yasujirō Ozu and many more.

New Wave and European cinema had such an impact on the direction students coming out of FTII that as soon as they left the institute and came into the industry, most of them were unable to adjust to the world of Hindi cinema because most of it was about entertainment and not cinema at all! The technicians were absorbed into the industry over the years but most of the FTII-trained directors chose not to make the kind of cinema they abhorred.

While we were still at the institute, Vikas and I fell in love with each other. It was not love at first sight. We started off as good friends, respecting each other's thoughts and ideals. We grew to love each other. I still remember every time Vikas walked up to me, he was preceded by a strong waft of the Old Spice aftershave which was quite heady. He was roly poly like a teddy bear and was very comforting to be with. He often spoiled me silly and called me 'Raje'. I think he was my best friend for a long time and our marriage also worked because of the strong foundation of friendship.

Though he was only a year and ten months older than me, he looked much older. I was petite and slim and people often mistook me for his daughter. I was not surprised that I had gone in for a fatherly figure and not a 'chocolate' boy to love because I missed my own father. Though I was my father's favourite, he had little time for the family, keeping himself overly busy with his office or social work. Later, when my parents separated and quite bitterly too, I had no access to my father at all.

My mother was an amazing person. She brought us up in the absence of our father and gave us everything any child could wish for. Things had gone horribly wrong for her. She had given up a lot for the man she married and had been left with four children to bring up. So it was quite natural that my father's name would not be taken in our house.

I had grown up immersed in intellectual pursuits and had even been nicknamed a bookworm for my addiction to reading. I did not have much practical knowledge of the world and would very easily score a zero in culinary affairs. Vikas taught me how to make tea, boil eggs and even how to cook rice. I then started enjoying cooking and since both of us stayed outside the campus we would often cook together.

Vikas spoke to his parents about us and they were happy to go with his choice. I spoke to my mother but she was not happy about it. She thought I was making a mistake and said to me in no uncertain terms that she disapproved. However, at the time she did not give me any specific reason for her view.

In the summer of 1968, I was spending time with my family at our farmhouse in Hanumanmatti, north Karnataka. Vikas and his family decided to come and formally ask for my hand in marriage. I was afraid that in the face of my mother's refusal, relations would get strained and Vikas's parents might even feel insulted. I shared this with Vikas but he decided to take the chance. I told my mother that I would not go against her wish, but that I would never marry anyone else ever. She was too precious for me and I could not think of making her unhappy.

Vikas's parents and his uncle, Fatfati Mama (that was Vikas's name for music director Vasant Desai), drove down with Vikas. They stayed for two days and my mother was very hospitable but I was under great stress. Throughout their stay the matter was not discussed at all. Hanumanmatti had a little Hanuman temple on the hillock behind the house. I went and prayed, a la Hindi film style, to 'Him', to grant me my love.

Finally, on the third day, after breakfast, when they were about to leave, the matter was brought up. I already knew what my mother's response would be and was worried about theirs. But to my utter shock my mother accepted their request for my hand. Everyone seemed happy and they left but I was puzzled. I asked my mother what made her change her mind. She just said that she wanted me to be happy.

The engagement followed. Shobha Gurtu's recital, which was part of the celebrations, was attended by the aficionados of classical music. Musical concerts were a regular feature in Vikas's house. Bhimsen Joshi or Kumar Gandharva would perform during the Ganesh Chaturthi festival which was celebrated like a mini wedding. The event would stretch over five days and every relative and friend of the family would drop in any time of the day to seek Ganesha's blessings and partake of coffee and snacks or lunch or dinner along with the mandatory prasad.

Though we had a live-in cook, during Ganesh Chaturthi my mother-in-law would wake up at 4 a.m. to make modaks. As a young bride I would join her. I had no cooking skills then and she taught me the art of making modaks. We would have a lot of relatives visiting us and by 7 a.m. they too would join in. We used to end up making hundreds of modaks, the best I have ever eaten.

Vikas was very keen that we get married while still at the institute and pass out as a couple. We got married in Bombay in January 1969, just before our graduation. However, it was not a pleasant experience for me at all because there was some misunderstanding between the two mothers in the months before our marriage.

It made me very miserable and, unable to take it, I told Vikas that we should call off the marriage and even tried to return his engagement ring. But Vikas was very firm about going through with it and, despite the bad start, it was his commitment that saw us through. After marriage too, he supported me in every way to adjust to my new family and surroundings.

Since we were still working on our diploma film, there was no time for a honeymoon. We came right back to the institute to complete the film. Both of us passed out of the institute a couple of months later, having won gold medals in our respective disciplines.

After our graduation, we had an opportunity to come back to the institute and work on a feature film – *Jai Jawan Jai Makaan*. The film was being produced by the institute for the acting students who were graduating. Among them were Jaya Bhaduri, Anil Dhawan, Rashmi and Danny Denzongpa. The film was to be made by a film director who wasn't associated with the institute: Vishram Bedekar. The toppers of that year in different disciplines were the chief technicians. Vikas and I were direction assistants on the film set and I was the editor.

The film was shot in Pune and Bombay and when in Bombay, Jaya often stayed with us. During that time Hrishi-da was looking for a young girl to cast in the film *Guddi*, in which Vikas's uncle (Fatfati Mama) was the music director. Hrishi-da visited the institute, saw Jaya's diploma film and decided to take her on. That Ganesh Chaturthi, while Bhimsen Joshi or Kumar Gandharva sang, I cannot remember who it was, we had the whole team of *Guddi* – Hrishi-da, Jaya, along with Amitabh – attending the concert. According to a report in some magazine, Amitabh was quoted as having said that it was at this concert that he and Jaya fell in love.

In October 2015, when I was sitting with Jaya at the release of Smita Patil's biography, she reminded me of something I had quite forgotten. It was Vikas's and my first wedding anniversary and Jaya had come down to Bombay from Pune. Since the guest room was already occupied, she spent the night with me in our bedroom and Vikas had to sleep outside. But both of us did not mind that at all. Both of us loved people and were always happy to play hosts to them, especially when it came to friends.

Jaya was playing a school girl in *Guddi* and Fatfati Mama was keen to use a new voice for her. Hrishi-da agreed and Fatfati Mama got Vani Jairam to sing. Vani was a great find. Vani immortalized her first song, '*Bol re papihara*', which is extremely popular. The other *Guddi* song, '*Humko mann ki shakti dena*', is sung in many schools all over India as a morning prayer.

One thing Fatfati Mama never did was compromise and I think I learnt that from him. No short cuts, no selling short – work like a purist within the integrity of the raag, that being the context or paradigm that you have chosen.

4
EARLY DAYS

I think it is important, when you are learning something new, to know what not to do. In my view, it is perhaps more critical than knowing what to do. That way you save yourself from some possible disasters, especially if you are working in an expensive medium like films.

Unlike many other art forms, films were and still are expensive for many reasons. Until a few years ago, most movies were shot on celluloid as against digital today. A single frame on celluloid film lasting one twenty-fourth of a second cost a few thousand rupees, the processing and printing further escalating the cost. With digital technology, the medium on which you capture images is cheaper but the equipment is very expensive, as also the final finishing of the exposed images like digital imaging and colour correction.

But whatever is the medium on which you capture your images, the equipment, the actors, the technicians, locations, costumes, music – background and/or songs – all that cost an enormous amount and if there are high production values like stars, opulent sets, historic or period recreations, dancers or crowds, special effects, etc., the movie is going to be a hugely expensive affair. Meticulous planning, organized execution and discipline in all areas are critical for completing a film within budget and on time.

While working on *Jai Jawan Jai Makaan* (1971), I found that the director of the film, Vishram Bedekar, had scant respect for continuity and cinematic discipline. There was a scene in which Rashmi, one of the protagonists of the film, opens the door. This was shot from both sides but on two different days. On the first day, Rashmi was wearing a certain pair of earrings. The next day she left her earrings behind in the hostel and wore a different pair. When I asked her to get the earrings from the hostel, which was only five minutes away, and there was still time for the shot to be taken, the director intervened and almost shouted, 'Do you want to spoil five thousand feet of a beautiful face for some earrings? Nobody will look at the earrings!' He thought that the second pair of earrings made her look prettier than the first. And he went ahead and shot the scene as is.

The audience is very discerning and observant and quick to catch mistakes, even things like number plates of cars. As for the earrings, being large ones, the break in continuity was very noticeable and distracting. Even if you think something looks better than something else, once you have established the character wearing a particular costume or jewellery you cannot change it in the middle of the scene. No wonder then, with directors who thought like that or just didn't know better, many Bollywood films used to have a large number of continuity jerks. It was not rare to see the make or model of a car change during a chase scene or the colour of the hero's jacket change from shot to shot, not to mention the colour of the heroine's lipstick or her jewellery or sometimes even the hero's moustache! A 'continuity girl' who looks after all kinds of continuity – props, costumes, action, etc. – is critical in a film unit. I certainly learnt not to compromise on continuity, no matter what, because such mistakes distract the audience from the narrative.

There was another issue with Mr Bedekar that I as a woman technician had to face. I wore jeans and T-shirts for the shoot as I always did and still do. He would insist that I attend the shoot in a sari. I did try it for a day but gave it up. As an assistant I needed to be active and agile, ready to run or climb a ladder or steps and the sari was not the most appropriate attire for the job. In fact, there were times on that shoot when I had to climb over the gate of a bungalow we were shooting in because it was forever locked. And having been a tomboy, I could do that without worrying about managing a sari or for that matter even a dupatta. Mr Bedekar himself wore a thin dhoti for the shoot which, according to us, was not the most suitable piece of clothing for a film shoot.

Some days later, while we were at his house chatting informally, some of us raised the question about Indian and Western clothes and dressing suitably for any occasion. We had thought he was just old-fashioned and did not like Western clothes when he had given me the directive to wear a sari through the shoot. His answer shocked the daylights out of us when he declared that a woman's body was the most ugly thing God had made and needed to be swathed in cloth. We were horrified at his views and insisted that a woman's body was God's most beautiful creation, and that it had inspired art and artists all over the world!

While we were working on this film, we were called to Mysore to edit Girish Karnad and B.V. Karanth's maiden Kannada film, *Vamsha Vriksha* (1972). We were asked to leave almost immediately. It seemed like an adventure beckoning us and we were keen to go. *Jai Jawan Jai Makaan* was almost nearing completion, and we informed them that we could join them only a couple of weeks later. They reluctantly agreed.

Things don't always go as planned and there were some delays on the film. As a result of that, we found ourselves working day and night to complete the film. Finally, *Jai Jawan Jai Makaan* was completed and we returned to Bombay.

Vikas and I had planned to drive down, so we got our Ambassador car serviced and left for Mysore. We had lunch at Pune and continued on our way. Accompanying us were my stepfather and my editing assistant. Vikas was driving and I was sitting in the front with him, knitting something to keep myself awake.

Somewhere near Kolhapur, Vikas fell asleep on the wheel and drove into a tree after which the car fell into a deep ditch. It was a major accident and I lost consciousness. When I came to my senses I was shivering inside a truck and bleeding all over. The truck apparently took us to Vikas's uncle's house in Kolhapur from where I was taken to a hospital. While being wheeled in, I remember asking for Vikas, who was right there holding my hand. I thanked God, then and there, for keeping him safe. Vikas told me that the others were OK too, before I passed out again. When I regained consciousness, there were bright lights on my face and a doctor was sewing it up. The smell of the anaesthetic or whatever it was hit me and I could not stop myself from vomiting all over the doctor. I passed out again.

The next time I came to I was in a special room and in great pain. My legs were broken and my face smashed. I had been taken to Wanless Mission Hospital, I think in Miraj, and was thankfully under a dedicated team of doctors.

I had to stay there for a few days. My face was covered with a mask with two peepholes for the eyes. I was told that they had had to stitch my face after administering local anaesthesia because they were afraid to risk general anasthesia, as the head injury I had suffered might have caused damage to the brain. I looked like I had stepped right out of a horror movie!

After a few days I was shifted to Kolhapur where Vikas's aunt and uncle lived. The doctor took off my face mask about three weeks later and I was allowed to look into a mirror. I saw myself and I wished I had not survived. Imagine a face without a nose! Everyone had envied my nose, it was supposed to be one of my best features along with my eyes, and it was gone! I felt like such a freak! I wished desperately that I had died in the accident. Vikas consoled me that we would put it right with plastic surgery. But it was hard to accept – to live each day with the way I looked.

A few days later I was shifted to Bombay. Both my legs were still in plaster and for my face, I had now a makeshift mask to be removed at night while sleeping. Though I was at home and in the comfort it provided, it was a difficult period. Relatives, friends and acquaintances came visiting. And they were sorry for me. I had hardly been married for two years, and was now bedridden. No one could tell what the future had in store for a girl like me. Even I was not too sure whether I would be able to walk again and, even if I did, if it would be with a limp. My face after the accident didn't have any resemblance to my earlier so-called pretty one. My frustration began to mount and I began to slide into depression.

Soon after the accident we had informed Girish Karnad about my condition. They asked us to give an update in a few days. After a couple of weeks we told them that my condition was quite bad and that they should take another editor to work on their film. But the producer, G.V. Iyer, decided to wait. Despite our repeatedly telling them that there was no certainty at all of me editing their film, for some reason, they chose to wait.

The flowers, the conversations to cheer me up, the visits, were all becoming unbearable. Vikas and I strongly felt the need to get away. Besides, there was also the fact that the producer was waiting for us in Mysore to start the editing. We thought it might be a good idea to go and edit the film if I could work from a wheelchair. Soon enough, the wheelchair materialized and we informed our family of our plans. They were aghast. We kept insisting until they saw that they could not stop us from going. We informed Girish that we were coming. Little did he know what he was about to get!

We took a flight to Bangalore and drove down to Mysore, taking wheelchair and all. When Girish saw us at the studio, he was horrified. I still had my face mask and the plaster on my legs. The editing rooms were on the first floor and going up and down every day was out of the question. Even staying in a hotel did not seem plausible. Then someone had a brilliant idea. Maybe it was Vikas. The idea was to convert the editing room into a bedroom – luckily it had a connecting door to the second editing room where the editing could take place. There was a bathroom right next to the first room and that could be kept exclusively for us. It ended up being a suite of sorts!

Perhaps only a film student who knows the history of film-making, would know how films were edited fifty years ago. A movie was shot on film negative. This negative was processed in a laboratory and a print was made from it. This print could run in projectors and editing machines which were called moviolas. A more sophisticated version of an editing machine was called the Steenbeck. This machine had a screen on which you could see the film which came in rolls of 400 or 1000 feet. For editing and projection we joined the film bits and made 1000-foot rolls, which ran for a little over ten minutes, given that the speed at which the film was run was 90 feet per minute. The machine had a mechanism to go backwards and forwards and stop wherever you wanted it to. That way you could choose the exact frame where you wanted to make a cut. The sound was on a separate roll – it had to be matched to the picture and threaded on the machine. When the coupling was done they ran together in sync and when it was uncoupled you could do whatever you needed to do with each separately.

This machine, the moviola, was at the other end of the corridor. The process involved threading the film with picture and sound loaded on spools and viewing them. Shots were seen and marked for beginnings and ends with a glass marking pencil. After the whole reel was marked we would come back to the editing table. The equipment here was a set-up to load the spools on a rack on the left side and a winding mechanism to receive the film on spools on the right. In the centre of the table was a light box with ground glass on it so the frames would be lit up from below for better viewing. The sides of the tables were cut like big windows to accommodate two cloth bins on either side, so the film fell in the bins and not on the floor.

On the glass was another piece of equipment, a synchrometer, which had four tracks that ran parallel to one another. So with every roll of picture you could edit three more tracks of sound film. Looking at the marks, you actually cut the film with a pair of scissors going from the end of the first shot to the beginning of the second shot that you had marked. The unwanted cut portion was put away in a separate bin and then rolled up and stored in a tin.

How we joined the film was another process altogether. When you edit now, you can 'do', 'undo' and no matter how many times you do it or how many versions you make, it does not affect your picture. In those days you had to be very precise – every cut meant losing a frame. And no one could afford to do that. If you changed your mind, too bad, the frame was gone and you would need to put a blank frame instead and it would affect the flow and, therefore, impact of the picture.

Whatever type of cut, it was imperative you got it right the first time. Once the cut was finalized we had to scrape off the emulsion on the film covering one perforation or the gap between two frames. Scraping the emulsion off meant scraping the picture or image off, leaving only the transparent celluloid piece underneath. Then you would put a strong-smelling chemical liquid, the film cement, between the overlapping parts of the two pieces of film with the perforations matching perfectly. You held it tight, pressing on it, until it became one continuous piece. Sometimes the film would tear but the joint would not give way. Some innovative editor had improvised the tools – the brush used for the delicate work was a nail-polish brush and the container for the film cement, a nail-polish bottle.

My entire day would go in working on the moviola or the editing table. Vikas was amazing through that period. He took care of me and my needs so well – whether it was sponging me, taking me to the loo and cleaning up afterwards, helping me to dress – anything and everything. It must not have been easy for him. He was brought up as the only son of a very well-known industrialist, whose grandfather was supposed to be one of the founders of Bombay and whose picture used to hang in the Prince of Wales Museum. (I don't know if it still does!) Ours was a love marriage and Vikas was a real hero at that time.

A strange thing happened in Mysore, which was to happen over and over again in Bombay too. People found me an oddity. They would come and peep into the editing room or stare at me as I worked, whispering among themselves, 'It's a girl, it's a girl.' Every day people came to watch – I was a novelty for them as a woman editor and technician. Another conversation that went around was, 'How can you learn film-making in an institute? It can't be taught and these students can never fit into the industry.' Yet another conversation in Mysore was, 'They have brought these people from Bombay – as if we couldn't have done the job here. Let's see what they will do.'

Vamsha Vriksha, the film we edited, was shot in black and white and based on the famous writer S.L. Bhyrappa's novel. It was in Kannada, my mother tongue. I had spent most of my life in Bombay so my Kannada was very basic.

There was a strange reluctance on the part of Girish and Karanth to come to the editing room every time we called them. Later, they admitted that they were afraid to come – it was their first film and they were not sure how it would turn out. So it was left to us to do whatever with the material they had shot to give shape to the film.

One of the problems I encountered was that the female protagonist of the film, L.V. Sharada, was acting for the first time.

In the initial days of the shoot, she was overreacting by raising her eyebrows high every time. She was supposed to be a Brahmin widow in a small town in Karnataka, very suppressed and reserved. Her interactions were mostly with her father-in-law, a very stern knowledgeable Brahmin with a strict code of conduct. Girish had found it hard to control her and said that he had wanted to draw a line round the room saying, 'No eyebrows to go up beyond this point.' I knew I had to do something about it. I looked at the rushes again.

When we shot on film, the practice was to order the sound to go first, followed by camera and then ask for the clap. The clapper boy announced the scene, the number of the shot and take and moved out from in front of the camera. The director would then take a moment and say 'Action', after which the actor would perform. It was necessary to take that time for the film camera to get into its speed of twenty-four frames per second. After the clapper boy went out of frame, I found Sharada looking blank with no expression on her face, literally waiting for the director's instruction. This part was a little longer than usual because the directors took time to give the order because they thought they had to give more time for the camera to catch speed. I cut out the waiting bits, where her face was still and used those bits to show her listening to her father-in-law's rant. The bits with the raised eyebrows were cut out and the new bits pushed her performance up a few notches.

Most of the actors in the film were first-time actors and, as the shooting had progressed, all of them had settled into their characters. However, I had to innovate and create as we went along, doing away with things and moments, small and large, which did not fit in and looked incongruous or out of place. It could be the actors' actions or speech or a piece of 'property' that did not belong in the frame.

In fact, I remember wisps of smoke in a couple of scenes which didn't belong there and was horrified to find that the source was from the cigarette the cameraman was smoking while taking the shot.

Then there were light stands, cables and the boom mike in the frame. I had to somehow minimize the usage of those shots without it affecting the narrative. In one shot, of which there was only one take, the cameraman himself was in the frame with the elderly Brahmin character emoting. Apparently the assistant had been operating the camera and had not asked his boss to move out of the frame. In any case, it is the job of the editor to correct everyone's mistakes and have the smoothest possible narrative with no distractions.

Finally we got the cut done and it was worth all the trouble. The film won L.V. Sharada the Karnataka State Award for Best Acting, the directors got a National Award and we also got the Karnataka State Award for Best Editing. There is a famous saying that 'performances are made on the editing table' and in this case it proved the point.

For me it was like going back to the basics. In his book *Film Technique,* V. Pudovkin, a Russian director, had formulated a theory of film editing which was like a basic guide. This was way back in 1929. According to him, the raw material in a film was the shots taken by the director, exposed and printed on the celluloid film. So the material of the film director was not of real processes happening in real space and time but of those pieces of film in which the processes or content of the shot or action were captured. And that the celluloid was entirely subject to the will of the director who edited it. He felt that for a narrative to be continually effective, each shot, each cut must make a new and specific point. (*The Technique of Film Editing* by Karel Reisz and Gavin Millar, 1953).

In fact, when teaching editing, we often give students a lot of shots not connected with each other – just random visuals. The same material edited by different people has a different impact with every version being the creative output of that particular person. It's only in the way the shots are assembled and then cut precisely, that a new meaning, mood or understanding emerges, which was not inherently present in the individual shots.

Pudovkin arrived at his conclusions partly from his own experiences and partly based on the experiments of his senior colleague, Lev Kuleshov, also a film-maker and film theorist, one of the founders of the world's first film school, the Moscow Film School. He demonstrated by examples that by suitable juxtaposition, shots could be given new meaning that hitherto they had not possessed. He argued that if one were to join a shot of a smiling actor with a shot of a revolver followed by the terrified face of the actor, people would take it as the actor was scared and cowardly. If the actor's shots were now reversed the audience would see a different effect and consider the actor to be heroic.

In another experiment, Pudovkin and Kuleshov actually shot close-ups of the actor Mosjhukin with a neutral expression and intercut the shot with a) a shot of a plate of soup on a table; b) a shot of a coffin with a dead woman; and c) a shot of a little girl playing with a toy. When these three experiments were shown to the public, the reaction was amazing. The audience raved about the performance of the actor, pointing out the heavy pensiveness of his mood over the forgotten soup, were moved by his deep sorrow over the dead woman and admired the light mood as he watched the little girl at play.

Of course, the audience did not know that the shots were all one and the same and completely neutral in expression. Kuleshov elaborated that in every art, first, there must be a material and, second, a method of composing this material specially adapted to that art. He maintained that the material was the shots of the film, while the composition was those pieces of film joined in a creatively discovered order. He emphasized that film art does not begin when the artists act and various scenes are shot – this is only the preparation of the material. According to him, film art began from the moment the director joined the shots in various combinations and different orders and obtained different results.

Editing *Vamsha Vriksha* at that time did two things for me: one, it kept me from thinking about my physical condition and worrying about it and worse, getting depressed, and second, it gave a fillip to my creativity, which was great for my soul and which helped me heal faster.

But we ran into another major problem during the completion of the film. In those days the picture and sound were on different pieces of film. And for the re-recording of the film, i.e., getting one final track of sound that would include clean and clear dialogue, incidental sound effects, general ambient sounds and the background music – all in the right perspective and volumes to match the content of the picture – we needed to have the dialogue track married to the picture so that both could be on one strip of film. For that we had to cut the picture and sound negative and give it over to the laboratory to make what was called the R/R print (re-recording print). The music and effects recording and re-recording were to be done in a Madras (now Chennai) studio and we left for Madras for the last lap of the film. By this time, I had abandoned the wheelchair and had started walking with the help of crutches.

At the re-recording studio a shock awaited us. We were told that the R/R print was out of sync – the picture and sound did not match and we would need to get another print. This was out of the question for the producer of such a low-budget film! Naturally a blame game started. Vikas, I and indeed the entire film Institute were criticized by the old guard who did not believe in film education. I said to them that if it was my mistake I would pay for the entire print, but I had to examine the print and see where the mistake lay. I checked the print. I saw that the laboratory guys had not matched the leaders called 'standard' leaders which have numbers on them in a descending order – 9, 8, 7, 6, 5, 4, 3, 2, 'start'. These are standard for the editor, recordist, re-recordist and the laboratory. They had just printed it, mismatching the numbers, but whether it was deliberate I would not know.

However, as an editor and a trained one at that, from FTII, I knew my job. I talked to the recordist, Mohansundaram, and checked with him what tracks he had for mixing. We found that he could spare a magnetic track. We transferred the printed track on to a magnetic roll, after which I re-synced the picture to the magnetic track and we were, literally, back on track. Those guys who wanted us to fail must have been quite disappointed for they had been pretty vociferous about their opinions on film education and girls working as technicians.

We did not have good Foley facilities for recording incidental sound effects in those days. It was very primitive, unlike what we had learnt at the institute. The effects were recorded randomly while the picture ran for ten minutes. We actually had to decide amongst ourselves what roles we were going to play – be a crow or a dog or a cow and make those animal sounds and then take on some other effects like walking, running, falling, different kinds of footsteps, a match being lit, water being poured, the tinkle of cups and saucers, and so on, everything that could be done in that stretch of ten minutes.

In very professionally made films, sometimes there would be twenty-four tracks or more just for effects, with each track having only a particular kind of sound. Lighting a match could not be in the same track as a train or a bird or even a knock on the door. But given what was available, we did whatever we could.

The film got completed a couple of weeks later. The producer had, by then, run out of money. So we did not get any money for the work we did. But I was grateful to be working – it was good for my morale and an experience to cherish – to be able to create something that was thrown in my lap. And most joyous of all was the fact that by the time the film was completed, I had begun to walk!

On returning to Bombay, we got in touch with a plastic surgeon for my broken nose. The first thing he asked us for were photographs of my face so that he could reconstruct the nose similar to the original. Vikas was an avid photographer and he had taken innumerable snaps of me which came in handy at this juncture. What the doctor did next was to make a mould of my face and create a cast of it in plaster. He then took a plasticine kind of material and built the nose on it. We were then invited to see if the construction looked accurate.

After our approval, he created an identical piece in 'cylastic' to be placed where my nose had gone missing. We fixed a date for the surgery and I went to the hospital. What the plastic surgeon then did was make a small longitudinal slit at the base of my nose, just above the lips, and push the piece of 'cylastic' all the way up my nose till the forehead. He then closed the slit and that was that. In a few days I woke up to a brand-new nose, almost as good as the original one!

We were keen to work on a feature film but meanwhile we thought it might be a good idea to do some short films. My father-in-law put us in touch with Durga Khote, a star from the very early black and white era. She was doing character roles in Hindi movies and had a production company which she ran with her Polish daughter-in-law Tina Khote. Together they produced advertisement shorts, documentaries and corporate films.

We met Durgabai, as she was known, and got our first ad film. We did that pretty efficiently with no hiccups. At the end of it, we received a cheque of Rs 500 each. We were shocked, to say the least. We promptly returned the cheques to Durgabai, saying the money might be of more use to her. She understood immediately, and gave us another cheque for a more acceptable amount. That was the start of a great rapport with both Durgabai and Tinabai in Durga Khote Productions (DKP). Our work with them helped them develop faith in the technicians who had trained at the film institute and word began to spread in the short film industry. We brought in a lot of people to DKP and it was a good place to start for new graduates coming out of FTII.

We made a lot of films for them, mainly corporate ones. But wherever we went I was stared at, whether it was Rajkamal Studios or Bombay Labs. Often, when we were shooting in factories, being slim and agile, I would climb ladders, two or three floors high in the working bays, to take top-angle shots with the cameraman. At such times all work would stop as the workers would watch me as if I was a stunt queen and it would take some doing to have them get back to work.

One huge problem I faced in those days was the lack of toilets for women. Drinking plenty of water was considered healthy but it would mean going to the loo. Initially, Vikas would stand outside the men's toilet after making sure it was empty and I would go in but we couldn't do that all the time. I began to drink less water and finally got to a stage where I would leave home for a 7 o'clock shoot and come back at midnight without using the loo even once in those long hours.

Initially it was fine but as I grew older, it began to take a toll on my health, especially my bladder and kidneys. I got a strict warning from my physician not to abuse my health. If it was outdoors and in the fields it wasn't such a problem, but when I was in my late thirties and forties, it was especially hard for me as a woman, working through my periods, with heavy bleeding and fibroids etc., and somehow managing to do what I needed to do with the least amount of fuss. It may sound strange but the most expensive room in my house was always the toilet, every time I got my house renovated.

Unfortunately, toilets have never been a priority for most Indians. This sounds like a general statement but those of us who have lived long enough even in a city like Bombay could vouch for that. It is common knowledge that most of India lived in the villages and openly defecated. In Bombay, around the '70s and right into the '90s, as I remember, there were very few pavements which one could walk on. Most of them were like public urinals and it was quite a common sight to see men peeing against the compound walls. The stench was unbearable but people did what they did. In order to stop them from relieving themselves in such a disgusting manner, a lot of buildings had on their walls painted tiles of gods so that men would hesitate to pee on the gods.

Early mornings on the beach or alongside the local train tracks there would actually be a 'bum' show with people squatting to relieve themselves. I still remember a shot we had in a documentary about the state of the country, hundreds of people on the beach shitting openly with their bottoms bared. Later, a social movement started in the media and on the streets, to stop people from peeing in public and spitting 'paan', and Sulabh Sauchalayas too began making their presence felt. No wonder the current prime minster has put so much emphasis on this aspect if we are to be considered a powerful developed nation.

In Famous Studios in Mahalaxmi, where the major film production companies had their offices, the stench emanating from the toilet would waft out till the entrance of the building. Since we worked quite regularly in the editing rooms of that building, we had to somehow insulate ourselves. We were lucky that Vikas and his family were members of the Willingdon Club, opposite the Race Course, and we could go there when we needed to use the loo. Even in Naaz Cinema building, where major film distributors had their offices, and for whom money was no issue, they had dirty stinking toilets and lots of paan stains on the staircase and walls.

Another important part of my film education during this period was learning the use of music in films. Vikas's uncle Vasant Desai was highly appreciated for his background music. Vikas and I were always invited to attend his recordings, whether it was for features or documentaries, and we got to learn a lot from him. He always composed for a film keeping its context in mind and his changeovers were very accurate to the frame.

In those days we did not have what was called the 'rock and roll' system and the whole piece had to be done in a flow, without breaks, with the whole orchestra playing. Even for songs the situation was the same. The singer sang along with the musicians as they played from beginning to end. Then came the rock and roll system that allowed the film to be rolled back. Later, as digital recording came into effect, you could do just about anything bit by bit. Now it is possible to record just a word or phrase, or a line bit by bit, add or subtract instruments and the song finally evolves from the recordist's console after all the manipulating and tweaking is done.

5
FIRST STEP FORWARD

Vikas and I were considered 'whiz kids' and, often, difficult or challenging assignments came to us. One such film was an ad film for Arvind Fabrics where the models had to walk on sheets of cloth as they rolled out of the looms, instead of the ramp. Unlike now, when you can combine and blend images on your computer or even your cell phone, doing special effects on film was a difficult process at the time. It meant exposing the two different visuals separately and then overlaying one on the other by making special inter-negatives and inter-positives before bringing the two images together, frame by frame, with perfect synchronization and composition. Most often the effects never turned out right and had to be done a few times to achieve perfection.

There were just a handful of people who did special effects. There were no courses for special effects and many of them had worked hands-on in the field, to train themselves, here or abroad, experimenting over years. Today, people cannot even imagine how painstaking a process it was to create a special effect back then. It was a huge drain on the budget as well, as inter-negative and inter-positive films were very expensive. Even a simple superimposition of titles on a visual or a simple dissolve left a lot to be desired because after all the multilayering and processing, the background visual never looked the same; most often it looked washed out or 'muddy'.

Another challenging film was an ad for Goodlass Nerolac Paints. The client wanted it done with puppet animation. Hardly anyone had done that and cel animation was usually the norm, though even that was uncommon.

People were familiar with animation mostly through the cartoons that came out of the Walt Disney Studio. The process was painstaking, expensive and time-consuming. If a movement consisted of ten still pictures or frames, it meant drawing or painting ten of those frames and shooting them on a stop motion camera one frame at a time. In the early days the backgrounds were bare and simple, giving prominence to the characters in the foreground. The painting was done by hand on thin transparent sheets of cellulose acetate. Since there would be more than one character and lots of movements of those characters, what was required was a lot of cels. It was a very demanding, precise and delicate job, painting hundreds of cels and the Disney Studio is known to have hired a lot of women to do the paintings. In time, multiple layers were used; backgrounds became more interesting and complex as the layers increased. When computer animation came in, it was much easier as the visuals were done on computer which could easily duplicate a large number of cels.

The basics of animation were the same for the puppet film but it meant working in three-dimensional conditions unlike the two-dimensional flat plane of regular animation. To begin with, we had to find a puppet-maker who could create Goody the Tiger, the mascot of Goodlass Nerolac. Our search led us to a lady, Indira Iyengar. Our requirement was a tall order because she had to not only make a puppet that looked like Goody but make one whose joints in the limbs, tail and jaw could be moved a little at a time and could sustain a given position. It needed to have a skeleton that was an armature so that not only was it stable but movement could be controlled. It took a lot of tests and Indira had to keep going back and working on the puppet till we got what was needed. Goody was about twelve to fifteen inches tall. The little girl puppet, who was supposed to interact with Goody, was much smaller and making her had been simpler.

The next thing was to get a 'shooting set' of the little girl's house in proportion to the two puppets. The art director worked on the design and finally we got the little house with all the little furniture in place. It was placed on a large table and of course, the ceiling was removable because that was our access to manipulate the puppets in the house and to light up the house as well.

The shoot to create a one-minute film took eight days. We had a camera that exposed one frame at a time and each action was carefully broken up into the number of frames required to complete the action. The number of frames required to bring Goody's paw to his face or take a step forward was precisely calculated. But it was not so simple because as his paw came to his face, Goody's tail too had to go up (it had its own number of frames to complete the action) and his eyes had to roll and his eyebrows arch. Each movement had its own beginning and end – it was quite complicated to manage five or six elements at a time, starting and finishing at their own pace. A very detailed log had to be maintained. And when both the characters were in the shot it was doubly difficult because the girl's movements were also not just one action. When she spoke and made a movement, her eyes moved, as did her lips and her plait that flew up and came down and her skirt that swished and so on.

The dialogue track had been pre-recorded and it also was broken up into action frames. It was very precisely done – the number of frames calculated for every word, when the lips meet and when they need to part or even how wide the mouth opens. When the film was completed it was considered quite an accomplishment.

Another film that broke new ground was the ad we did for a cold drink called Double Seven. It was the first ad film made in Cinemascope and was shot by the veteran ace cinematographer R.M. Rao who specialized in ad films. The film was two minutes long with a song/jingle and was shot with special colour filters that added different colours on the same visual. This drink had the then government's backing and had been created to counter the popularity of Coca-Cola.

Even as we kept making advertising shorts and corporate films, we were constant in our efforts to find funding for a feature film. We found a story that we liked and had read some years ago, and adapted it to Indian conditions and emotions. We approached N.B. Kamat, who was a distributor and a producer operating out of the Naaz building. At some point he was the vice-president of the Indian Film Distributors Association and, in 1976–77, president of the Film Federation of India, the apex body of the Indian film industry.

Vikas's father knew Mr Kamat and so we approached him and narrated the story. He seemed interested. He proposed that we become his partners and co-produce the film. That is how the banner 'AVIKAM' came into being. It stood for Aruna, Vikas and Kamat. Those days the most important thing for a film was to sign on the actors/stars and get some advance or commitment from the distributors. So we walked the line.

Vikas and I were clear about the choice of our actors for the lead roles – Amitabh Bachchan and Waheeda Rehman – who were essentially good in their craft. But Mr Kamat was dead against Amitabh because his films before 1972 had not done well. *Zanjeer* (1973) became a super hit but we had missed the bus. We had faith in Amitabh's acting skills then but no amount of persuasion had worked with Mr Kamat. He had no idea of Amitabh's potential as he judged him solely from his previous box-office returns and much as we tried, we could not convince him. We were pressured into finding someone else. We tried taking a newcomer, even did a photo shoot, but again Mr Kamat was not satisfied.

Meanwhile, we had narrated the script to Waheeda Rehman. She liked it and agreed to do the film. Our interaction with her was fantastic. Very rarely do you come across someone so unpretentious, and so natural and gracious, especially in the film industry. Since our film was a low-budget one and we did not have much money, she was generous enough to let us use saris from her personal wardrobe. We wanted a natural look, not the painted faces with a heavy pancake foundation that most films had those days. We asked Pandhari dada, one of the ace make-up men from the industry then, to do a make-up test. We took a lot of stills and were more than satisfied with the outcome.

The next name to come up in our pursuit of a hero was Vinod Khanna, suggested by Mr Kamat. We accepted his suggestion and he fixed up an appointment with Vinod for us to narrate the script. Vinod liked the subject and finally we had found our leading man. But the pairing with Waheeda did not work. Mr Kamat suggested we take a new girl. We went to Waheeda's house, and even before we could tell her what was happening, she gave us the go ahead to move on without her. She said, '*Tum aane wale log ho aur main jaanewali, aur aane wale log nahin rukte jaanewalon ke liye*,' ('You are the guys coming in and I am on my way out, and those who are coming in do not wait for those who are going out!') We were floored.

We did not have to look very far to find a new girl. Vikas used to go to FTII in Pune, on and off, to teach while I stayed behind. I had just delivered our baby girl Gaagi, a few months ago, and I needed to be home with her. Vikas had been interacting with a new batch of students and having seen Shabana, who was studying acting at the institute, he suggested her name to play the lead opposite Vinod. I met her too and liked her, and thankfully, Mr Kamat agreed to take her on. By the time we shot this film Shabana had done Shyam Benegal's *Ankur*.

When we wrote the subject we had thought of calling the film 'Shayad'. But Mr Kamat thought it was too arty. So we found another name and called it *Shaque (*Doubt*).* For a lot of people in Naaz building this title was not commercial enough. There were many horrendous suggestions like 'Khooni Mera Pati', etc.

One day Mr Kamat wanted to know which camera we were planning to use. When we said Arriflex, he was quite shocked. He suggested that we use the Mitchell camera. We said we were shooting on live locations, meaning in real houses, offices, roads, etc., and not sets and therefore did not need the big heavy camera which was more suited to shooting inside studios. 'Vinod Khanna is so tall and big, how will you shoot with a small camera?' he countered. Of course, we did not point out that the size of the camera has nothing to do with the size of the subject! Those were the days when technical know-how, by and large, was very limited even with the people in the trade.

Most feature films in those days were shot on constructed sets in the shooting studios which had catwalks and 'tarafas' – planks tied across the set to facilitate lighting from above – and heavy cameras and lighting equipment. It was the FTII technicians who popularized live locations on coming into the industry as they preferred real locations, which looked authentic, and lighter equipment. The offshoot was that with the popularity of live locations, by the '80s, many bungalows were built or renovated with well-furnished interiors and hired out for film shoots.

The character played by Shabana was that of a well-to-do middle-class Maharashtrian housewife, and her saris and jewellery were very typical. While we were doing the costumes of the film, we ran into a bit of a disagreement with her. The type of character she was playing, when at home, mostly in the afternoons or night, commonly wore what was called a 'housecoat' or 'duster-coat', which was a knee-length cotton light coat often worn over a petticoat. Shabana argued that no one wore clothes like that and challenged us to convince her. Right across our building lived Kiran Shantaram and his wife Jyoti who were good friends with us. We went to their house one afternoon with Shabana, without prior notice, and rang the doorbell. Jyoti opened the door dressed exactly like that – in a housecoat worn over a sari petticoat. Shabana conceded graciously and wore whatever we thought was appropriate for the film.

Those days stars worked in many films at a time. There were no bound scripts except maybe a handful of the few hundred films made annually. Most of the time, scripts were written in hotel rooms and dialogues written invariably on the shooting floors. Vinod was quite surprised when we had a couple of sessions with him working on the character, to help him understand who he was in the film – the back story, the beliefs the character had, behavioural traits, motivations, etc. We called those sittings character-imbibing sessions and went into pretty minute details, including even the kind of underwear the characters wore. Once the background work was done the actors were free to perform.

The first day of shooting that Vinod arrived for was at a live location – a penthouse apartment done up pretty conservatively, suited to the characters living in that house in the film. When he came in, we showed him into what was supposed to be the make-up cum resting room – a spare bedroom with an attached toilet in the house. When he asked us about the costume, we got him the clothes ourselves, ironed and on a hanger ready to wear. When he asked for a drink we got him a Coke too. Vinod was quite taken aback to see his directors doing such tasks.

When he saw our commitment to detail and everything happening inside and outside the shot, he told us that he had not done the necessary preparation and that if we let him off that day, he would come fully prepared the following day. And he was true to his word, delivering a powerful performance in the film. He spent a lot of time with us and the unit on the shoots even when he was not required. He often brought chocolates for the unit. Having him around helped a great deal in bonding.

In the mid-seventies, the zoom lens was a pretty new tool for people, or so it seemed because the zoom was used so indiscriminately and thoughtlessly in Hindi films. Perhaps as a reaction, we made the entire film using block lenses, without the zoom, except in the last shot of the film when the end title comes on just so to make a point that we do know what a zoom is.

The editing of *Shaque* was talked about a lot – critics opined that it broke new ground. Those days, the editing pattern of most Hindi films was pretty stereotyped. A character 'X' would be speaking and the shot would cut when he finished and 'Y' would then take over and speak. So both just kept speaking to each other and it looked like no one was listening. There were hardly any pauses either. It seemed to me that the black and white films which were pure narratives were better cut.

What we did was overlap chunks of dialogue on the listener so that we could see the profound impact the information had on him or her. Especially given the subject of the film, where the character of Shabana thinks that her husband may be a murderer and is keenly listening for any information that anybody could provide about the involvement of her husband in the murder.

The story of *Shaque* revolves around Shabana's doubts that Vinod may be guilty. Since she loves him, she is driven to investigate by reading the old newspapers in the archives and meeting people from his past. When she finally meets the person, played by Utpal Dutt, who aroused her suspicion by sending her a letter, what he says is very critical to how she deals with it in her life.

He describes the murder and his own plight as Shabana listens and her belief in her husband is gradually destroyed and the spectators get to witness it in a scene so ably performed by Shabana. Utpal-da was brilliant too in the way he played that scene, weaving the web of lies around her, so low key, gradually demolishing the trust of a wife for her husband.

Another aspect of *Shaque* that was different from the films of those days was the love scenes. There were no couples running around trees, no gyrating bodies, or women dancing in the rain. There were no semi-nude bodies writhing either or songs with double entendre and hidden 'sexy' meanings, all of which began in the late '70s and became the trend in the '80s. Justifying that kind of content, which had nothing to do with the stories they told, there were some film-makers who openly claimed that they were not social workers and not responsible for how the content in their films was received by the public at large.

The scenes in *Shaque,* whether in bed or in the sitting room, were intimate; it was like the husband and wife had been together and their bodies too were comfortable with each other and it was apparent whichever frame they were in.

In fact, early in the film, there is a scene in which Vinod and Shabana are in bed together, asleep. The alarm rings. Vinod shuts it off and wakes up Shabana in a cosy, intimate way. Just before the scene, Shabana turned to us and said, 'I don't know how married couples behave ... show me what you want.' So Vikas and I actually got on to the bed and demonstrated what we had in mind for her and Vinod to do. They did the shot very well and we got feedback from many people saying that they loved the love scenes and at the end of the film many couples said that they walked out holding hands.

But we had problems with the CBFC. The committee of the CBFC is made up of normal people but when they sit in a censor's chair something weird happens to them. It was so then, has continued to be that way even now and considering how things are, it will continue to be the way it is in the future too.

We had a scene in the film wherein Shabana walks into the sea, wishing to end her life as she cannot bear to be with her husband who she thinks is a murderer and yet cannot leave him because divorce is not an option for her. She loves him and, unable to deal with the situation which renders her helpless, she chooses to give up her life altogether. Just at that moment, Vinod finds what he has been searching for – the proof of his innocence – and as he comes to the beach looking for his wife, he realizes she has walked into the sea. He jumps in, swims up to her and rescues her.

He carries her back to their beach house, puts her on a 'divan' and covers her with a quilt since she is shivering. He then lies down next to her and revives her. He caresses her and kisses her forehead and ear and neck while a song is playing in the background. The whole song was done in four trolley shots, with the camera mounted on a trolley.

The CBFC asked us to cut large portions of the scene which, if cut, would cease to exist because we did not have any spare shots and we could not keep cutting in and out. According to them, in their words, in the letter they wrote, 'the couple is performing coitus', and that needed to be cut. There was no way that Vinod and Shabana could be deemed doing that, given their physical positions but the guys at the CBFC were adamant. Finally they chopped a bit of the entangled toes and the beginnings and ends of the shots.

Those days, and they had the gall to do it, they would run the film on the Steenbeck and tell you what to cut and where to resume from. They did not have a clue about movies or continuity but they had the power to bring even established film-makers to heel.

When we had about ten days left of the schedule, Vinod had to cancel the shoot for some reason. It took a few months, maybe a year, to make up for the lost time. Meanwhile, I got pregnant and had my second child. Then we got the dates to complete shooting the climax which was on the terrace of a building called Donald House in Colaba. It was an all-night shoot and my baby was only a few months old. I was still nursing him and, in my effort to be the best mother in the world, I did not want to put him on the bottle. I had breastfed my daughter and weaned her straight to the cup and wished to do the same for my son. So we decided to take him along.

We managed to get a spare room in the building in a flat that was empty, had it cleaned up and set up a kind of resting room. We hired a nurse to accompany us to the shoots. But Vikas's mother was not happy with the arrangement. So she came along with us for about two weeks, staying up all night to be with her grandson while we shot. I was feeding my son every three or four hours and I would set up the shot and go down to feed the baby while the lighting was going on. Then I would come up again, take the shot and go back down when it was feed time. It was not easy at all, but I was determined to fulfil both my responsibilities and commitments and Vikas was a great support right through.

Once the shooting was over, it was easier to manage the other post-shooting processes. We edited the film at Famous Studios, which was close to our home, so going back and forth was not a problem. But the atmosphere in the studio building at that time, in the '70s, was a bit strange. There were a lot of production offices as well as editing rooms in Famous. We would often see girls walking about in the corridors, entering the offices or leaving them, accompanied by their mothers or some seedy-looking men. We wondered what it was all about until one day somebody told us what was actually happening.

We knew that hundreds of girls from all over the country came to Bombay to become film stars. Somebody would take them to meet the producer in his office. The producer's office typically had, apart from the desk and chairs and a sofa, a large noticeboard on the wall, very often done in velvet and pinned on it would be photographs of the company's old and new productions. There would be close-ups/portraits of stars, the producer posing with them, some working stills and production stills for publicity.

Every girl who entered that office must have visualized herself in the portraits in place of the glamorous stars. The producer would sweet-talk the girls into believing that they might be chosen as the next star in the making. To make the act even more convincing to the mother and daughter duo, he would pick up the phone, dial a number and pretend to talk to 'Kaka', as Rajesh Khanna was called, and tell him that he had found the perfect girl to co-star with him. He would describe her in a flattering way, so much so the girl and her mother would believe that they had arrived on the first steps to stardom. Some producers even signed on the girls, giving them a small advance as a token of their commitment.

What followed, we were told, were script sessions in hotel rooms, screen tests and such exercises done to convince the girl to give her virginity to the godfather-producer just to see her name in the limelight. After he had had enough of the girl, the producer would concoct a story of the film being delayed and would send her to another producer friend. He would speak flatteringly of the girl and when the girl went to him, a similar scenario would play out.

The girl and her mother, probably thinking that if not this producer maybe the next one would surely give the girl a break, kept doing the rounds of office after office because no one would reject the girl outright. They would just use her and dispose of her too. After being passed around from producer to producer with her hopes dwindling and desperation rising, the girl, jaded and tired, would finally end up as a junior artist or as commercial sex worker in the red-light area; or perhaps, if she had enough style, she would end up as a call girl in Colaba.

Many of those producers never came into the industry to make a film and many of the films they launched never got completed or released. But they got what they came for – a brush with the glamour world and all the fringe benefits that the industry provided, at the expense of the star-struck girls.

Those days a kind of dance or cabaret number was an important box-office ingredient in Hindi movies and luckily enough we could have a character who could be an authentic cabaret dancer in a restaurant in the film. But we were clear that we were not going to do a typical Hindi film dance number. Our quest for authenticity led us to a restaurant called Mandarin in Colaba, where cabarets and striptease numbers were performed twice a night. I was advised not to go and Vikas was warned against taking me along, but I insisted on going. So off we went to do our research.

The women who performed were not very young nor shapely either. They stripped and danced, marching around naked but what disturbed me was not the women so much but the men at the tables, drooling, tongues hanging out, not even blinking their lust-laden eyes, making obscene gestures and trying to grab the girls. I did feel sorry for the women who had to do that to make a living, but this blatant exploitation of women sickened me so much, young and impressionable as I was, that I actually fell ill. I was down with a severe bout of diarrhoea and vomiting for the next few days. Of course, people got a chance to say, 'We told you not to go!'

Years later, watching the cabaret, strip dancing or body show in Moulin Rouge or Folies Bergere in Paris was different. The presentation was impeccable, the detailing and coordination mind-boggling! They brought a certain class and polish to the performance as against the crude stuff that was churned out in India. The women in those shows looked like they were proud to show off their assets while in the Indian version, the women looked helpless and desperate and their make-up could not hide that.

Coming back to the film, Bindu had been finalized to play Rosie's character and we chose to do the striptease a la Mandarin. She was very cooperative and professional. The striptease was designed in a way that allowed for the many layers of clothing to be taken off. We had Bhanu Athaiya and Mani Rabadi to do Bindu's costumes in a realistic mould. We got all the other costumes of the film made by the regular tailors because we did not want filmy-looking clothes but what real, normal people wore. We wanted a special prop for the striptease which was a shaggy carpet for Bindu to writhe on and almost make love to. We searched all over Bombay for such a piece and finally found it.

We now turned our focus on the customers in the restaurant. Those days junior artists were called extras and there were agents who brought them for the shootings according to one's requirement. As per the association rules, we could not have non-card holders like one's friends in the film, because they would be doing someone out of their legitimate earnings. Most of the junior artists in Hindi movies did not look like they belonged in the scene, especially the party ones where they would stand in the background holding glasses. They did not look educated or rich even when they stood against fancy sets or in posh bungalows. We decided that we would select them so that they looked like real customers. We were told that every day the junior artists would meet at the office and we could select them there. So off we went accompanied by the junior artist supplier, as he is called.

It was certainly not what we expected. The junior artist situation was pathetic, to say the least. Apart from a little cabin with a desk and two chairs, the place was designed like a small arena or stadium with tiered seating all around. The junior artists would be sitting on the steps around us and we would be in the centre picking and choosing who we wanted, off the shelf as it were. It almost felt like we were pointing at animals or even inanimate objects. We felt very uncomfortable doing that because the selection process was so undignified. The entire set-up suggested scant respect for the obviously less-privileged fellow beings. Most of the junior artists looked bedraggled, bleary-eyed and hungry, even destitute, as if they had been picked off the streets. There was no way we could place them in a fancy restaurant. We shook our heads sadly and said we needed to see some others.

The guy who had shown us the junior artists told us that there were many more shooting at different studios whom we could go and meet. We visited four or five sets before we could find enough artists to represent the customers. We had a nice Parsi family, some who looked like people who were out for a pleasant evening, some who looked like bachelors and some Punjabis and Sikhs, who looked like they enjoyed food and fun. It seemed like the cosmopolitan crowd one sees in any posh Bombay restaurant. We selected some more people who were basically musicians to make up the live band and a young girl to play the crooner.

Since it was a striptease we decided to shoot it in a studio. We had our art director build a circular set for the restaurant with steps. We made sure we used regular building material for the finish, including straw matting that was popular then, because we wanted the set to look like a real restaurant and did not fancy a shiny, filmy, unreal one.

The dance was quite sensuous and certainly not vulgar. In fact, what I thought vulgar were the huge larger-than-life cut-outs of Bindu dressed minimally, at a couple of theatres, with her arm moving up and down, dangling a bra or bikini top. These were put up by the distributors when the film was released. It was extremely embarrassing and the film wasn't even about the sexy dance number or titillation. If Vikas and I would have known beforehand, we would never have approved that kind of publicity.

We had layered the film and it worked at three different levels. At one level it was a murder mystery, at another, a love story of a man and his wife and the concept of trust in a relationship and, at a still deeper level, about a woman who has her own opinions and choices – a woman for whom a compromise is not possible as she thinks no matter how much she loves him, she can't live with a murderer.

During the making of this film, a terrible tragedy struck us. Vasant Desai, our dear Fatfati Mama, passed away in a horrible freak accident inside a lift.

One evening, Vikas and I were supposed to go out but for some reason I was hesitating. Suddenly, Fatfati Mama's secretary came running up three floors, mumbling, 'Something has happened and saheb is not OK.' It was difficult to comprehend what he was saying, so Vikas and I rushed down with him.

We could not believe our eyes when we got there. Fatfati Mama's head was stuck in the elevator between two floors while his body dangled in mid-air. Vikas moved in quickly and held him up, supporting him from below. He told the secretary to tell my mother-in-law to call for the doctor and instructed our Man Friday, Gopal, to call the building caretaker to manually bring the lift down so that his head could be freed. Someone also went to call the fire brigade. In a few minutes, as we watched and prayed, the lift shook and shuddered as it moved up freeing Fatfati Mama, who fell into the pit. People jumped in and brought him out. He was rushed to Jaslok Hospital, which was just ten minutes away. As we waited at home, still praying fervently for his recovery, we got the news that he was gone. He had been dead on arrival. Vikas said he had felt Fatfati Mama's life ebbing away when he was holding him up.

According to his secretary, all Fatfati Mama did was open the collapsible door of the lift and place one foot inside. At that very moment the lift shot up with the door open. Fatfati Mama lost his balance and fell backwards and his head got stuck in the gap between the doors and the wall.

His demise was a huge loss for us because he was the one who held the whole family together with his good cheer, humour and encouragement. Every evening, when he came back from his music room or recording, he would share with us what he had done during the day. We got to learn a lot from him.

When Fatfati Mama died there was still one more song to be recorded. *Shaque* was his last film and we did not want anybody else's music in the film. So we thought of a novel idea. We took an old song of his which had been recorded but not used and asked Gulzar to write new lyrics for that composition. The words Gulzar wrote were some of the most romantic that I have ever heard. The song '*Ek dil hai ek jaan hai …ek jaane jaan…*' was sung by Vani Jairam and Mohammed Rafi and they brought out the romance with every word.

We recorded it afresh with Enoch Daniels who had worked with him earlier, keeping in mind Vasant Desai's style of orchestration. It was a background number and I wonder now if we wasted it by keeping it in the background.

When it came to doing the background score, once again we wanted to use only Fatfati Mama's compositions. We sat with his assistants and selected some melodies after listening to some of his old compositions. Enoch Daniels put it all together and did a fabulous job.

Vasant Desai had a place in his heart for everyone and people called him God's own good man. There was no challenge he would not take up. Once when Pandit Nehru remarked to him that there were no common songs children sang in India like in other countries, and bemoaned the fact that not many could even sing the National Anthem together in one tune, he decided to do something about it. He began teaching the National Anthem to schoolchildren in Bombay and covered hundreds of primary and secondary schools. The following year when Nehru visited Bombay, he had more than one lakh children singing the anthem in one voice at Shivaji Park. Nehru was very moved by this vision of a strong, united secular India of his dreams.

Films and film music have always been able to reach the masses and there have been some people in the industry who have tried to utilize that to transform society. Vasant Desai was one of them.

During the Chinese and Pakistani aggressions he taught patriotic songs to school children and also created brass bands playing martial tunes with musically inclined mill workers. He organized mass singing choirs and rallies and reached into the interiors of Maharashtra to create unity and oneness in the rural areas under the movement 'Ek Sur Ek Taal'.

During the Gandhi centenary, in 1969, he created a song out of Gandhiji's letter, '*Hey namrata ke samrat*'. Making a song out of prose, that too a letter, was a big challenge, but he rose to the occasion so ably. Manna Dey sang the composition brilliantly and it is a hugely inspiring number.

Though Fatfati Mama was in the movies, he did not hanker after popularity nor did he cultivate people to get ahead in life. He was a purist and pursued his work with integrity and left no stone unturned to achieve excellence. He was very encouraging and loving and so proud of me, I could not have had a better person to be inspired and influenced by at such an early stage in my career. It is not surprising therefore that I do workshops, often gratis, to empower people, on a range of topics, be it in film-making, or just life, covering subjects like women's issues, self-discovery, gender sensitization, sexual harassment and safety for women, and so on.

6
DELVING INTO THE UNKNOWN

After the success of *Shaque*, Vikas and I got offers to do a remake or do something similar. But we wanted to do something different that would really excite and challenge us. We had always been inspired by Ayn Rand (I still am!), so we zeroed in on *Night of January 16th*. We got the funding organized and the casting was done; we signed on Vinod Khanna and Zeenat Aman. We discussed some basics about the set design with Bansi Chandragupta, a very well-known art director from Calcutta who had worked with Satyajit Ray, because we did not want the typical Bollywood look.

But things took a different turn when Vinod decided to follow the spiritual guru Bhagwan Shree Rajneesh, also known as Osho, to Oregon in the United States. Vinod and a lot of film folks, namely, Mahesh Bhatt, Vijay Anand and Sural Sanim were followers of Osho in those days and often spent a lot of time in Pune at his ashram.

For some reason we could not or did not pursue that subject and our partner distributor suggested we make a quickie. Back then and even now, I have always felt that there is no dearth of subjects to draw upon from real life. I have always been fascinated about black magic and witchcraft, the spooky and the mysterious, the unknown and the unpredictable, from childhood. As a little girl, I had watched my family, particularly my mother, deal with lemons with kumkum on them in our compound, or little figures with weird marks and signs of worship with the tell-tale smears of haldi and kumkum buried in the garden in Bangalore. Until we moved to Bangalore I had never heard of such things, but apparently it was common in the south to do black magic and put a hex or spell on some family to create obstacles in their life. Obviously those things were planted by someone to create problems for our family. Since we didn't believe that stuff, my mother would throw those things in the garbage or have them burnt.

I had shared an idea for this film while we were working on *Shaque*, which had enthused Vikas, but our partner, Mr Kamat, had put it aside as not viable commercially. Meanwhile, *The Exorcist* had been released and its runaway success prompted all of us to look at this subject again, in the Indian context.

We decided to make a real scary, horror film, definitely not fantasy or make-believe. We were neither believers nor people who were just fascinated. Having the film grounded in reality meant doing a lot of research. We had to delve into the practices of witchcraft, mantra and tantra and study their effects and implications. We got the well-known playwright Vijay Tendulkar on board. Thus began our journey into the unknown.

It was not easy tracking down black or white magicians – the victims were comparatively easier to find. But they led us eventually to all kinds of practitioners, from the deeply spiritual and knowledgeable to the charlatans. The people we met spoke about seeing ghostly apparitions on moonlit nights, or at high tide or on new moon days. Some people had a strange experience like when they were about to take the first morsel of food from their plate, the food would turn to worms and maggots, sometimes even turd, as a result of which they would be repulsed and not eat. Many of them fell ill, eventually dying of starvation and weakness. There were also highly dramatic stories of how business deals were broken or marriages destroyed because someone had put a curse on them. Fascinating stories of how a woman would be drawn to a man who desired her, because of a magic spell like vashikaran, and submit to him, totally and mindlessly. There were incidents of out-of-body experience, souls taking over bodies, in fact a whole gamut of them too difficult to enumerate.

However, we culled a handful of stories that we altered to create the backbone of our script for *Gehrayee*. The central theme, of a girl being possessed by another soul that had entered her body and have her take on a new persona, came from the experiences of two people.

There was a Christian girl, I think a Protestant, who was the sister of a well-known regional-language writer. This girl was sixteen years old and went to college with her friends. One day, while they were going home they came across some lemons and chillies with haldi and kumkum on them along with a few flowers and betel leaves under a tree. It looked like these things had been a part of some puja. As they were about to step over it, one of the girls remarked that it wouldn't be safe to do so and that they should go around it. It was pure superstition for the Christian girl. She disregarded her friend's advice and stepped over it.

When she reached home she was very, very quiet. After some time she began to speak in Urdu in a male voice. Initially her mother and sister did not understand what she was saying but when they realized that she was not play-acting, they became very nervous. They were scared to say the least but the male voice calmed them down and asserted his presence. He told them not to worry and that he would be around for some time. They were so afraid of what people might think they did not dare tell anyone what was happening.

They found the Urdu of the man who had possessed the girl very sophisticated and cultured. There were many words they could not understand and the character actually took the trouble to explain the words to them. The whole family was in a tizzy because they didn't know what to make of it. Was she really possessed? Did such things actually happen? They thought they should talk to the priest and figure out a plan of action.

That night the girl was attacked by some mysterious force. There were bruises on her body the next morning. It was apparent that the unknown invisible force had beaten her up the previous night. The girl was in terrible pain. A priest was summoned. He prayed and said he would talk to a senior as he was not an exorcist and could not really do much. They knew they had to get help somehow and the search for white and black magicians began.

From what was revealed, it was found that the soul belonged to a professor from Lucknow who had died in an accident. The professor was very courteous and well-mannered and insisted on speaking in Urdu, as a result of which the family began to learn the language and understand its nuances. He even taught the family the finer points of Urdu poetry and sher o shayari.

All that was not much of a problem, if it wasn't for the beatings the girl got from time to time. The professor began to apologize in chaste Urdu and talked of his majboori (helplessness). The other weird thing was that she would ask for biryani and consume large quantities of food. But strangely enough, she began to lose weight and became very skinny.

The worried mother and sisters finally found a black or white magician. The time was set. They waited anxiously but the man did not show up. Who showed up instead was the professor, chuckling that the magician would not make it – he had been warned enough and would not dare come to the house. The efforts to find a mantrik, someone who would succeed in casting out the soul that possessed the girl's body with the help of sacred chants, continued.

One day, a highly recommended mantrik arrived. He did the exorcism ritual puja and got into a conversation with the professor. The professor told him that he would not be able to get rid of him. He had come to stay and he would, until his time was up. He challenged the mantrik to do his best. Eventually the mantrik was forced to concede defeat.

On another occasion, the whole family went for a Bollywood movie. The professor was quite agitated throughout the film and when the family returned home, he shred the film to pieces in an elaborate critique, chastising the elders of the family for showing such crap to the youngsters. He waxed eloquent on culture and tradition.

By now news of the girl being possessed had spread far and wide and people came forward to help with all kinds of solutions. One of them was taking the girl to a temple, somewhere in Maharashtra, where snakes lived in the inner sanctum. They were told that the best way to get rid of the possession was to have a snake bite the girl. The family steeled themselves to go through the ordeal and went to the temple. Just as they were about to enter its inner sanctum, the professor came on. He said he could not enter the holy sanctum of that temple but he would wait outside for them because he was sure that they would not be able to do what they had come to do. The family entered the temple but when the snake showed itself, they could not go through it. No sane, educated person would want to risk the poor girl's life – what if she died? They came out to meet the joyous professor who accompanied them back home.

A friend of the writer was a philosopher who also dabbled in spirituality. He would often come over and interact with the professor, discuss poetry, life and philosophy. One day he challenged the professor and questioned his credibility. The professor then gave him the details of his name and address in Lucknow. I don't remember now if they checked it out. The philosopher friend then dared the professor to reveal himself in a physical form. The professor turned down his request as impossible. But the philosopher was not going to take no for an answer.

After a lot of pestering, the professor agreed to show himself but warned him that he would lose his sleep for good if he saw him. That night the philosopher friend was in his house, sitting by the window writing. He heard a sound and looked up, out of the window. What he saw was a bloodied, disfigured face of a man. He seemed to have been run over by a train. The sight was so horrendous that the friend continued to have nightmares for a long time after that and lost his peace of mind just as the professor had predicted.

A few months had passed. The possessed girl's health was deteriorating so much that the sister took her to a doctor. The doctor conducted various tests and told the family that he was surprised that the girl was still alive. He said there was hardly any intake of food for months and her intestine had shrunk so much that it could not accept any food. He recommended a long series of treatments.

The professor had become like a member of the family but they felt helpless and were sure that they were going to lose their daughter. By now, there was no hope and they had almost given up. Out of the blue, one day, news came that there was some possibility still of saving the girl. Desperate now, the family decided to go to Ganagapur in north Karnataka.

Ganagapur, situated on the banks of the river Bhima in Gulbarga district, is the holy place of God Dattatreya who is known to fulfil wishes and provide cures for all afflictions. So off they went and followed the instructions to the tee. They were told to stay in the temple premises and live off the alms – whatever they got from people's contributions. The professor was unhappy with the arrangement because he could not go into the temple most of the time where the girl stayed. After a few weeks of rigorous hardship, the girl's health began to improve and there was no sign of the professor.

They returned to Bombay. The possessed girl had no recollection of what had transpired in her life in the past year. She got back into a normal routine and even got married the following year.

Another incident which we found relevant and useful happened in Bangalore. A young Roman Catholic boy, around sixteen or seventeen years old, the nephew of some good friends of the family, had an accident and was taken to Vani Vilas Hospital in the city. When they got into emergency, there was no free bed or stretcher available to place the boy. A staff turned to the occupied table on which lay the body of a dead man, lifted it and put it on the floor and placed the young boy on the table.

When the young boy regained consciousness he started speaking in Tamil, which he had never done before. He talked about his wife and children and how they would be worried. He talked of the bus accident in which he had been injured and brought to the hospital. The boy was taken home after some treatment but continued to talk about his family in Tamil Nadu. A Catholic priest tried exorcizing the spirit but the matter was not put to rest until the spirit met his own family and decided to find peace. For that to happen, the family had to go all the way to a small town in Tamil Nadu and get the closure they were seeking and freedom for the young boy.

Vijay Tendulkar, Vikas and I met a lot of victims and practitioners of this magic and had some strange experiences as well. One night, while we were discussing the script, a young maid in our house had a fit, blabbering stories of another time, another life. She cried, beat her chest and rolled on the floor, leaving us completely stumped. We had no idea how to deal with her. The male servants brought out onions, had her sniff them, rubbed her hands and the soles of her feet, etc., until she calmed down after a couple of hours. But it appeared to be more out of sheer exhaustion than anything else. Of course, we were warned not to dabble in these matters and play with dark forces but we continued on the trail we had chosen to walk on.

We decided to set the film in Bangalore – we felt it would be more credible with a family from the south. A few months later, the script of *Gehrayee* (1980) was completed. Simultaneously we had started work on getting the cast in. We had Padmini Kolhapure as the adolescent girl who is possessed. Dr Sriram Lagoo was to play her father Chennabasappa, with a scientific outlook, and Indrani Mukherjee her mother Saroja, who was god-fearing and religious. Anant Nag was to play the elder brother, attached to his sister, willing to go to any lengths to protect her, very emotional and vulnerable. We had a good supporting cast as well with Sudhir Dalvi playing the good mantrik, Suhas Bhalekar as the poor, broken, battered soul out to seek revenge and Rita Bhaduri as his daughter who brings the story to its horrific climax. Amrish Puri played a dangerous black magician, a tantrik. He was so threatening and evil in the film that when Steven Spielberg was casting for *Indiana Jones and the Temple of Doom*, the reference we sent of Amrish's performance and look in *Gehrayee* was bang on and landed him the role.

Bangalore lent itself perfectly for the film we were making. Cubbon Park with its countless hundred-year-old trees was spooky, especially when the weather was overcast. We had the scene where Padmini is walking with her cycle and senses a strange presence, somebody following her and nobody actually there in physical form. It gets so eerie that she drops her cycle and runs like the devil is after her.

The scene was shot with a handheld camera and it was a challenge for the cameraman who had to run not only forward but also backward. Having graduated from the film institute in Pune we were all very much at home with the handheld Arriflex camera and we pushed the boundaries of what we could do with it. *Gehrayee* was not an easy film for a cinematographer, and Barun Mukherjee, the cameraman and a very dear friend, brought a lot to the film, doing everything that we asked for and more in lighting and executing the shots the way we had designed them.

The scene in Cubbon Park, even silent, was very scary, with a sense of foreboding and dread. But adding sound to it intensified the feeling by several notches. Laxmikant–Pyarelal were composing the music and when we were doing the background score, Pyarebhai, who is an absolute genius, thought of some unconventional inputs, one of which was the Tibetan singing bowls and the other, a visiting musician from the United States of America who played different flutes. What was interesting, however, was that this musician was able to produce strange guttural sounds from his throat which didn't seem human; they sounded like they were from some other dimension, perhaps from an alien world, another galaxy or what seemed like a supernatural world of spirits, beyond the normal scope of the human eye and ear.

The scene looked perfect with the music and effects, but it is amazing how every single technician adds something to a scene. We were mixing the film with the re-recording pioneer Mangesh Desai at Rajkamal Studios and we had almost done the final take when Mangesh Dada had a brainwave. He got sounds of Grand Prix racing cars from his library and added them to the track. I cannot describe what it did to the scene – we had our audience so gripped that they were literally afraid to move.

At this point, I am very tempted to share an anecdote of Mangesh Desai. He was a demanding technician and verbal abuse came naturally to him. Most people who worked with him were afraid of him, especially his own staff and the editors whose tracks were not perfect. But he was the best in his field and people came from all over India to work with him, including Satyajit Ray. Once, there was a foreign director who had made a film in India and got his mixing done with Mangesh Desai. Mangesh communicated with his staff in the projection room through a talk-back system and instead of addressing them by their names he would call them gadvano (donkeys in Marathi). When the foreign director was leaving he thanked Mangesh profusely and the gadvanos too, not realizing that it was Mangesh's word for them and meant donkeys.

The film *Sholay* was mixed in London and the industry was rife with stories about Mangesh's interaction with the British technicians. Apparently the use of abusive words was banned in the London studio and Mangesh Desai could not restrain his colourful language. We were told that he had been fined many times and with foreign exchange being dear, paying in pounds had become an expensive affair for him and the producer.

Another tool we used effectively in *Gehrayee* was the crab dolly, which is a camera dolly that has the ability to move in any direction and does not need rails like conventional trolleys. There was only one available in Bombay, maybe in India at that time, and it belonged to Merchant Ivory Productions. Booking it was as difficult as getting a star's dates. We used it to move from room to room with speed when something was afoot (with the spirits). The house we shot in had thresholds between every room and we had to lay a platform of plywood over all of them to facilitate the movement of the camera which, in one scene, literally rushed from room to room.

Sometimes, the way we planned our shots, where we kept the camera, the lens we used, the field, the angle, the height of the camera and its movement, the characters' movement, all were very complex and were not very easy to light up. It seemed every now and then that we were just throwing challenges at Barun and making his life difficult. One day it so happened that, in one of the bedrooms, we wanted to take a 360-degree shot. Since all sides were exposed there was no place for the lights. Barun shook his head and said, 'Not possible, you have to give me some place to keep the lights.' I was adamant. 'No, it has to be this way.' Then I said to the others in the room, 'Everyone, please leave this room. Let Barun-da figure it out.'

I said to him, 'I don't know how you will do it, but find a way. We'll come back in half an hour.' Before half an hour had passed, Barun had found a way to do the lighting.

Overhead lighting can be done easily in a studio because the studios are designed for that but in a live location it is very difficult unless there are beams or some such contraptions. In those days we did have what were called 'king poles', again brought in by Merchant Ivory Productions, not commonly available in the industry. Also called auto poles, they were poles that could be fitted vertically or horizontally across the room, wall to wall, and lights could be hung from them. But they came in a certain size and it was not easy to fit them anywhere. Besides, one had to be careful not to put too much weight on those bars. Lights falling from above and causing injuries to people even in studios was quite common and dangerous. But Barun found a way to fit them and we took the shot as designed.

A disastrous thing happened at the end of the shooting schedule, when there were just a few more days left. The owners of the house we were shooting in suddenly demanded a huge sum of money, without which they would not allow us to continue the shooting. We had already paid them the rent for the entire shoot in advance. We were in a tight spot. There was no way we could change the house as it was already established as the protagonist's house. Continuity in the film demanded that we somehow make it work and complete that part of the shoot in the same location. There was no time for negotiation either as it was a tightly planned rigorous shoot and the actors' dates and travel arrangements were fixed. We eventually coughed up the extra money somehow and completed all the scheduled work in that house. It was certainly a drain on our resources as the film we were making was a low-budget one.

One thing that we had learnt was whatever location you may be in, it is only what is in the frame that matters. Though a major portion of the shoot was done in the protagonist's house, there were still many other locations to shoot at. We managed to save a lot of money by shooting at my mother's house, which was a large sprawling bungalow, set in six acres of land with mango trees and a guava orchard, as well as a thickly wooded area. The compound even had a silk cotton tree and I remember that just one tree produced so much cotton that it was enough to make cushions for the entire household. I still have some cushions made from the cotton from that tree.

We used thirteen areas in that same compound and house as different locations. There's no way anyone can guess that it was all part of my mother's house and compound.

A scene that drew a lot of attention was the one where Amrish Puri as the evil black magician had hypnotized Padmini through vashikaran and was invoking the Goddess in her so that he could have sex with the Goddess, amassing enormous power in the process. That's what tantriks do to achieve siddhi, we were told. The background was a broken-down temple where the yoni pooja was being performed. Padmini was supposed to be nude in that scene and though unintentional, a lot of curiosity got generated, the buzz being whether she was actually nude or not during the shoot.

To begin with, the scene was very much an integral part of the script. I had personally promised Padmini's parents that Padmini would not be uncomfortable in any way and she wouldn't be exposed. And though she looked nude in the film, she was not actually so.

Films are all about make-believe and simulating reality, not having something actually happen in the frame except maybe in documentaries or that genre of film.

But journalists can be strange. Looking to create a sensation, they wanted to find out if Padmini was indeed nude in the scene while the shooting was happening. They kept asking me the question again and again, not willing to believe what I was saying.

Finally, I sent them to Amrish. Amrish laughed at their question and said she hadn't exposed at all. I had used my mustard-coloured shawl, fixed halter-style with a ribbon, to fully cover her from the front so that even if a little bit of the shawl was visible, it blended with the fire in front of her. Her long hair covered most of her back – the nude effect was simulated. It was just smart shooting without the use of any special effects.

People often wondered how Vikas and I actually worked together because two people directing is very rare, perhaps as rare as two people painting a canvas or writing poetry. We did everything together. How can two people think so much alike? Were we pretending to be on the same page on most of the things? To check this out for ourselves we decided to do a small exercise. We took a scene from *Gehrayee* and told each other to do the shot division, after which we would compare notes and see how similar or different we were. In that scene, we had ten shots and of that nine were exactly the same. We were quite surprised by the result.

When Padmini is possessed by the spirit and it speaks in its own voice, we used Jalal Agha's voice and when Suhas Bhalekar speaks from the body of his daughter, played by Rita Bhaduri, we used her voice along with Bhalekar's. The effect was not only very different but also authentic and created a powerful impact.

In the film industry they say that any publicity is good publicity. Before the release of *Gehrayee*, Prince Charles had visited India and had gone to Rajkamal Studios to see a film shoot. Padmini was shooting for another film there and she had kissed Prince Charles on the cheek when she met him. That became hot news and our distributor used that to promote *Gehrayee*. 'See the girl who kissed Prince Charles in *Gehrayee*', read the newspaper advertisements. To put it mildly, we were extremely embarrassed.

We had a premiere of the film for Vasant Swar Prathistan, founded to promote Vasant Desai's music and values. The film was premiered in Eros at Churchgate in Bombay and was attended by Amitabh, Jaya and many other celebrities. It did really well as people found it scary and spell-binding.

One habit we cultivated and I still do follow is visit the theatre at different times where one's film is showing to see the reaction of the audience. I remember one such instance towards the end of the film. It was the scene in the cemetery where Anant Nag is trying to get a spirit to talk to him amidst the shrieking of ghosts. The scene was dark and there was pin-drop silence in the theatre. It was very, very scary. For a moment my heart stopped beating. It was as if I was all alone. I could not see anybody else in the audience – I seemed to be stranded in the empty theatre with the ghosts. But it was only in the next scene that I breathed a sigh of relief, when the picture was brighter and I could make out the heads of the audience in silhouette.

After the film we got hundreds of calls from people asking for help, sharing their stories of how magic spells and hexes put on them had affected their lives. They asked for solutions and names of the magicians who could undo the bad effects of somebody's evil design. We used to hear them out sympathetically but did not give any names of the people we had consulted or interacted with. It is very difficult to figure out who is genuine and who is fake and we did not want to misguide them.

We were asked a lot of questions about our personal belief in the phenomena. We did not have any such beliefs but at the same time could not deny that the phenomena existed and affected people. At least during the making of the film we had become temporary believers, I guess. We had a line in the beginning of the film which is self-explanatory. 'No explanation is needed for those who believe and for those who don't, no explanation is possible.'

There were a lot of people who told us not to make the film. They warned us that dabbling in such subjects would have an adverse effect on us – it might even destroy us. Well, within the next few years, a lot that was precious to me was lost – my daughter, my marriage, etc. But I don't think it had anything to do with the subject or making a film on it. People go through difficult circumstances in their lives anyhow and it would be ridiculous to look for cause and effect. I can buy the theory of karma but not this.

7
A REAL-LIFE TRAGEDY

Both Vikas and I loved books and we had a huge collection. The other thing we were passionate about was equipment. It didn't take us a moment to decide what we were going to do with the gifts in the form of cash that we had received at our wedding. Vikas was an avid photographer and we invested the money in getting ourselves a printer and had a darkroom set up. What followed were many nights in the darkroom playing around with the pictures we had taken and getting some phenomenal results. That hobby lasted for a long time but the interest petered out as we got busy and began to raise a family.

The next piece of equipment, which almost literally walked into our life, was an old editing machine, a horizontal model, supposed to be a precursor of the Steenbeck. The Union Table, as it was called, had reportedly belonged to Paul Zils, a famous German documentary film-maker who lived in India. It needed some major repairs before it could function with precision. A guy known to Fatfati Mama had come to sell it to us and we bought it trusting that we could make it work.

We spent time, energy and money and got the machine working to our satisfaction. We had it installed in our bedroom since we stayed with my in-laws and we had to accommodate our stuff in our room. I remember working on it to edit Girish Karnad's documentary on Dattatreya Ramachandra Bendre, the famous poet from Karnataka. When our first child Gaagi arrived, we moved the machine into a little office space in Tardeo. We would hire out the studio with the machine when we were not using it ourselves.

My father always said work is worship and for me, who followed in his footsteps and still lives by that, the workplace is sacred. I was very fastidious about keeping the equipment in top working condition; a fact that attracted many to use our studio and editing facilities. Mani Kaul edited his film *Duvidha* (1973) on the machine in Tardeo, as did many FTII graduates.

Though we had been directing films, we did not let any opportunity to edit films by other directors go by. *Vamsha Vriksha* had been a good experience and we had used it to hone our film-making skills. I think more so because we had a lot of freedom to give shape to the film and experiment with the material.

Shekhar Kapur, whom we knew well, approached us to help him with his film *Masoom* (1983). We were, in essence, his sounding board and he would go back and forth between us and Gulzar, who was writing the film, to get clarity on what he wanted.

Before Shekhar left for the shoot, he worked with us on shot divisions and misc-en-scènes. We spent quite some time with him on the 'imaginary line', which most directors get confused about.

The 'imaginary line' is actually an invisible line connecting two characters or more in a scene. Say, you have A and B. A is on the left side of the frame, looking to the right, and B is on the right side, looking to the left. The imaginary line helps you to maintain that orientation. If that is not taken care of, you might find A sometimes on the right and sometimes on the left, or both looking in the same direction, leaving the the viewer confused. This distraction does not allow the spectator to be with the scene as he starts trying to fix the location and direction of the character.

The situation gets worse with chase scenes. If A is running from the right of the frame to the left and B is chasing him, he too would have to run from the right to the left so both would have to run in the same direction, one behind the other, right to left. After establishing this, if you have a shot showing A running from the left to the right of the frame the viewer would expect him to bump into B because B is still running from right to left. When the imaginary line is crossed, it seems a contradiction to what is already established and the whole tension and momentum is lost. It's imperative that the screen direction and orientation is maintained while shooting so that the spectator gets to see a logical seamless depiction of the scene.

The imaginary line is not carved in stone. It can be crossed if done intelligently. What is important is that at no point is the audience distracted from the narrative because of a film's grammatical mistakes. If the basic grammar of film-making is not followed what the audience gets to see is a shoddy, disconnected, illogical piece of work.

It is critical to maintain the continuity and get the undivided attention of the audience because at no point do you want to lose them. When I talk of continuity, there are many types of continuity that need to be maintained rigorously throughout the shoot. Apart from the direction or orientation continuity, location continuity, costume continuity, make-up continuity, action continuity and so on, are critical – all in the cause of making the audience believe the truth of that moment without getting distracted.

Even now while editing I find many problems with action continuity during shooting. An actor in one angle of the shot uses his right hand and in the next uses his left. It is the editor's skill to cut in such a way that the audience does not notice that the hands have changed doing a piece of action. I remember in *Rihaee*, Naseer puts down a cup with his right hand and in the following shot he uses the left hand to put it down and bring his hand up. But I was able to cut it in a way that nobody noticed the mistake.

We warned Shekhar about all the problems he would face as a first-time director, including continuity and imaginary lines. But to hand it to him, he came back with good material. Shekhar was an eager learner during the edit. Having taught students of mass communication at Sophia Polytechnic and Xavier's Institute of Mass Communication and edited their continuity exercises, I had this habit of raising questions about where the cut should be and why, which would allow the students to apply their minds. Sometimes I would agree with them and sometimes not and then I would decide on the cut and demonstrate to them why it worked better.

With Shekhar, I was not asking questions, he was! He would ask me what if we cut here or there, or why I was choosing a particular frame. At that time the teacher in me would come to the fore and I would go out of the way to explain the fundamental concepts of editing or explain why I was making a certain aesthetic choice. By then, the tape splicer had arrived in the editing rooms, replacing the scissors and cement, and though we cut the film strip physically and joined the two strips with cello tape, we did not lose any part of the frame. So I could actually show him some alternative cuts to demonstrate a point.

I believe that a director who knows editing, or at least understands it, makes for a better director and often a more efficient one. Because at the end of it the final shape is given to a film on the editing table. Also a director with a good editing sense will not shoot his scene from every possible angle and with every lens, as many directors who are unsure of themselves tend to do. An editor-director when sure of his editing pattern will shoot the scenes accordingly and very precisely, not wasting time, energy and resources duplicating material.

However, I found that most assistant directors do not like to attend the editing sessions for some reason and lose out on the huge opportunity of actually understanding how to put a film together and make it work. They then perforce have to rely entirely on the editor. I believe that one of the best places to learn film craft is in the editing room. David Lean, Hrishikesh Mukherjee and now Raju Hirani are fine examples of editor–directors.

Satish Kaushik, basically an actor from the National School of Drama, was assisting Shekhar and he was an exception. He would attend the editing sessions religiously and it is no wonder then that he became a director and went on to make his own films.

Zaakol (1980) was a Marathi film directed by Dr Sriram Lagoo. He acted in it as well along with Tanuja and a Marathi actress Sarla Yeolekar. Govind Nihalani wielded the camera and we edited the film. It was a very dramatic film and it won us a Maharashtra State Award for editing.

We also edited *Phaniyamma* (1983), a Kannada film, directed by Prema Karanth, an alumnus of the National School of Drama and wife of B.V. Karanth. In the '70s and '80s, we had every kind of film: the commercial potboilers, parallel cinema, middle cinema, the NFDC cinema and those literally made on a next-to-nothing budget. *Phaniyamma* was like that, made on a shoestring budget. Shot on 16mm, it was a simple, bare film about a young Brahmin widow in a village. Madhu Ambat was the cameraman and Sharada played the protagonist. It was Prema's sheer passion that drove the film. There was literally no budget for editing and in my commitment to promote good regional cinema I did the film gratis and even gifted Prema with a tape splicer when she returned to Bangalore. The film went to festivals and also won National and state awards.

The editing was not exactly as Prema had envisioned. Sometimes following the script is the worst thing you could do to a film at the editing stage. You need to look at the material from a different perspective. The script is a guide but it cannot be the film. Not everything that looks good on paper, works in the audio-visual medium. This was one such case. I have often done it in my own films too; changed the order of scenes or even cut out my favourite scenes if they held up the narrative in any way.

First, there was a dearth of material, and even with what we had in hand, there were problems. My job was to have Prema tell the story about a widow stuck in a cruel unsympathetic society and tell it well. Prema was willing to shoot a little patchwork and maybe shoot for a day and I told her what I needed to strengthen her narrative. She brought the additional bits, after which I turned the whole film upside down, reshuffled whatever I had and made it work.

Many years later I had a similar experience with the Marathi film *Gabhara* (1999) made on a shoestring budget and directed by Raju Khandagale. There too I worked with the material I had and created a narrative that was not exactly as per the written script. Given that it was Raju's first film there were a lot mistakes but the strength of the acting and the editing saw the film through. It won many Maharashtra state awards and was well worth the effort.

As an editor I always looked at what the director wanted to convey because I believe it is finally the director's call. I would often say to my directors, 'Tell me what you want, not how to do it! It is my job to give you what you want but how I will get that for you is my lookout, considering I am supposed to be the expert.' Even as a writer, I was clear about following the director's lead. Eventually whatever role one plays in a film, one needs to make the film win because when the film wins everyone wins.

We did quite a few things in those days – features, documentaries, corporate films, advertising shorts, editing for other directors, etc. We were particular about the feature films we wanted to make and were looking for the right projects. After the success of *Gehrayee*, we got a couple of offers, ones that we could actually consider. One of them was a project for Mr F.C. Mehra. We finalized the script and did a recce in Delhi for the locations.

The hero, a newcomer we had selected, was also approved by the producer and he was none other than Jackie Shroff who was in those days advertising Char Minar cigarettes and lived in Walkeshwar. The film got delayed and we lost Jackie, who would have debuted with us, to Subhash Ghai.

At that time Vikram, an actor, also an acting graduate from FTII, approached us to make a film. The film *Situm* (1984) was supposed to be based on a real story. It had the background of football and had three very good roles for the lead actors. Obviously Vikram wanted to be in the film and we cast Naseeruddin Shah and Smita Patil in the other roles.

We were not that familiar with football. Cricket was our game and so we started our research. We had to get not only the game and its nuances right but find teams and people. There was another aspect to the film, the medical one – the way in which Naseer dies in the film. Beyond that there was psychiatry involved too.

Naseer and Vikram were the two football players in the film and there was no question of faking it. They needed to be trained and we found a coach who was in the Tata team. Naseer was very enthusiastic about the training and for many months Vikas, Naseer, Vikram and I went at 6 a.m. every day to the football grounds in Chembur just so that the actors could train. To begin with, they had to run around the field a few times followed by exercises and then the training with the ball would follow. Another thing we included in our schedule was watching football matches at the Cooperage ground to get the nuances of the game played by professional teams.

In the film, during a match, Naseer, who is the goalkeeper, gets hit on the head by a ball kicked by Vikram. Naseer collapses, is taken to the hospital, and dies thereafter. We had to get this situation right and after consultation with the medical experts we came to the conclusion that Naseer's character would have something called berry aneurysm. On being hit on the temple, the aneurysm would rupture, leading to his death.

In the film Naseer's wife Smita blames Vikram for the death of her husband. He feels guilty, though he is not really to blame and in spite of asking her for forgiveness, she refuses to forgive him. Vikram's guilt wreaks havoc on his mind, he goes into depression and ends up in a mental asylum. Through hypnosis it is discovered that Vikram blames himself for his parents' death, though he was directly not responsible. The experts advise that if Naseer's wife can absolve him of his guilt, he may improve and begin to lead a normal life.

Smita, who loved Naseer, finds herself unable to deal with her husband's death and struggles to console and comfort their only child. Their child, played by Hith, our son, misses his father and his grieving mother. When Vikram's boss approaches Smita to let Vikram off the hook, she downright refuses. He begs her to at least go to the asylum and meet Vikram. He emotionally blackmails her, waxing eloquent on what her dead husband would have wanted.

She goes to the asylum with Hith and cannot but feel sorry for the man who had caused her husband's death. He is a pale shadow of the confident and aggressive football player she had seen. Hith makes friends with him and as Smita and Hith continue to visit him, he begins to improve. At some point, Smita realizes that she is getting attached to him and has begun to react as a woman does to a man.

She withdraws and stops going to the asylum. Vikram, who has become completely dependent on her, begins to regress. His boss, however, encourages him to go plead his case and declare his love for her. Vikram does that only to have the door shut in his face. He leaves her home dejected but Smita on the other side of the door is heartbroken too, having discovered her feelings for him.

Soon after, she hears the sound of an accident on the road. Thinking it might be Vikram who may have been run over by a vehicle, she rushes out, calling him by name. She pushes herself through the crowd to where the victim is lying under the car and on finding it to be someone else, calls out to Vikram. She sees him, he turns around and they come together in an embrace and the end credits roll.

We had to set up an asylum which was not easy and we wanted a live location. We found a bungalow in Pune near the Osho Ashram and got some actors to play the role of mentally ill patients. We had to work on each one so that they looked credible – which meant a lot of case studies and rehearsals before the shoot.

For the psychiatry and depression angle we had to get an expert. We worked with Dr Ashit Sheth and in the course of our research did some interesting things. Vikas was playing the medical expert who hypnotizes Vikram and has him reveal his background and childhood trauma. For that we needed to see Dr Sheth in action.

Dr Sheth demonstrated both hypnosis and the power of auto suggestion to us. The entire unit was there and when he asked who would like to do an exercise with him, Sushma Tendulkar, the daughter of Vijay Tendulkar, volunteered. She was playing one of the inmates of the asylum. He hypnotized her and, taking a needle, began to stitch her fingers. Though we were squirming at the pain she might have felt, she did not even wince and there was no sound at all from her! When he got her out of the hypnosis she was surprised that she had experienced no pain.

A student of ours from Sophia College, who was assisting us, had a fear of lizards. Following Dr Sheth's instructions we got a rubber lizard that looked like the real thing. When he asked her to hold it she recoiled in horror and when he tried to get her to hold it, she ran around the room trying to avoid it. Then Dr Sheth sat her down and hypnotized her. I do not remember the exact words he used but when she was in a state of hypnosis, he gave her the lizard. She took it in the palm of her hands, caressed it lovingly, stroked her face and body with it, even putting it in her mouth. Oof, I experienced utter revulsion because I don't like lizards either, though I am not afraid of them. After he got her out of the hypnosis, she continued holding the lizard – the fear and revulsion had disappeared!

When a production is on and a shoot is about to begin, a list of props is given to the producer in advance with enough reminders. Usually, no director will compromise when it comes to getting the required props right.

Once, we were shooting in Pune and we required a white Ambassador car in the asylum compound. It was an absolute must on that day, because the actor who was in the scene with the white Ambassador was going back to Bombay and we could not recreate the asylum and its 'actors' in any other place. We had waited almost the whole day and evening was approaching. We had no choice but to voice our frustration to Vikram.

He said, 'Give me half an hour and I will organize it.' Of course we did not believe him. How could he organize something in half an hour what he could not in two weeks? But in about twenty minutes a white Ambassador showed up with Vikram at the wheel. He asked us to hurry and we quickly took our shots. Just then some people turned up and started to create a ruckus. We realized then that Vikram had literally stolen a parked car and brought it for the shoot. We often say on the sets when we need something, 'Beg, borrow or steal, but get it.' We did not know that Vikram had taken our instruction so literally. Of course, it took some appeasing but when it comes to shootings, most Indians are happy to oblige as long as they can take pictures with the stars.

I remember another incident vividly. Smita Patil loved to drive. After pack-up she would sometimes drag me and drive at great speed. On one such occasion, we reached the hotel where we were staying, which was a simple budget hotel in Pune, the best that the production could afford, and found that there was no place to park the car. There was a scooter which, if moved, could create space for the car. Finding no one to help, we looked at each other and then almost simultaneously nodded. Obviously we had a plan! We went straight to the scooter and without batting an eyelid picked it up and put it somewhere else. Then we parked the car in its place and went into the hotel as if nothing had transpired. Smita was such a simple and practical person with no star airs.

Smita could also be truly funny. I had fallen ill during the shoot and had fever. A doctor had been called and Smita found that he was paying more attention to her than me, his patient. She did not hesitate to tick him off sternly. The poor star-struck man was so embarrassed that it left all of us in splits.

During shoots it is quite common for people to drop in and watch a bit of the shoot or interact with the cast or crew. One day, while we were shooting in the asylum bungalow, we had a visitor, Baba Majgavkar, on the sets. He was a film-maker, also from the FTII, but he was junior to us. He was an expert at reading signatures. Of course it was a major preoccupation for all of us that afternoon to have him look at our signatures and predict the future. I do not remember what he told me or Vikas but I certainly remember what he said to Smita. He told her she had a short life but in an aside he mentioned to me that she may not live beyond thirty-one years. Of course, we did not believe him then but his prediction was bang on!

Both Vikas and I loved Shammi Kapoor and Vikas was good at acting out his songs. We had Naseer's character created in that mould and he did a great job of it, singing those songs to his wife Smita in the film. But we used the song, '*Akele akele kahan jaa rahe ho*' in a totally different context, in what seemed a contrary manner. It would have been a song Naseer would have sung for Smita but in the situation, the way we used it, the song was to highlight that he was the one who had abandoned her by dying. Though the song in the original was a kind of courtship song for the beloved, in the way Rafi had sung it with so much passion, we used it when Naseer's body is being taken for cremation and Smita is left alone. The song, as it was recorded originally, had a lot of reverb and echo and seemed perfect for the situation. It left all of us grief-stricken though Smita was the one emoting the scene in the film.

In those days, we did not have a monitor to see what was being shot. We set up the camera where we wanted it, discussed the lens we wanted, fixed the frame, explained the movement, if any, to the cameraman and then left him to create the magic on the emulsion after we had taken some rehearsals looking through the eyepiece. We stood right next to the camera to get almost the same angle at which the camera was trained on the actors. I remember working with Smita, the invisible thread that connected us – she in front of the camera and me behind. When she emoted, I emoted too and often found myself in tears at the end of the shot. On the sound of 'cut' she would look at me and she would know that the shot was OK.

Our daughter Gaagi was part of the film too. She played Hith's friend, the neighbour's kid. She talks of death and God in the film and explains to Hith what happens to people when they die. It was so uncanny because she herself died a year later, leaving us just with her explanation. There is a shot in the film where Naseer, Smita and Hith leave for Bombay and Gaagi is standing waving goodbye to them. It was like the 'goodbye' captured on film was actually for us, though we did not know it then.

The film got delayed. We were dealing with Gaagi's cancer for a year but we did manage to complete it a year later. However, the film had its own problems and did not get released for ten or eleven years.

During the shoot, Gaagi would often complain about pain in her legs. The initial tests revealed nothing alarming. But when the pain persisted we consulted another doctor who led us to check beyond the area of the pain. And that's when we were told that a biopsy needed to be done.

Vikas got the biopsy report and was the first one to know that Gaagi had cancer. Instead of coming home, he went to our friend Dr Ashit Sheth to ask him whether or how he should break the news to me and if I would be able to deal with it. Dr Sheth told him to break the news as directly as possible and that I would be able to deal with it. I remember shutting myself in the bathroom for some time and crying my heart out.

The first question to hit anyone, when one is suddenly faced with such a calamity, is 'Why me?' 'Why us?' And there is no answer to that. It had been a bolt from the blue, totally unexpected, since no one in the family had any history of cancer. I knew though that I had to be brave and strong for my daughter and for the rest of the family too.

We set about gathering all possible information about cancer, particularly about Ewing's Sarcoma, which Gaagi was inflicted with. We also had to get the right oncologist. Our search led us to Dr Asha Kapadia who had returned to India after a long stint in the US. Her last assignment had been at the Memorial Sloan Kettering Cancer Center in New York.

Gaagi was a very bright kid and she was quick enough to guess something was seriously wrong. She asked us what she was suffering from. We wanted to be straight with her. So we told her it's cancer. She looked it up in the encyclopaedia and even shared some information with us.

Gaagi underwent her first chemotherapy in St. Elizabeth's Hospital, the same hospital where she was born. We had her take all the successive ones at home because we did not want her to feel isolated in a hospital. Also, we felt that at home, with family and friends and the food that she liked, she would heal faster. We took great care, however, to make sure that the room set up for her was sterile and hygienic. Everyone who entered the room wore face masks during the chemotherapy or when her white blood cell count was low.

A number of friends and colleagues would drop in. Smita, Parveen Babi, Jagjit and Chitra Singh were among the regulars. My sister Uma, who is a painter, was there almost all the time too. Irene and Sushma, teachers at Gaagi's school, were unflinching in their support. After the first chemotherapy, Gaagi could still not go back to school. She was prone to infection and needed to be in a protected environment. It was going to be a long haul. So she started doing school work with Vasanta, another teacher from Cathedral and John Connon School who would visit every evening.

Smita was very good at mimicking and she would keep quacking like Donald Duck and both Gaagi and she would burst into peals of laughter. Gaagi had many Barbie dolls and Parveen played with her. She even got Xerxes, her dress designer, to make special dresses for the dolls like the ones she wore in her films. Xerxes had done such a fabulous job with them, I remember particularly the one in the '*Jawane jaaneman*' song.

Another time, Chitra made up her face, the full works with heavy eye shadow and all. Jagjit, meanwhile, told funny stories and made both Gaagi and Hith laugh. Gaagi was totally a people's person and she was at home with all our friends and colleagues.

We had nurses round the clock during the chemos and, at other times, just during the day. Once a nurse made a mistake and the drug spilled over on Gaagi's forearm and burned the skin badly. Of course, we were hugely upset and after that I decided to take over the nursing myself. We still had nurses in attendance and I had told them to just watch me and correct me if I was about to make any mistake.

A few months later, we took Gaagi to Memorial Sloan Kettering Cancer Center. Our doctor accompanied us. Gaagi was a cheerful, happy human being and though she was in pain, she bore it really well. At the hospital, she soon became very popular and was nicknamed Smiley. They operated on her leg and when we left she had to be in a plaster cast waist downwards right to the toes. This meant she couldn't go to Disneyland as planned. But we resolved to return to the US just for that.

We returned to India about a month later with a clean chit, after the American doctors had done what is called 'bone resection' and put her on medication to keep the cancer out.

Gaagi was doing pretty well after our return to Bombay, despite the plaster cast which had to stay for about two to three months. She had wonderful messages on the cast written by all the friends we had made at the hospital and people kept adding to those messages as time passed by. Her chemotherapy protocols continued as before, though the cast was kept on for much longer.

She was so 'cool' that every time a test was run after her chemo, she would ask, 'What is my white blood cell count?' She felt she could handle whatever and we shared most of the information with her except the doctors' prediction about her lifespan. The success rate for the treatment of Ewing's Sarcoma, we were told, was 85 per cent. Unluckily we fell in the 15 per cent and Gaagi's leg got infected.

The cast was removed. The infection was pretty serious, with something oozing continuously out of it and needed dressing round the clock. It also meant that she had to have additional antibiotics. In the last few months the poor child had a lot of medication/chemicals pumped into her. Yet she took everything in her stride. The doctor recommended amputation and said if we did not get it done, we would lose her very soon because the infection would spread.

He assured us that if we did amputate we had, without question, at least six months. We were greedy and wanted her to live longer so we decided to take the second option, hoping the six months would maybe extend and she would have a chance to live longer. We thought maybe she could even go to Disneyland as she had wanted to!

But to tell Gaagi that she was to lose a leg was the most difficult thing for us. Once again we went back to Dr Sheth for help to break the news to Gaagi. He came over and she chatted with her Ashit uncle. At the end of their chat she declared, 'If something is rotten or bad we cut it out, right? My leg has gone bad, so it has to go.' After Dr Sheth left, Gaagi hugged me and cried and cried like she never had in all those months. I felt helpless, like we had betrayed her trust somehow. All along she had believed that her mom and dad could do anything and now it seemed that nothing was in our hands and we were helpless too.

We went ahead with the amputation in Dr Bacha's hospital and even while we sat there waiting, a hospital attendant carried Gaagi's amputated leg across the room, wrapped in a newspaper, completely oblivious to what her family may feel. We had not needed to see that but that's life. We met the doctor and to our horror and even anger, he said the operation was successful but he felt that Gaagi would not last more than ten days. If we had only known that earlier, we wouldn't have put her through so much emotional and physical pain. We would have let her go gracefully, in one piece.

We took our daughter home as soon as we could. We wanted to give her the best ten days possible! We fed her food she loved – one day, Chinese, another day, Continental or Punjabi. Everything she liked. We had parties every day with all her friends around and I made her favourite waffles and lemon tarts, while her grandmother too cooked her favourite dishes.

Gaagi loved watching Amitabh's movies – she watched one every day. In fact, it so happened that Amitabh was in Breach Candy Hospital recovering from his accident on the sets of *Coolie* and when Gaagi needed to go to that hospital, we took her to meet him. He wrote such a beautiful message for her, it made her day!

The ten days the doctor had predicted stretched to forty.

Gaagi got fed up of what her life had become. She declared that she wanted to study – she had not given her exams that year. We got Vasanta, her teacher, to start coming again. Gaagi insisted on giving her exams though she was in a terrible state.

During that period, her condition deteriorated. The cancer spread to her lungs and the rest of her body, even to her head, where there were little tumours like horns. The pain was excruciating and the painkiller doses had to be increased. To add to it all was another pain, the 'phantom pain' she experienced in her amputated absent limb.

She would often ask me, 'Is there no justice in this world? Why do I have to suffer?' I had no answer to that. All my prayers to God to give me her pain had gone unheeded. All I did those days was chant, 'Love you, darling, love you, sweetheart, love you, pudding, love you, honeypot,' and all the endearing sweet nothings I had for her. She would reciprocate and give me that million-dollar smile and mumble, 'Love you, Mom.'

That whole year, people brought her small Ganesha idols, God's lockets, holy ash from various temples and even the Lourdes' holy water as blessings. All of it was on a tray in Gaagi's room and one day she told me to take it all out of the room. On another day, she talked about a dark tunnel and light at the end of it. I sensed that her end was near, but we never spoke about it until one day, when she told me that she didn't want to leave me and go and promised me that she would catch up with me sometime somewhere. After she was gone, for years I kept trying to find her somewhere, to see a glimpse in someone maybe.

During the day there was always something to be done and at night I would sit and watch over her. Suddenly in the middle of the night I would wake up having dozed off. With my heart beating loud enough so I could hear it in the room, I would go up to her, bend over and see if she was still breathing. I was afraid to lose her just like that. Finding her still alive, a wave of relief would wash over me and I would return to my seat and look at her. I was completely unwilling to let her go.

She was also put on steroids and one day we had a straight conversation with her doctor. We asked her, 'If there is no cure why are we keeping her with a false sense of well-being, when her systems are beginning to fail one by one?' Her doctor said that there was nothing we could do to end her misery but we could withdraw the steroids. As her nurse, I was administering the steroids by injection about six or eight times a day. Her doctor told me to reduce the dosage and the frequency gradually and I did, according to the plan she gave me.

Gaagi's condition was getting worse by the day. However, she insisted on writing her exams even though holding the pencil had become difficult for her. About a week before she left us, her teacher told us that Gaagi had passed her exams with a distinction. Immediately Gaagi shot back, 'What's the percentage?' The school decided to award Gaagi a prize and the principal and teachers came and gave it to her at her bedside. Gaagi passed away after two or three days of this incident.

Morphine was recommended in case Gaagi's pain went beyond being bearable, even after the heavy dosage of painkillers. It acts directly on the central nervous system to relieve pain. It was a drug that was not easily available and to be able to administer it to someone, you needed special paperwork and we had got that organized too.

The last few days must have been hard for Hith, with all of our attention on Gaagi. He had become quiet and subdued and I would try and find time to be with him, get his homework done and play with him.

On that fateful fortieth day, Vikas went to work after a long time. That morning, I had given Gaagi the last of the steroid. I fed her breakfast and was right beside her, chatting with her, and I also had Hith on the other side, who was building a temple with his Lego set. Gaagi said to me that she was feeling sick and as I was comforting her, she asked for the tray with the gods to be brought back. I asked my mother-in-law who was also in the room to do that since it was kept in her room. I felt then the time for Gaagi to go had come. She wanted to make peace with the gods she had rejected and sent out of the room.

A little later, she said she was in extreme pain and she could not take it anymore. I felt it was time for the morphine to be administered. But I was afraid that if she slipped into an unconscious state Vikas would not be able to meet her. I had someone leave a message at the studio for him to return at once and delayed giving the morphine. Gaagi's hand was in my hand, I was looking at her and she went away quietly with every breath shorter than the previous one. Just then Vikas walked into the room – he called out to her but she did not respond.

Many months later someone asked me that if I had a choice would I have chosen to have Gaagi in my life with all that had happened to her and I said 'yes'. She was like an angel, if angels ever come to earth, and she was a special gift to me. She taught me courage, strength, fortitude and what they say in cricket – playing full out until the last ball!

8

FINDING ONESELF AGAIN

I cannot describe how it was when Gaagi was gone and she lay lifeless and people came and went. There was so much hustle and bustle and then they took her away. I had known that death was coming, had willed it to come and save her from another day of pain. That night someone gave me a Calmpose and I drifted into a deep sleep, like into the land of the dead where there is no pain, no pleasure.

It must have been around 7 in the morning when Vikas woke me up. All I wanted to do was cling to him and cry my heart out. I wanted to hear his soothing endearments which I had not heard in a while. But that was not to be. He held me firmly by the shoulder, looked into my confused, sleepy face and said, 'I want a divorce.' I thought I was having a nightmare and tried to shake it off, reaching for him. He still held me firmly and repeated that he wanted a divorce. He then left me sitting there trying to make sense of what I had just heard.

I knew it would come, sometime someday. Our marriage had been vulnerable in the past year and a half and my friend had made inroads into it pretty successfully. But I did not know how and when it would come. Though deep down I had hoped it wouldn't come at all. In fact, I had tried to explain his involvement with my friend as a distraction he probably needed, away from the scene of seeing his daughter suffer.

This phase was the most difficult one of my life. Losing my daughter, husband and friend, almost all at the same time, in the span of twenty-four hours, had shaken the very foundations on which I stood.

To wake up to a new day every day was torture. The only anchor that kept me alive and connected with life was my little son, Hith, for whom I knew I had to live and for whom my heart used to cry. I had said 'no' to the divorce but had not imagined what it might be like living on sufferance.

Looking back, I remember that during Gaagi's illness, maybe even before and after, there were other influences on Vikas. There were some well-known Bollywood personalities that Vikas was interacting with and they were shocked that he was a one-woman man and faithful in his marriage. They made him feel that he had missed something, not having played the field, and encouraged him to be adventurous. And he surely seemed to have taken the cue.

I think it was just four or five days after Gaagi had left us when we got a call that Parveen was not OK. Her secretary told us that she was behaving weirdly and we should look in on her. When we went over to her place, she looked frightened and scared. She had an attack of paranoia and told us that there were bombs planted at her place, in her sitting room, bedroom and in her cupboards too, so much so that she was unable to move. She also said that 'they' were trying to poison her so even the kitchen was not safe. She had apparently not eaten for a couple of days and sat crouched and hungry in her living room.

The first thing we did was listen and not negate anything because it was real for her. After she fell silent, I asked her if she trusted us, trusted me. She nodded and I told her that I would personally go into her kitchen and make something for her to eat. I made her an omelette and she ate it.

After that we offered to take her home to our place on Peddar Road. We took a change of clothes and brought her home. We contacted Dr Sheth, who came over and gave her some medication. She began to relax and was quite at home until she saw one of Vikas's friends who had come for a condolence visit. She freaked out saying that he had come to kill her. I took her into our bedroom and had her lock herself in so she felt safe. Of course, I had the key to the bedroom so there was no cause for concern and she needed to feel safe and secure.

Within three days there was a marked change in Parveen. She became quite normal and told us that she wanted to go home. We let her go and the next morning we heard the news that she had left the country the previous night.

Vikas kept asking me for the divorce and I kept saying no. I was going through the motions of living and taking care of Hith. During that period, a few weeks after Gaagi had left us, I ran into Shiamak Davar, one day, at the Willingdon Club. He talked to me about connecting with departed souls. I was not sure if I wanted to do that. But Shiamak was very persuasive and asked me to meet the Bhavnagris anyhow – they could perhaps help me reconnect with Gaagi.

So I went one day with him to meet them. Khorshed Bhavnagri shared with me how she had lost her sons, Vispy and Ratoo, when they were still young and had found a way of communicating with them regularly. She had learned to do auto-writing and through that she was able to know about the world of spirits and what happens to people when they leave the earth and their physical bodies.

I was not convinced but since I was brought to this situation by the powers above, I decided to give it a go. But even after a couple of sessions I could not really connect and all I wrote was 'love you, darling' over and over again. A few years later, *The Laws of the Spirit World*, written by Khorshed, was published. I felt that if there was another world and Gaagi had gone there, as her mother I didn't want to pull her back and disturb whatever was there for her. I just wanted her to be happy in whichever world she was. But I do appreciate Shiamak's commitment to bring peace to grieving, bereaved people.

Life seemed utterly hopeless and I just didn't know what to do with myself. One day, my depression overtook me. I tried to end my life but failed miserably. I think I was far too responsible a person to actually succeed in that endeavour. I went to Dr Sheth but ended up crying in every session. He put me on some medication but I was so afraid of getting addicted to it that I would cheat and not take the prescribed dose.

My consistent 'no' to the divorce led Vikas to take a drastic step to precipitate the divorce anyhow. He moved out of the house to live as a paying guest a few buildings away. That completely upset the apple cart as far as my in-laws were concerned. Whatever little sympathy they had for me ended because their own son had left home, just to get rid of me. And now it was my turn to go.

Those were perhaps the most miserable years of my life when I was relegated to my room and all the civilities and privileges that I enjoyed as a family member were withdrawn. I was alienated and the family I had taken to be mine was no longer mine to stake claim on. The way it was, where I lived did not seem like my house anymore either.

It got to a stage when my eight-year-old son decided to intervene. He told me bluntly, 'Mom, everytime they say something you just cry and cry. You can't give them tit for tat. Your old Gandhian principles will not work here. Why don't you and I go away somewhere and stay by ourselves?'

I was moved to tears and told him that I really did not know what to do. I had said 'no' to the divorce only for his sake. I did not agree with him right away but promised to think about it.

If I were alone, I would have left my marital home without taking anything and started life from scratch. But I wanted my son to have a home with both parents and grandparents. I was willing to be a persona non grata, wife-only-in-name and keep the home from breaking up. After all, there were so many marriages that were marriages only in name and mine could be another. When my ex-husband mentioned that we couldn't work together anymore (as a director duo), I offered to give up film-making altogether and let him be the director. I was confident that I could channelize my creativity into writing and told him that.

But, of course, my marriage was beyond redemption. Vikas looked forward to a new life with a new wife. Amidst all this, I would like to put on record, not once did we have ugly scenes or slanging matches, though there were plenty of tears from my side. It took us a lot of time but we worked it out and finally parted in 1988.

During that time, I remember when I prayed I did not ask for my husband to be given back, but for strength and courage to face whatever was in my destiny. Maybe I felt that our marriage and relationship was irretrievable, considering all the indignity and humiliation I had suffered. Perhaps I had realized at some point that my life and happiness could not depend upon another's whims and fancies. I had to take life the way it came at me, good, bad or ugly.

I got further insights into human behaviour. I found that in times of suffering, some people get closer to you while there are others – friends and colleagues – who avoid you like the plague. The common refrain was, 'It was too much to deal with …'

The first reaction to that had been anger. What too much? They did not have to deal with anything. We were the ones that were dealing with disease, death and divorce. Were they so fragile that they would fall apart if they saw someone suffering? Or if they spoke to us?

There was just too much to deal with and I knew I needed help. Some friends were a great support. I went back to work, which was both my escape and my therapy, not to mention perhaps the only future I had, to be able to bring up my son and give him a good education. My family was away in Bangalore and whenever anything happened to me, the numerous times I was hospitalized, it was always my friends who would be there, their hearts full of generosity and love.

Life had to go on and I took it by the horns. One of the first things I did when my marriage broke up was get a bank loan and buy a Steenbeck, the best film-editing machine ever. It had to be imported from Germany. I set up my editing studio in Rajkamal Studios. When I was not using it, I hired it out for other editors to use.

About five years later, when the loan was cleared, I took another bank loan and bought an office space on Linking Road in Khar. I shifted my editing studio there where a lot of commercial Bollywood films were edited. I was not making big money, just enough to put petrol in my car and food on the table and provide for my son who lived with me. But somehow I was OK with all that.

When my friend T.S. Ranga wanted to make *Giddh* (1984), I helped him with signing Smita Patil and the other cast. I had even attended part of the shooting, to be with my dear friend Smita, and helped Ranga with the shooting of some jatra scenes. Vikas was there too as an actor in the film but we didn't have much to do with each other, with the issue of the unresolved divorce hanging between us. Ranga was very organized and committed and brought in good material to edit and so there were no major hiccups during that film.

The biggest issue I had to deal with was a lot of unwanted attention at that time. A majority of men think that a woman whose marriage is broken, or is in the process of divorce, is an available commodity. Almost all the men I knew, barring a few exceptions, kept propositioning me. They offered me their shoulders to cry on and also support in various ways, but in reality all they were offering me was the exalted position of 'mistress' or girl-friend who was not to be seen with them during the day but was expected to spend the nights with them.

I am not exaggerating, but almost every Tom, Dick and Harry

With Family

With her mother (1955–56)

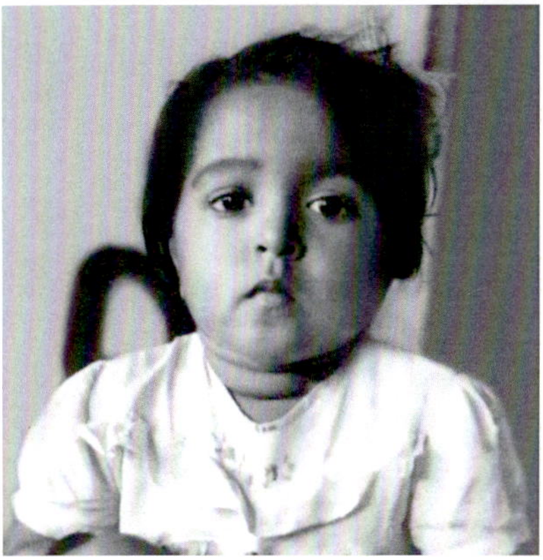

Early days (1951–52)

Aruna's father with Queen Elizabeth and Prince Philip (1961)

With her parents, siblings and family friend (1959)

Marriage and Education

Vikas and Aruna at their marriage reception while studying at FTII (1969)

Aruna receiving the Diploma in Cinema at the FTII convocation (1969)

Children

With her daughter Gaagi at a beach resort (1979–80)

Hith and Gaagi at home (1977–78)

Gaagi with Aruna's mother at a family function (1975–76)

Shaque (1976)

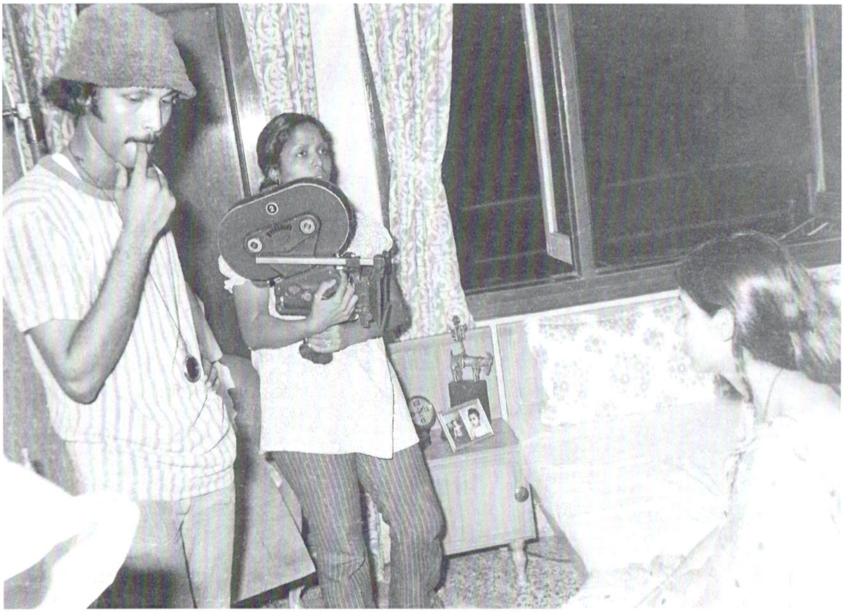

Shooting with A.K. Bir (cinematographer) and Shabana Azmi (1974)

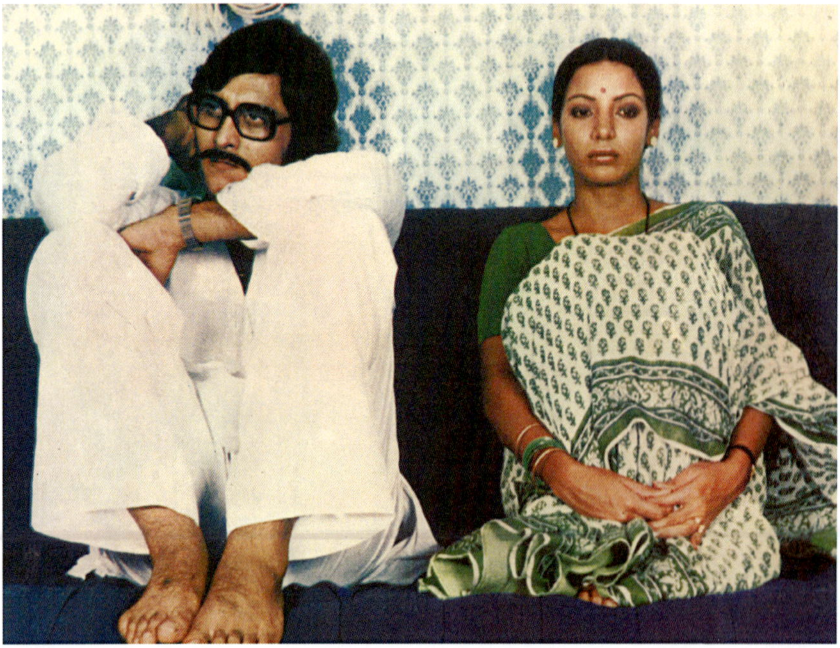

Vinod Khanna and Shabana Azmi (1974)

Gehrayee (1980)

Amrish Puri and Padmini Kolhapure in the controversial vashikaran scene

Anant Nag and Padmini Kolhapure with Amrish Puri as the evil tantrik

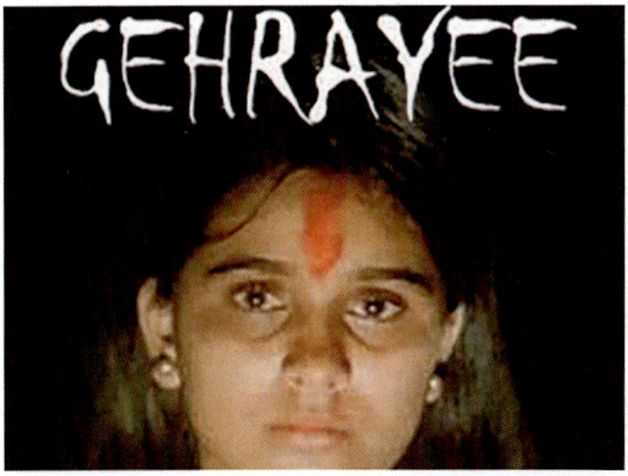

Padmini Kolhapure in a still from the film (1979–80)

Aruna and Vikas setting up a shot with Padmini Kolhapure

Situm (1984)

Naseeruddin Shah, Vikram and Smita Patil (1982)

Aruna and Vikas during the shooting of a football match (1981)

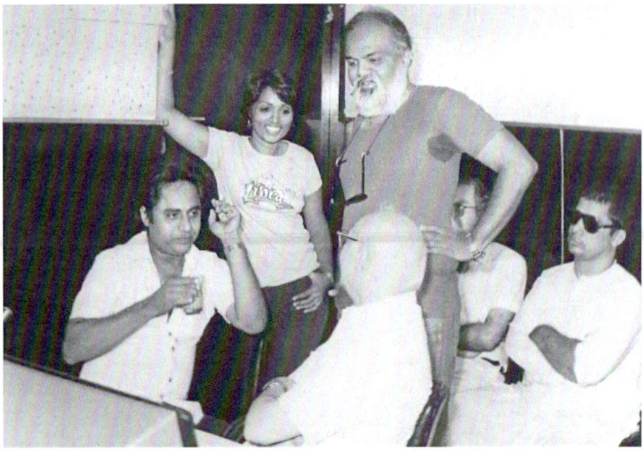

Aruna and Vikas at a song recording with Jagjit Singh at Film Center

Difficult Days (1982–83)

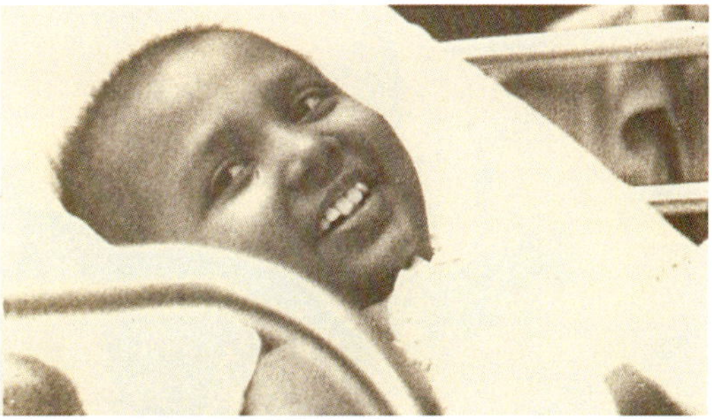

Gaagi at Memorial Sloan Kettering Hospital in New York (1982)

Aruna's son Hith playing alone at home

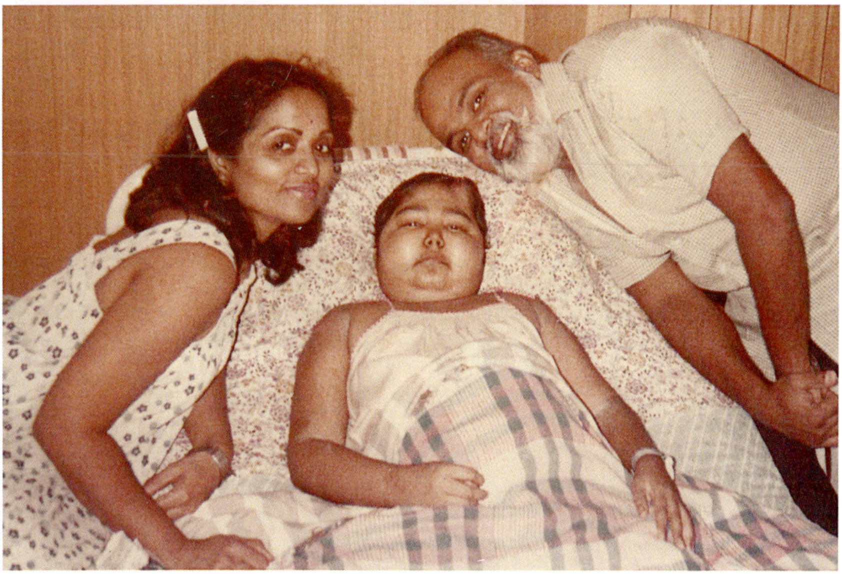

With Gaagi and Vikas during Gaagi's last days (1983)

Rihaee (1988)

Hema Malini while shooting for *Rihaee* in Vadnagar (1987)

Going over the climax scene with Vinod Khanna and Hema Malini (1988)

Naseeruddin Shah and Hema Malini at the Hatkeshwar temple in Vadnagar (1987)

Vinod Khanna and Mohan Agashe in Vadnagar (1987)

Patita Pavana (Marathi) and *Patita Pavani* (Kannada) (1992)

At a song recording with music director Vijay Bhaskar and playback singer Vani Jairam (1991–92)

Shooting in Kamathipura with S.R. Krishnamurthy (cinematographer) and actors Raju Khandagale and Bharati Patil in the foreground

Sukanya Kulkarni and Dayanand shooting in a village near Saundatti in Karnataka (1991–92)

Sayyaji Shinde shooting in the red-light area of Kamathipura (1991–92)

Bhairavi (1996)

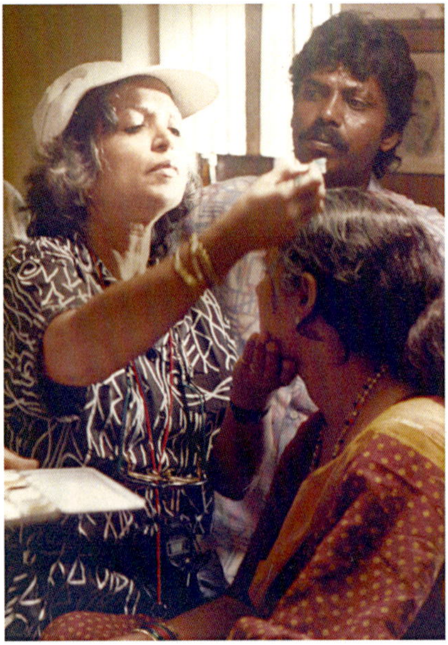

Touching up the greys for actor Anjana Mumtaz

The *Bhairavi* booklet with Ashvini Bhave and Manohar Singh

Sridhar and Ashvini in a romantic scene at the Gaganchukki Falls in Karnataka

Setting up a shot with Barun Mukherjee (cinematographer)

Keh Do Na – A Telefilm (2001)

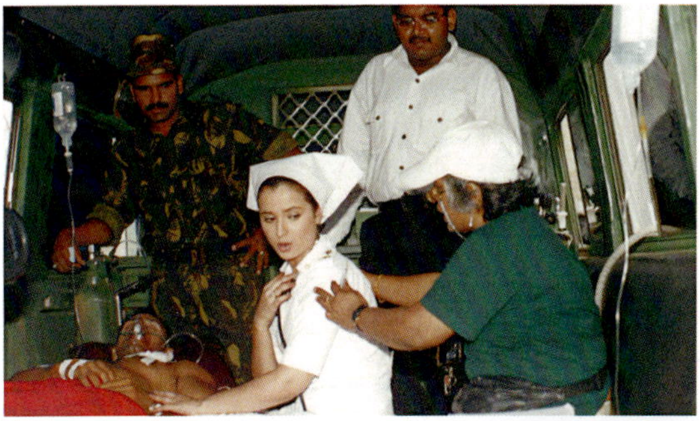

With Parveen Dabas and Simone Singh in an army ambulance

With Simone Singh during the shoot

Kothri No. 42 – A Stage Play (2003)

Arvind Panday and Vishwajeet Pradhan as the two convicts

Vishwajeet Pradhan and Arvind Panday performing as King Creon and Antigone in a play within the play

A Few Other Films

Om Puri and Smita Patil in *Giddh* edited by Arunaraje and directed by T.S. Ranga (1984)

Naseeruddin Shah and Shabana Azmi in *Masoom* edited by Arunavikas and directed by Shekhar Kapur (1983)

Suniel Shetty in *Red Alert* written by Arunaraje and directed by Ananth Mahadevan (2009)

Tum? (2004)

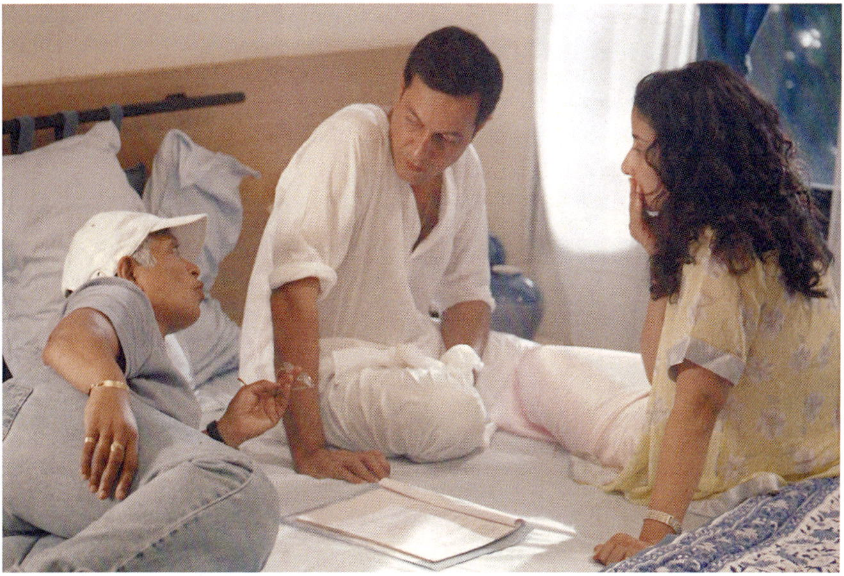

Discussing a scene with Rajat Kapoor and Manisha Koirala (2003)

Manisha Koirala and Rajat Kapoor enacting a scene in Mauritius (2003)

Talking About Films, Transformation and Women's Issues

Speaking at a lecture

Presenting a paper at a conference

With her son Hith on a family holiday

Awards and Recognition

Receiving the Star and Style Gold Medal for Best Editing Student at FTII (1969)

Receiving the Karnataka Rajyotsava Award (gold medal) for Contribution to Cinema (1992)

Receiving a National Award for the documentary *Mallika Sarabhai* from K.R. Narayanan, the then President of India (2000)

Receiving two National awards as director and producer of the documentary *A New Paradigm* from Dr A.P.J. Abdul Kalam, the then President of India (2002)

Receiving two National awards as director and producer for the documentary *Behind the Glass Wall* from President Pranab Mukherjee (2014)

thought he stood a chance and tried to get me into his bed. And the list included not just the Casanovas or Romeos of Bollywood but colleagues, friends, common friends, family friends, fathers of my children's friends, professionals who were part of my infrastructure and acquaintances too. The most demeaning proposition was when a very rich and famous astrologer from Singapore, recommended by none other than a family friend, was visiting Bombay and came to see me. Instead of predicting my future, he offered 'to keep me like a queen, wanting for nothing' in his very own words. I cannot even begin to express how disgusting I found it all. I became a recluse, too scared to meet or interact with any male during that time.

But I could not stay at home forever; I would go further into depression. I started working gradually and figured out innovative ways to handle unwanted attention. I would not take someone's declaration of love seriously and laugh it off like they were teasing me, or appreciate their wife and marriage or pretend I had someone else in my life. Sometimes I would even sit down and explain how I was a 'wrong number' and at other times righteously declare that I was not going to break up another woman's home just like somebody had done mine. There were times when people tried to act funny in my own house, in my sitting room, with my son asleep in his bedroom and the maid asleep in the kitchen. I had to then throw them out of my house.

I am surprised, however, that men wanted me then despite my sad face, tear-laden eyes and distrustful demeanour after the betrayal I had experienced. For years together, I was plagued by nightmares of my mother-in-law, whom I had been scared of, and Vikas too. They were unpleasant dreams and I had to keep overcoming them to have a normal day. There was no joy anymore and I was not even pleasant company. I found it hard to even eat because all food tasted like sawdust in my mouth and I had to wash it down frequently with water. I had lost a lot of weight too and had become very quiet and pensive, hardly ever smiling. In short, I had become dead wood. But

I realized that when a man wants a woman, he doesn't care about all that. It is not the woman but what he wants from her that matters to him.

But in all of this, I came across a strange creature. I say creature because he was different. He too wanted me but there was a big difference. Whatever I said or did, he would not take 'no' for an answer. I think I had become a huge challenge for him and he persisted and pursued me all over the country and abroad too. He tracked me down while I was shooting a documentary down south, and everywhere I went, he would somehow reach me. He had tremendous depths of tenderness and love that can only be experienced.

I kept running away from him. I ran and ran and ran until I could do so no longer and, one day, I succumbed. I had no feeling, no desire, no reaction, nothing, and whatever was going to happen was going to happen. I was just too tired. It was unbelievable what did happen though. As he slowly and gradually and lovingly seduced me, the dead wood began to come back to life. I could actually feel blood throbbing in my veins, my heart beating umpteen times faster, becoming breathless and the sweet pain that followed. And the deep dreamless sleep I could have after a long time.

He was an expert womanizer, a real butterfly that moved from flower to flower. Our affair, if you may call it that, lasted for a brief period, maybe a couple of years, but it gave me back my life. He moved on and that was fine. The universe had sent me healing in whatever form that I needed to be able to get on with my life – to become whole again from the dead wood I had become. Thank God that I did not fall into the wrong hands and experience further misery! I am saying this because it was therapeutic for me. I know of so many women in a similar position, used, abused and exploited. Knowing who and what he was, I had not imagined any future with him, so there was no expectation or disappointment. I am eternally grateful to him for giving me back my life and making me feel whole and complete again.

There were serious proposals of marriage too but I was focused on two things only: bringing up my son and making films to express myself. I got better at handling men but I was never rude or arrogant with anyone as I was afraid of the consequences. I had heard men boasting about the women they had been with and most often it was when they did not get what they wanted or were spurned. I had to let them down gently, for the male ego, I believe, is fragile and there was no point in inviting more trouble.

Almost everyone in the industry knew me to be extremely tough. I wasn't frivolous. They also knew I did not suffer fools gladly and gave me a wide berth. Being the sole woman editor-director in the industry at that time (apart from Sai Paranjype), I would travel alone to the studios in my own vehicle and return from Film City at 3 a.m. It took guts to do that. I went to film functions, marriages, chauthas, premieres, parties all by myself and was known as the lone ranger. However, they respected my talent and integrity. I did not owe anyone any money and all transactions were clean and above board.

One very persistent character was a well-known personality from Bollywood who pestered me quite shamelessly for quite a long time. There came a project when I was supposed to work with him and initially I refused. But with pressure from the producers I gave up, telling myself that I needed to be professional and get the job done and to make sure that I was always with someone when he was around.

One of the times we met, the guy sent off all the others present on various errands and manipulated things in such a way that I was alone in the room with him. I was afraid and had no clue what would happen, but I decided then and there to face matters head-on and deal with whatever came up bravely. He then declared his amorous intentions, stating how he had fallen in love with me years ago when he had first set eyes on me. One thing I did was not to interrupt him while he spoke until he finished what he had to say. Seeing that I was not reacting to his words, he asked me to respond. I said vaguely that it depended on a lot of things…

He then began to talk of his exploits with other women, giving graphic details of them – the foreign women with white skin, huge breasts and rumps and much more that I am loathe to describe, and how long he had sustained his erection, and so on. A thought struck me that I was neither white nor buxom. Repulsive as it was to my ears, I just let it flow, all the crap that came out of his wretched mouth. Once again, when he was spent emptying himself telling me about his puerile manhood, he looked at me.

I looked at him, somehow not afraid anymore. My reputation had certainly preceded me and he was afraid to touch me without my consent, though he did inch closer to me. He asked me to be his and how he could give me a time I would never forget, make me ever so happy. He said that our union would result in such heights of creativity that it would leave the world spellbound.

At this point, I actually smiled wryly and I don't know if he noticed that. I told him having an affair was no big deal – I was my own master and not answerable to anyone but … He asked, 'But what?' I told him that in the past I had had such extraordinary experiences of lovemaking that those memories would last me a lifetime. If I did not have sex for the rest of my life, I said, what I experienced, had been so satiating that I would not miss it. I looked at him and said that only if I felt anything new, something that would go beyond those superlative fantabulous experiences, would it be worth considering. I didn't want to indulge in the ordinary and mediocre.

At this point of time his face was worth looking at. He was downright nervous and must have thought, 'Wrong number! Why did I have to talk to her? I should have just jumped on her and risked a slap or two.' He was so afraid of not measuring up, he backtracked and even called me 'sister' before I left. I can't tell how much confidence this little victory gave me in living my life on my own terms; single and happy by choice.

A lot of Bollywood personalities like him, over the years, have kept claiming that there is no 'casting couch' and yet taking full advantage of vulnerable women all the time. That's not true at all! I have met several girls over the years who shared their stories about the molestation and sexual harassment that takes place in the film industry. To be fair, it is not only in the film industry that this happens – it is present in the corporate world, in politics and many other spheres of life. A few years ago I found that it was not only the girls who had horror stories to tell but the boys too. Many young male actors at the time, after an audition or acting workshop, would share with me how even they were subjected to the 'casting couch'.

During this phase, I kept going to Europe. I was always drawn to Paris which I did visit after I broke up with Vikas. I got a chance to go to Paris again when *Rihaee*, with a French voiceover, was shown in Creteil, a suburb of Paris. It received a standing ovation and for me, people seeing my films, appreciating them or discussing them has always held more importance than awards that gather dust in some corner of the drawing room.

Another time, in November 1989, I had to go to East Berlin for a conference on women audio-visual workers. I was selected to go by the Indian Film Directors' Association and I had prepared my paper on the 'Portrayal of Women in Films', which I was to read. There was a lot of anxiety as the ticket had not arrived and the visa formalities needed to be taken care of. Finally everything was done and I left for Berlin.

On landing in Berlin, I found that no one had come to receive me. I did not have any details of where the conference was to be held so I had to track down the organization somehow. I did not know German, did not have any German currency and I had landed at 6 or 7 in the morning so there was nobody around who could help me. I went to the phone booth and looked up the directory but it did not have the name I was looking for. The few people I saw and tried to talk to, shook their heads or put up their hands. I was stuck.

To add to my troubles I had a huge bag, because after the conference I was going to Paris and I think to the US after that. I always carried lots of gifts for friends when I went abroad and while coming back, used up the space in my bag for my shopping.

Those days I always travelled with a Berlitz guide which facilitated basic communication. There were no cabs and I could not even get myself to a police station to track down my hosts. I did manage to change some money however.

Finally, after a couple of hours, somebody told me to take a bus to Checkpoint Charlie. Getting on to the bus with the bag was not easy but somehow I struggled with it and boarded the bus. The air was fraught with people looking suspicious and on edge and I did not realize what it was until I reached Checkpoint Charlie. The Berlin Wall had just come down and there was a lot of tension and anxiety.

I went into the office and there too, I met with nodding heads. Finally, somebody directed me to a police station a little distance away. Off I went, dragging my bag but it felt like a sequence from some European surrealistic film. At the police station, after what seemed like an interrogation, I was directed to Checkpoint Charlie again. They told me in bad broken English that I had to cross over to East Berlin and then try to locate my hosts. When I asked them how I could go across, they shook their heads again – there was no service yet but private vehicles did go and I could try to go with someone.

I just wanted to sit on the pavement right there and bawl. Once again I dragged myself and the bag and reached Checkpoint Charlie. While I was trying to make myself understood to the German guys manning the place, by sheer chance, an Englishman happened to be around. I spoke to him and he told me that he did business across East and West Berlin and was about to go across. On my earnest request, he agreed to give me a ride. At that time I thought my troubles were over, but a lot more was to come.

He had two more associates who joined us after some time and I must admit that they did not look respectable in the least. This increased my anxiety but I kept my fingers crossed. We stopped at the barrier/gate for our papers to be checked. My papers were thankfully in order but theirs were not. My mind raced. Was I with smugglers or drug dealers? What were these guys up to? I could rot in a prison for the rest of my life and no one would know. The Englishman got down and the three of them kept arguing back and forth with the armed guards for what seemed like hours. After a while the officers checked all the baggage and let us go.

What a relief that was! But I was not sure of my fate with the unsavoury companions I had chosen for my journey. We crossed the border into East Berlin and drove straight to Hotel Metropole, an old-style edifice with a large lobby and chandeliers. The Englishman was very friendly and helpful and while he checked in I was at the reception trying to find my hosts. The guys at the reception were very supportive but we kept drawing blanks everywhere we phoned. It was already late and I was not sure what my next step would be.

The Englishman who had a room now insisted that I go up to his room, freshen up and have a drink, maybe just a glass of wine. That scared me even more. Those days and right through college, I used to carry a flick knife, but while travelling, it had to go in the baggage. I did not have that with me now, in case I needed to use it. He wouldn't take no for an answer so I went up, used the loo and told him I simply had to get back to the reception and find my hosts.

All along the trip we had talked on and off and he had been paying me compliments and he tried to take that further and have me stay. Thankfully he was not aggressive and wanted whatever he had in mind with my consent. Anyway I went down and he came with me, not willing to let me off so easily.

I went back to the reception and had them try again. On his insistence, I did have a glass of wine and a snack, having been hungry all day and then just as I was wondering what next, we had a breakthrough! The guys at the reception had made some connection with one of the organizers. They said they would contact the responsible person and get back to us. The call came and they gave me an address. It was about an hour and a half's drive into the interiors. They asked the hotel to arrange the taxi and asked me to pay for it, which they would reimburse later.

I left thanking the Englishman profusely for his help and really grateful that he had not laid a hand on me. Of course, he took my details – address, phone numbers and all. I didn't ask for his because he had already given me his card when he offered me a ride. For years afterwards he sent me cards and good wishes but I kept my responses to a minimum and that was the end of it.

It was midnight already when I got into the cab. We seemed to drive endlessly and soon were into the interiors, amidst thick forests. I did not know where the cabbie was taking me but I was not so worried now because the organizers knew I was on the way and the hotel knew about me. It was 3 a.m. when we arrived and I was let in and shown a room. There was already a schedule on the desk – breakfast at 8.30 and conference at 9 a.m. I crashed into bed extremely relieved to have landed safely in one piece.

Next morning, the organizers told me that they had not received any details of my flight or confirmation of my departure. There were quite a lot of women representing various countries. Of all the discussions and papers that were read, I was most shocked by what I heard about Japan. Japan has been such a leader in the world, in what its people have accomplished after Hiroshima and in rebuilding their country, that it was quite surprising to hear about the status of women in that country. I thought that in India women were second-class citizens and got a raw deal in the patriarchal chauvinistic society but I found that the status of women in Japan was much worse; pathetic to say the least!

The venue of the conference was a palace, by either a river or lake I am not sure which, surrounded by thick forests. This, we were told, was a secret pleasure palace, a hidden resort of the communist leaders, who enjoyed such luxury for all that they preached, propounded and advocated.

We were in Berlin at a very historic time, when the Berlin Wall had come down, but the ground reality was that East Berliners and West Berliners were very wary of each other and an atmosphere of distrust prevailed. When we reached what used to be the border, there were crowds collecting pieces of the historic Berlin Wall. Some of my colleagues collected some pieces too. Later in my travels, I found that pieces of the demolished wall were sold in the United States and Britain as souvenirs.

I visited Berlin again many years later for another conference, and this time the unification of East and West Germany and Berlin was complete. I was fortunate enough to visit the Babelsberg studio outside Berlin, which was the largest studio in Europe, producing films from 1912. The German classic *Blue Angel* (1930) was shot there and Marlene Dietrich's room was still maintained as it was from the early black-and-white era.

9

DISCOVERING POVERTY AND DEPRAVITY

In Bollywood, trying to make authentic stories about real people dealing with real situations is as hard as trying to find an oasis in a desert. Regional cinema tried to hold on to its roots but sold out some years ago to bad remakes of Hindi films with a high entertainment quotient. There were exceptions, however, but they were a minority. However, Bengali and Malayalam cinema continued for a long time to make authentic, realistic films rooted in their region or ethnicity. Unfortunately, there was no one to follow in the footsteps of Satyajit Ray – I don't mean his style but the way he made his films, the meticulous detail, the authenticity, subjects pertaining to real life. Marathi films in the last few years have been re-establishing their identity with what is colloquially called 'class' cinema. In Hindi cinema I cannot think of anyone else except Shyam Benegal who consistently made films about real people and real issues. I wouldn't call them issue-based films but they were well-told stories with well-etched characters navigating through life, dealing with various issues.

Organic integrity, by which I mean a harmonious relationship between the elements of a whole, with subject, situation and characters, became a hallmark of art films referred to as non-commercial films. Actually, the term 'commercial films' is a misnomer because all films are made for an audience with expectations of some commercial release. The more accurate word for them would be non-formula films. However, they had no scope for theatrical exhibition because they could not draw huge crowds and therefore did not have any takers. Distributors, exhibitors and theatre owners were and still are not interested in films that tell real stories of real people. They prefer to buy or invest in Bollywood films made with stars and songs and dance numbers. The art films invariably won National Awards, even awards at prestigious foreign film festivals but that did not improve their business or box-office prospects.

What was missing was marketing. One has been around long enough to know that anything can be sold by a clever marketeer and there are takers for every kind of product in a country of one billion plus, not to mention the Indian diaspora abroad wanting to connect with everything Indian.

However, today Marathi films like *Killa* (2014) and *Court* (2014) and many others with English subtitles are pulling non-Marathi audiences to the theatres. The shift has become possible for two reasons. One, the audience has much more exposure to all kinds of world cinema thanks to the numerous television channels and, second, the availability of small theatres in multiplexes with limited capacity for niche audiences.

The world of Hindi films, even before it got the new name Bollywood quite some years ago, has been a strange one. Heroes in films I watched, right from my childhood days, never had any surnames, most of the time they topped the class and if uneducated, would have hearts of gold and take a stand for the poor or downtrodden. Sometimes they carried deep pain in their heart and took revenge to compensate for the injustice or humiliation meted out to their parents.

The heroines simply had to be virgins in the films even if their roles were of prostitutes or 'tawaifs' who lived in the red-light area, genteelly called 'fallen women'. And if they had lost their virginity, they were considered 'tainted' or 'spoiled', more like second-hand or damaged goods.

Indian society has set much store by women's chastity from the time of the Ramayana and films only seemed to follow that trodden path. And the women could not be in love with two men ever! Often they had to be sacrificing and have the ability to shed copious tears. And, most important, they had to conform to the male perspective with no real opinions of their own. A man could give up his beloved for a friend and often no one ever bothered to find out what the girl in question wanted, or whom she loved. She could be passed around like an object! Except for a few odd women like Draupadi or Sita who had their 'swayamvars' and chose their mates, the average Indian woman did not have a choice. Films invariably perpetuated these concepts in society.

Today there is a conflict – there are women who are obedient, subservient and dependent on the men in the family and there are some who are independent with opinions of their own, and self-reliant too. Both exist in the same time frame today – even in movies and television serials. It seems to have confused and angered the men though and they are often at a loss to deal with the new kind of woman.

In the old Hindi films of the '60s and '70s, there were two characters that were an essential part of a film – the vamps and the comedians. By the '80s, they underwent a major transformation. The vamps merged with the heroines, carrying with them the revealing clothes with deep cleavages and 'dangerously' high hemlines. All one has to do is go on the net and look up item numbers. They are all there for everyone to see. The comedians literally disappeared as the heroes took over their antics and belted out the comic punchlines. If it wasn't for television, comedians would be in serious trouble, but luckily, over the last few years, they have had a platform to express their talent for comedy and make a living.

There are hardly any women-oriented films or issue-based films. But the girls have become more bold as compared to the earlier heroines. It has become quite a fad to produce remakes and sequels of successful films and the trend continues. What is shocking is that almost every Indian language is a treasure trove of amazing stories and yet there are no takers for them in Bollywood.

Another strange thing is that the men or women in Bollywood films do not represent any region. Certain stereotypes inhabit the Bollywood make-believe celestial firmament and are accepted as Indian men and women but they are far removed from the real people. The weirdest ones are the tribals shown in Hindi films. The way they look and act is quite funny. There was a time when rape scenes were shown in almost every Hindi film. The solution that these films offered those days was getting the victim married off to the perpetrator with not a concern for the rape victim, even when she was the hero's sister.

Bollywood has always been on the lookout for a formula that works at the box office and that is one of the main reasons why the films lack originality and authenticity in every aspect, be it the selection of stories, the casting, the music, the costumes, the kind of dialogues, etc. The films literally had to have every possible ingredient of entertainment in them. It is not surprising therefore that such films were called 'masala' films.

Any serious film-maker committed to his art would find it hard to make films in such a scenario and hats off to those who have worked against the tide, against the pressures of the Bollywood business demands and emerged victorious, by which I mean, have made a work of cinematic art and succeeded at the box office as well. There have been quite a few films which have broken the Bollywood notion of cliched formula and emerged as sensitive narratives but Bollywood itself is essentially about box-office returns of hundreds of crores of rupees for the entertainment provided. The movie moguls, the producers who lay out large sums of money and the corporates, the stars and the wannabes – they are all listening keenly, ears to the ground, after the release of any film to know how much the film has grossed over the weekend and then onto the next week and so on. Everyone aspires to be part of the 100-, 200- or 500-crore (rupee) clubs which gives them an exalted celebrity status.

Bollywood is an entertainment industry and there is money to be made. It has made millions temporarily forget their woes. If it did not provide the escapist fare it does and ended up giving the real India with its problems back to the audience, it would probably go out of business. We often forget that a major part of India still lives in villages; they don't have electricity and potable drinking water and even connectivity in many areas; girls are not sent to school and married off early. The money provided by the government through various schemes for the development of those people never reaches them, with the middle man siphoning it off and so on. There's no justice. Worst of all is the plight of women. Even people living in cities, except perhaps for the top 10 or 15 per cent, don't have it easy. Their day is fraught with struggles and issues. Bollywood is completely wedded to the notion of serving movies with a high entertainment value and thus cannot think of any deviation.

The problem for film-makers is that the emphasis on entertainment has created a situation that crushes the small film, which calls itself cinema, where real people with real emotions living out real stories are shown. While in literature we have a spectrum of every kind of writing, in films it is not so. Even as I write this, a change is coming in, with the scope beginning to widen.

But one thing that has risen above the mundane is film music. Over time it has managed to create an Indian identity. You could hear the same song sung in the north-east or in the deep south of

India. Though film music was by and large more melodious in the first seventy years since films came into being, even today there are exceptional numbers. The diversity or spectrum one is missing in films is present in the music, though classical music seems to have almost gone out from Hindi film music. The music directors, musicians and singers have thankfully still remained creative.

It was in the '90s, as I was developing some subjects close to my heart after *Rihaee*, strictly avoiding formulaic film-making, when someone approached me to do a Marathi serial. I was not interested in television and had no affinity towards it. I also thought at that time, doing something in Marathi, with such a small reach, was like a waste of resources, because with the same amount of time and trouble one could reach larger audiences if one did a Hindi film. But when they told me it was written by Madhu Mangesh Karnik, the well-known Marathi writer, I decided to give it a hearing.

Listening to the subject of *Bhakri ani Phool*, I was inspired by its intensity, authenticity, ethnicity and human emotions. Spanning the pre- and post-Independence era, it is the story of a poor Dalit family living in the Konkan region and their journey to Bombay and into neo-Buddhism. I was blown away by the depiction of the dire poverty at the grass roots and the values they lived for and clung to, in the face of all odds.

Their simplicity, integrity and humanity were so touching, I fell in love with all the characters and this is one piece of work that I am actually proud to have done. There were sixteen episodes and the telecast was scheduled to coincide with Babasaheb Ambedkar's birth or death anniversary. The performers, mostly from the Marathi stage, were just brilliant. Suhas Bhalekar, who had also acted in my films, *Shaque* and *Gehrayee*, was outstanding as the downtrodden head of the family.

The budget of the serial was so meagre that there was no question of shooting in Konkan on the western coast of Maharashtra. Since I had been married into a family hailing from the Konkan region and had been going every year to Walawali for Ram Navami, I was familiar with what that region looked like. But finding such locations in and around Bombay to depict Konkan was not easy. After a great deal of hunting we found the perfect locations in Vasai. Since it was a period drama, it was a challenge to find the costumes and props for our characters. Shooting outdoors in public spaces was even more demanding.

Then came a project that caused in me a violent gut-wrenching reaction. It was about the devadasis of the Yellamma temple which is situated in Saundatti in Karnataka, close to the Karnataka–Maharashtra border. Once again I was confronted with the depravity of human beings.

I had known about it while helping my friend T.S. Ranga, during the making of *Giddh*, but now I discovered even more gruesome details. The films were called *Patita Pavana* and *Patita Pavani* (1992) in Marathi and Kannada respectively, meaning saviour of the fallen, referring to Goddess Yellamma. But, unfortunately, it was exactly the opposite, a total exploitation in the name of the Goddess. She should have been called 'Destroyer of the Innocent'!

Girls aged ten to twelve years were offered to the Goddess or 'married' to the Goddess. They were made to wear red beads in contrast to the black ones worn by married women and told that henceforth they would have to serve any man who approached them for sex, and live their lives by going door to door and collecting alms. So they had a nomadic existence and lived in abject poverty. They were easy to spot as they always carried on their heads a basket of Goddess Yellamma's face masks and heads made out of brass. Their routine was to scrub those masks and heads by the riverside or a well so that they shone in the sun. They then worshipped them with haldi, kumkum and flowers. They would hang around in groups near a temple or marketplace where they could be picked up for sex.

The ritual of giving the girl to the Goddess or the 'initiation' ceremony was sponsored by a local landlord or a moneyed trader/

businessman who also paid off the girl's parents. After the ritual, the girl was handed over to the sponsor to 'enjoy her' for the night and for as many nights as he wished. After that she was passed on to his friends or whoever would pay for her. Most of the time, a pimp, who would be on the lookout for such girls, or one who would be visiting from Bombay, would buy her off and resell her to another pimp or a madame from Kamathipura, the red-light area of Bombay, which was just ten hours away by road. All through, the little girl would be treated like a dispensable object to be used and discarded. Since Saundatti was not so far away and just an overnight journey, it was a regular source for girls to be put into prostitution.

The Karnataka government had banned the system some years ago but it continued clandestinely. Very often the local politicians, corporators and police personnel were involved too so it continued to persist. The government came out with the initiative of awarding five thousand rupees to anyone who would marry a devadasi and give her a chance at a decent life. Many would come forward, marry a devadasi, pocket the money and vanish, or sell her off again to a pimp. Under the guise of rehabilitation, mass marriages were also conducted in which the hapless, 'rescued' devadasis would be married off to convicts.

Not only patriarchy but also the feudal system is very deep-rooted in these areas, not to mention the caste system. A girl child is considered to be of the least value among a poor man's possessions or assets. If the crops failed, or a bullock died, or there was a famine or sickness in the family, the only offering the poor could make was their little girl, to supposedly appease the anger of the Goddess. This was drummed into the heads of the poor farmers and labourers by all and sundry, including the local priest. Once initiated, these girls were actually raped over and over again and sold and resold until they finally found themselves in Kamathipura with no hope of any escape.

The story of the film was based on a series of real incidents as narrated to me by the producer, Mr Sali, who was from Hubli, an industrial business town in north Karnataka. We discussed at length what language the film should be made in. Since the producer was an educationist and our intention was to bring about a difference in the lives of the local people and not make the film necessarily to share the horrors of the subject, we zeroed in on making a bilingual film in Kannada and Marathi. It meant research, location hunting outdoors and casting in two languages.

We decided to take the same actors as far as possible for both versions and chose a mix of Maharashtrian and Kannada actors. Once the casting was done, we planned rehearsals for three days before the first shoot. The Maharashtrian actor who was well known and had done some work in Hindi as well, and who was to play the protagonist, did not turn up – not on the first day or on the second. This was highly unprofessional and the producer and I, after a great deal of thought, decided to dump him. The studio was already booked and whatever alternatives we wanted were not available, so we decided to shoot with a complete newcomer. He was a young man from Pune – Raju Khandagale – who had approached me earlier for a role. He was delighted at the offer.

He travelled the night on a train from Pune, reaching Bombay at around 4 a.m. I asked him to sleep for a couple of hours after which I would explain things to him. I woke him up at 6 a.m., briefed him for a bit, gave him the dialogues in both the languages and said we would leave at 7.30 a.m. for the studio. The first part of the shoot was in Filmistan Studio in Goregaon, where we shot for locations like the police commissioner's office and a cheap lodge in Bombay.

Those days we were shooting on film – on celluloid. Since raw stock was expensive, we could not shoot too many takes and the rehearsals had to be good. The young man managed somehow on the first day and then had time later to practise Kannada, which he was not familiar with.

We did a recce in Saundatti where the Yellamma temple is located and we were all set for the outdoor shoot. There was also an important segment to be shot in the red-light area, specifically Kamathipura.

I had visited Kamathipura two or three times during the shooting of *Giddh* and *Rihaee* but this needed much more in-depth research. Initially I was advised not to go there but send a male assistant to do the research work. But, adamant as always, I found someone who could take me into Kamathipura and ensure that I was allowed to interact with the commercial sex workers. I made many such visits and came out safe and sound in one piece each time. I am saying this because it was believed that any woman who entered Kamathipura could never come out of the place. I could have been abducted also and it would not have been easy to find me. I had to go with proper personnel connected to high places.

I remember those dirty lanes with women standing outside the doors in their petticoats and blouses with cleavages and midriffs showing, faces heavily made up, calling out to customers. I also saw the devadasi women, vermillion plastered on their foreheads, carrying their baskets of the ferocious Yellamma faces glinting in the sun.

It was quite daunting, however, to enter the buildings. The staircases and walls were stained with betel-leaf spit, stains and heaven knows what else. They had obviously not been cleaned or painted in years. Even though the steps were steep, I hesitated to hold the banister because that too was so dirty. I walked right in the middle of the staircase, afraid to let any part of me or my clothes touch the sides.

But that was only until I started the shoot. Soon enough I got so used to it all that it didn't matter that we were sitting on those foul mattresses and beds in 6x4 cubicles where the women entertained their clients and sold sex. We even had our evening snacks and tea sitting there, all our snobbery or distaste of the place and people having vanished over time.

I was shocked beyond my imagination when my guide took me to some hidden places in the building. Holes in the floor with big drums on top to hide them from view; small cupboards in walls that held tunnels leading to neighbouring buildings and other secret hideouts. The guide candidly showed me all this and requested me not to shoot those places because they were used as both escape routes during a raid, and places for minor girls to be hidden from the police. I realized these mazes were so complex that if one got trapped in one of them, it would be impossible to find one's way out.

I was also surprised to see stacks of money being exchanged and people playing 'matka' (a form of gambling with numbers). I pretended to be invisible and kept my mouth shut, for this seemed to be going on openly and I had to focus on the film I was making. I had heard about the criminal–political nexus and here it was obvious and in full display.

As I got familiar with the life of the commercial sex workers, the madames and the pimps, I was filled with despair at the depravity of man. But the film needed to get done and we decided to shoot for almost a week in that place. We shot a police raid, some parts in the interior – in the cubicles, backyard, corridors and staircases.

We managed to get some documentary footage as well, walking around capturing things as they were. The mornings in those streets were completely unrecognizable. There was a dirty gutter with dark fluid flowing, the stench of which cannot be described. But that was for outsiders. The people of Kamathipura were quite oblivious to the smell and the dust and dirt. There were khatiyas (coir cots) on the street with old women on them who had lived their lives and had nothing more to give to the world, just waiting to die; children playing quietly by piles of garbage, their snotty noses running, but not generating any happy sounds of childhood; old men lying on the street, dead drunk in the middle of the day or else coughing and spitting; goats and hens wandering aimlessly and dogs looking hungrily around for some crumbs. In the middle of all this would be a stove with something cooking in it while a parrot in a cage would squawk, disturbing the deathly silence, which seemed like some hangover from the previous night. The whole scenario looked like a part of some surrealistic film until people began to wake up in the afternoon after toiling all night and sleeping off the first half of the day.

The streets began to breathe life in the early evening and came alive only after sunset which is when the flesh trade flourished and went on the whole night.

One evening, when we were shooting in Kamathipura, a guy brushed past me, touching my shoulder. It seemed deliberate to me. So I stopped working and raised a hue and cry. The person who was taking care of us sent his assistants, more like 'bouncers', scurrying down the lane and literally in five minutes flat, they brought the man and threw him at my feet. The scene looked straight out of a Hindi film. The fellow grovelled at my feet, asking for forgiveness, pretending he had touched me by mistake. I was so shocked, I wanted him off my feet. I told him to go, it was OK, but the bouncers controlling the area were not satisfied until he had grovelled enough and rubbed his nose into the ground. The poor man, petrified out of his wits, was too willing to oblige and not risk more severe punishment. That was when I realized that the bunch of guys who escorted us were dangerous and could not be crossed. It was no wonder that the system was pretty watertight and escape for any girl quite impossible.

The girls brought there are tortured and raped relentlessly till they accept the life meted out to them. Most of them send money home but never get to see their families again. Even when minor girls are rescued by police personnel and NGOs, the parents and families of those girls refuse to take them back so they are forced to return to prostitution as a way of life. They do not have any money of their own and the local moneylenders exploit them, charging high rates of interest.

As the prostitutes get older they are relegated to the back rooms or whatever space is available. I was told that the young girls cater to the customers from about 6 p.m. to 2 a.m. After that the older women get an opportunity. At 4 a.m., I was told by someone else other than my guide, when most of Kamathipura is asleep, the lepers come and the oldest women are forced, often at knifepoint, to service them for literally small change. I have heard such women cursing and praying that they be born as men or dogs but not as women in their next birth.

One evening one of the protagonists of the film, the actress who was playing a commercial sex worker, got propositioned. She was naturally very upset and broke down. It took her quite some time to recover. Her family was disturbed that she was playing the role of a prostitute in the actual locale and when she went home every single night after the shoot, she was asked to head straight to the bathroom and wash herself before entering the house.

I had a scene in which the sex workers are in a jail cell in a police station after a raid. For the sake of authenticity, it was decided that we would take real sex workers to Filmistan Studio, where we had ready jail sets. My art director had got the police station set attached to the jail ready but I was worried about bringing these women out and what might follow if something went wrong. We organized a special bus and they were on their way to Goregaon, which is a two-hour ride from Kamathipura.

Oh, it was a sight worth watching! They were like little girls on a picnic in spite of their ravaged faces and the depression that sat heavily on their shoulders. They chattered incessantly and many of them told me that they had not stepped out of the lane for years. But when they arrived at the studio they created a lot of tension for us.

As soon as the bus doors were opened they ran amok to watch the other films being shot. We had not anticipated this and the pimps who had accompanied them had a hard time herding them back to the floor on which we were shooting. We lost two hours of precious shooting time but for the girls who loved Hindi films, it was a dream come true to watch a film shooting.

On location, at Saundatti, right in the beginning itself, we had a breakdown. I had a terrible stomach pain which was unbearable and did not know what the source was. And tough as I am in not letting anything upset a shoot, I had to consult a doctor. The doctor advised rest and some tests. It meant that we had to shift to Hubli. Things took a turn for the worse and I was admitted to a small dingy hospital and administered saline. The diagnosis turned out to be appendicitis and immediate surgery was required. There was fear that the appendix might burst but I was clear that I would not get operated upon in that little town. There were no airports or flights from anywhere nearby going to Bombay or even Bangalore; going by road was not advisable; so our only option was to go by train in that condition, with the IV drip and all, to Bangalore.

The producer managed to get a berth on the night train and my cameraman S.R. Krishnamurthy was good enough to travel with me all the way to Bangalore. I have been very fortunate to have good technician friends and Krishna was and is one such. We have a long association as he shot my diploma film, as well as *Bhakri ani Phool*, *Shaadi ya ...*, (the television serial on marriage) and *Rihaee*. He is a thorough gentleman and a big asset to a director, taking care of a great many things. That is the beauty of teamwork where the 'I' disappears and the 'we' takes the lead. My mother had made all the arrangements and a car and an ambulance awaited us at the station early next morning. I was taken straight to Wockhardt hospital and operated upon in the next two hours.

Being at home with my mother and the rest of the family in Bangalore, and well looked after, I recovered quickly. After a gap of six or eight weeks, we were all back on location. Having the unit travel twice cost the producer an additional amount of money, but we do have provision for such breakdowns under the head of 'unforeseen expenses' and he was generous enough to take it in his stride.

We shot the jatra (fair) at the Yellamma temple in Saundatti and came to know more about the horrifying fate some young girls met with. The police personnel who were helping us took us to the actual locations in the hillside where some of the 'dedicated' girls were discovered, hidden from the eyes of the law.

There was one scene in the film which was very challenging – the rape of a young girl after the initiation ceremony. I had seen plenty of rape scenes in Hindi films that left nothing to the imagination. I don't remember the names of the films but I do remember the actors, right from Prem Nath and Pran in black-and-white films up to Amrish Puri and Sadashiv Amrapurkar. I was certainly not going down that road. I devised the scene the following way and it had a huge impact.

To begin with, the little girl in the film, played by Pronoti, does not know what the ritual of marrying the Goddess or being dedicated means and is happy to be the centre of attention. When the landlord smiles at her during the initiation ceremony, she sees in it the kind gaze of an elder. There is another, older girl, played by Sukanya Kulkarni, who has been to school and has resisted all efforts to dedicate her to the Goddess in the past. She watches the ceremony and asks a senior devadasi, played by Jayanthi, whether it can be stopped. The devadasi shakes her head and says that nothing can be done and the system will prevail.

Pronoti is then taken away to the landlord's farmhouse. Sukanya, wanting to somehow protect the girl, dashes after the car and, running cross country, reaches the farmhouse. She finds the servants and henchmen playing cards near the outhouse and, avoiding them, she stealthily approaches the main house.

It is very quiet and as she goes around the house she hears the sound of a man's laughter. She goes towards it and climbs on a window ledge. Though the windows are closed, there is a broken glass pane through which she looks in and sees a terrified Pronoti sitting on a big bed. The landlord asks the little girl to take off her clothes. She is even more scared now and the landlord approaches the bed saying that he will do it himself.

After that I show the entire rape on Sukanya's face as she watches in horror, with the little girl and the landlord heard only on the soundtrack. Sukanya, unable to take it any longer, collapses, followed by a close-up of Pronoti sobbing and the landlord moving away, wiping his sweat. Sukanya then picks herself up and runs across the landscape, until she collapses on the ground.

We completed the films and took them to the CBFC. As expected, I was summoned by the committee after they had seen the film. They said they were very disturbed by the rape. I said that was precisely my intention – I wanted people to be disturbed, shaken up, upset, the works! This could not be taken lightly – it had to be unbearable. 'But …' they tried to protest. I said, 'Tell me, what is there to cut? There was no visual or sound that was offensive…' They had to just let it be. My intention had been very clear – the rape was not meant for titillation or for entertainment of any sort.

The committee had another cut in mind. Sukanya has a young admirer who wishes to marry her but the girl turns him down saying she wants to be a teacher and does not wish to marry then. At that time the young man is abducted. Two days later he is found lying in a gutter. Some people pick him up and bring him to the landlord's house to ask for justice. He is limping and his clothes are dirty and bloodied, particularly his pyjama. The landlord is not around, so the young man tells the landlord's wife that his manhood has been taken away from him. The censor committee was very disturbed by the pyjama scene and asked me to cut it. There was no way I could do that. The dialogues of the man made no reference to his private parts or the castration. There was no close-up of the pyjama either. It was a composite shot and the issue was critical to the story. So that too stayed without a cut.

It is so strange that people will condemn and criticize anything in public relating to sex and yet would like to have a piece of it, whether it is some juicy gossip or non-vegetarian jokes as they are called, if not a full-on indulgence, all in private, of course.

Earlier, when a film had to be sent for the National awards, a regional committee would see it and send it on. When this film came up for screening, I was told that someone passed a comment, '*Inn raandiyon ka film kaun dekhega?*' (Who will see this film about whores?) When I heard it, I was furious and thankfully the person who said it was not there to get a earful from me. I said, '*Inn raandiyon ko banaya kisne?*' (Who made them whores?) I don't know whether they saw the film or not. It was not selected anyhow – it was too hard to digest, though it won three or four state awards in both Karnataka and Maharashtra.

During the shooting of *Patita Pavana* and *Patita Pavani*, I had another uncomfortable experience. As film-makers if you are open, sometimes adventurous or daring and willing to explore life, you could be surprised at what turns up and how society, with its secrets lying hidden, reveals itself. In this case I was just plain innocent and ignorant.

There was a guest on our sets who had accompanied one of our woman actors. He drove in very fast and swerved his car into the parking lot. He was heavily built, dressed in jeans and a jacket, with cropped hair and a stud in one ear. His gait was aggressive. He passed us on the staircase but I did not particularly notice him. Later that evening, my cameraman Krishna commented on the person, referring to him as a 'she'. I argued with him that there was no 'she' but a 'he'. Later on we got introduced and Krishna was right, it was a 'she'. Oh, I thought, another tomboy type of woman.

But until she approached me one day, towards the end of the shoot, declaring her love, I had no idea she was a lesbian. I knew very little about the LGBT community and could not understand her attraction for me. I told her about my sexual preferences and even conjured up an imaginary boyfriend. But she was not to be put off easily. I didn't know her, I hadn't spent any time with her, I had not even met her socially or even had a couple of conversations with her and suddenly this onslaught!

When I got back to Bombay, happy to escape the unwanted attention, every single day, for months together, I got pink, blue, green, yellow, purple and orange cards with love messages. It was so exasperating and I did not know how to deal with it. I did not know whom to turn to for help. I realized then how people feel when they are stalked!

I finally thought, let me tell her directly to end the nonsense. She was from Bangalore, and when I was visiting my mother there, I called her over and made it amply clear that she would never get what she wished. In my ignorance I even said I would recommend a good psychiatrist who could help her deal with her issue. I wasn't sure which issue I was referring to – her sexuality or her desperation to find someone. Later on, I educated myself and understood her plight. I felt very sorry for her, for her inability to have a life like everyone else, to have the freedom to be whichever way she was.

After that, I have been an advocate for freedom of sexual orientation and a supporter of the LGBT community. Thankfully, this community now has been accepted to a great extent but more needs to be done with regard to laws so that people from this community can live a life of their choice.

The films *Patita Pavana* and *Patita Pavani* were done but I wasn't. For over three years, the images and the stories of the girls in Kamathipura haunted me. I had the habit of putting down on paper things they had said, in verse form. It was not poetry, it was pain. It was not even verse and as someone told me once, just prose written like verse. I kept writing what could be called the 'red-light verses'.

I did not publish it because the content was too hard hitting and I was afraid of it being sensationalized. However, we did print a few copies to raise money for the NGO Prerana which supports, educates and rehabilitates the children of commercial sex workers. I would like to include a couple of examples here:

A Prostitute to Her Unborn Child

My child,
I beseech thee,
do not be born…

Your future lies
in the dark hole
between your legs…

The grey shadows of lust
will corrode your insides
to give birth to a million worms…

The red-stained tongues
with their pervading breath of tobacco
will smother you with their acrid fumes…

If you come armed with a prick,
the only lands you shall conquer, my son,
are the dark caverns of the unfortunates!

Funeral Rites

With every sunset religiously
I prepare for my funeral rites;
to die a million deaths
and rise again the following night.

Mourners come one after another,
to rejoice in my sorrow;
what is death to me is their spring of life
and a renewed strength for tomorrow.

As a trustee and treasurer of Stree Bal Shakti, a NGO run by Maa, I found that we had two balwadis in those areas. I would go there sometimes and see those innocent tots who were just like any children in the world but without a future. They would reach out and literally climb over me, starved as they were for a little attention and some kindness. It was at that time I discovered Prerana, doing stellar work in Kamathipura. They have a night shelter where the kids stay while their mothers are at work through the night. During the day they attend school and many have done very well, going on to college and getting jobs. Unfortunately, the stigma travels with them as we live in a 'holier-than-thou' cruel society.

I also tried to have someone teach Reiki to the women to heal and empower them but that project got aborted for some reason. For me, the women in the red-light areas are angels come to earth to deal with the bestial facet of human beings. It used to be said that it's only because of them that women are safe in their homes but today, even that cannot be said, because no girl seems safe anymore in any city.

There used to be a strong movement to legalize commercial sex workers some years ago. That would certainly save them from exploitation at the hands of pimps and madames. They would be in charge of their own lives and be regular citizens with a profession like everyone else, and enjoy the same rights.

Why is selling your brain, your skills, your talent considered superior to selling your body? Logically, if it's yours you can do what you want with it … People are selling their body parts, kidneys, while they are still alive. Women are selling their wombs … So why come down heavily on women who find themselves unable to earn a living or feed their little ones for lack of some skills, and resort to prostitution? It might surprise a few but some women have actually told me, '*Kaun ghar ghar jaayega bartan manjne ke liye – pair failaana jyada aasaan hai*', meaning, who would want to go from house to house washing utensils when it is easier to spread your legs.

If women choose prostitution as a career, I would accept it as valid as my own choice of film-making or anybody else's. But mostly sex trafficking and prostitution are abuse and exploitation. What goes on in these hellholes called brothels has very little to do with choice. Most of the little girls who are bought and sold do not even know what is beneath their skirts, let alone understand sex.

The tragedy is that society has become intolerant about another's religion and not where it really matters. Can we be intolerant, angry and militant about the exploitation and abuse of women, instead?

10

MARRIAGE, SEX, LOVE AND GOD

After *Rihaee* was released, *Savvy* did a cover story on me. It came out in March 1990 and people found it intense and moving. It added to people's image of me as a strong woman standing up for women, though I was quite oblivious to it. I got a lot of mail through the years from people all over the country, even from some unheard-of places.

Today, twenty-seven years later, people still remember the article and share how they were inspired by it.

A couple of years after *Rihaee* was released, I came in contact with an old colleague who was in advertising, Karuna Samtani. She was working with Zee TV as the programming head. Knowing me and my reputation after *Rihaee*, she proposed we do something compelling, provocative and bold.

At that time Zee was the only channel apart from Doordarshan (DD) and we had to create the kind of programmes that would enable people to discover the real scope of television – new ideas, new stories, new game shows hitherto not available on Doordarshan. The bold, contemporary and modern outlook of Zee TV had people switch their allegiance not only from DD but also from movies because of its new content. In those days, Subhash Chandra personally looked into the programming and created the brand that stood the test of time.

After a lot of discussion, we zeroed in on the topic of marriage. I had an abundance of stories – real stories I had heard from people and read about, after my marriage had broken up. *Rihaee* had also catapulted me into being a women's rights activist and I had become a voice for women. Stree Bal Shakti gave me a platform to do workshops for women, to empower them and stand up for their rights. In all of this, I got a lot of insights into the institution of marriage and man–woman relationships.

Every episode of the serial I did for Zee TV in 1993 had a new story, all based on real incidents. There was twenty minutes of drama followed by ten minutes of discussion with experts and others which was moderated by me. Each had a new title: Shaadi Ya _____?/Marriage or _____ ? e.g. Marriage or Bondage? Marriage or Compromise? Marriage or Legalized Sex?

The serial had all kinds of issues relating to marriage – social, legal, moral, emotional. There were stories of adultery, cheating in marriage, incest, trivial arguments and self-righteous attitudes leading to break-ups; others on issues like dowry, bride burning, bigamy, domestic abuse, 'joint family' issues, exploitation for gain and even themes like desire for unlimited sex, demand for producing a male child, use and abuse of a woman like a domestic servant; and yet some more on couples giving each other space, understanding, domination of one or another or sometimes the family, suppression of individual talent, disillusionment, compromise, parenting, couples ignoring each other's needs, peer pressure, men berated for being considerate husbands who helped their wives and the fate of dark-skinned brides.

The serial ran for six months and at the end of it, in the last two episodes, we had all the characters come in, and they confronted each other for their actions and brought in a new understanding of marriage.

The serial at one level was very welcome and people waited for the next episode, while at another level it made people squirm. It was as if marriage was not such a secret confined to the bedroom anymore and worms were being let out of the closet. Almost everyone could see themselves or their issues reflected in some scene or some episode of the serial.

Some people were squeamish about the love scenes too while the rest revelled in watching them because they seemed realistic as compared to the Bollywood fare of khatiyas, flowers and birds doing the work.

Given that our society is not only patriarchal but chauvinistic as well, I was accused of bias too, as most of the stories showed women getting a raw deal in marriage.

The process that had started in *Rihaee*, being a voice for women, escalated to another level. In those days, I was on almost every talk show on television representing women.

I used to get a lot of fan mail too from people who not only appreciated what they saw but also from those who had shared their stories. Since I was non-judgemental and did not hold a moral torch, girls and women felt free to discuss their issues, problems, transgressions and even fantasies.

There was one such case that, I vividly remember. A young girl of sixteen or seventeen kept calling me on my landline and most of the time I was not there to answer her call. She would leave messages with whoever answered the phone but she never left a number for me to call her back. Finally she did get me one day and threatened to commit suicide if I did not meet her at once. I was both alarmed and worried and called her over right away, cancelling whatever appointment I had.

She lived in Tardeo and came over pretty quickly to where I was at Worli. I could not imagine that the girl was having to face something so barbaric in Bombay of the '90s. Her father was a police inspector and she was brought up with a lot of love and affection.

When she was fourteen years old, she was suddenly told that she would not be going to school anymore and that her marriage had been fixed. She tried to talk her parents out of it but to no avail.

She was married off and sent to her husband's house. The husband lived alone and on the first night itself, he raped her. She was shattered and told her husband that she would complain to her father and her father being in the police force would take him to task and not spare him. In response to that, the husband had laughed and said her father knew exactly what he was going to do with her and had given her to him for just that.

The poor girl was subjected to rape every day and night, whenever the husband fancied her. She was not allowed to meet anyone and was locked up in the house when he went to work. She would stand at the window and watch life pass by. The husband began to be suspicious of her and started beating her as well, berating her for having a paramour who, he thought, she communicated with through the window. She had tried to escape but the father and husband got wind of it. She did not know anyone and was virtually a prisoner in her house. She used to watch TV, had seen some episodes of *Shaadi Ya* ... and thought if anyone could help her out of her misery it was me. It was not very difficult to get my number because those days many of the interviews in the papers, especially the vernacular ones, gave the address or phone numbers.

She was a minor married for two years, caught in a marriage that was illegal. She told me that her father had fudged her school certificate and had even printed invitations for the wedding. I could not imagine such a blatant disregard for the law of the land by a police officer in a city like Bombay.

She begged me to help her out. I made a few calls and got a promise from a women's support group that they would get her out as soon as possible. She warned us that we had to be careful because her father was a cop and all her attempts to flee had been unsuccessful in the past. Finally, in the following week, we did get her out to a home in the suburbs. She was there for a year or two.

Unfortunately, in situations of domestic violence neither the relatives nor neighbours intervene, leaving the woman to fend for herself. People shrug it off saying that the problem is between the husband and wife. And the wives, with no support, learn to take it in their stride. It was a constant problem with a domestic help I had some years ago. She would come to work every day, beaten and bruised, and would be unwilling to do anything about it. Once she came to work with ten stitches on her scalp and could have died but she refused to let me take her to the police station to file a complaint. She chose to stay with her alcoholic husband and get beaten up.

Women who are not powerful or don't consider themselves to be of any worth, prefer to stay with a known devil rather than face an unknown element which could mostly be a multitude of men wanting to exploit them. Though there are laws for women to get justice and even be safe or secure, in practice there isn't that much available to them.

I have heard it said, good times pass but bad times pass too. Thankfully I had recovered from my depression and found my equilibrium with my focus on other people rather than on myself. I continued to work and bring up my son.

One day, when Hith was about seventeen, he asked me how much I earned. I had no clue because being a freelancer my earnings changed from year to year and only my chartered accountant knew the figures. I asked him what he wanted but he persisted in finding out how much I earned. Since I was totally clueless we came to a dead end. I had provided whatever he needed pretty well until then and he needed to tell me what he had on his mind. On further questioning, he let out that he wanted to go to Switzerland to study hotel management and catering. I said, 'Done.'

He was shocked and blurted out, 'Mom, do you know how much it costs – three years in Switzerland?' I shook my head. Of course,

I didn't know but I was clear that whatever it cost, he would go. And I did everything that I could, using up whatever was saved for his future, and also working day and night on some projects to put together the money required. And he did go.

Johnny Bakshi, who had played the coach in *Situm*, and who was also a producer–director, called me up one day and asked me if I would like to do a film for Plus Films. Headed by Mahesh Bhatt and Amit Khanna, Plus Films had funding for twelve films and they were shortlisting names of possible directors. Johnny said the story had already been finalized and if I liked it, we were on.

The following week I met Kaamna Chandra, whom, I had met earlier and listened to the story. I liked the subject she narrated, and I was willing to consider making it but I had some reservations. I asked to be given a few days to make up my mind. The protagonist was a blind girl who sings and my dilemma was whether I would be able to do justice to a subject like that.

I did not know the world of a blind person and if I did not get under the skin of the character, it was pointless. The next few days, I tied a bandana over my eyes and walked around the house, getting a feel of how it is when you cannot see. Of course, I bumped around, bruising myself, as I had no idea about even the familiar space without my eyesight. I tried to listen to sounds carefully, and discovered another dimension in the daily sounds I had taken for granted. Pouring water in a glass is a very mundane activity but the sound as you pour changes from empty to full. I realized that if you listened carefully, even without sight, you could tell when the glass is almost full. My experiment gave me confidence. I told Amit and Johnny that I would do the film.

The script was already done, but I wanted some changes. We decided to set the film in Karnataka, near Mysore, near the Kaveri river, where nature is in its full splendour. It meant some rewriting and Kaamna and I worked harmoniously and got the script ready. We zeroed in on Ashvini Bhave for the protagonist. It was not very easy though to find the male character who had negative traits.

Bollywood is strange sometimes. Many stars/actors declare they want to do negative roles but when offered one, they shy away. Maybe it is because they lack the confidence to pull off a negative character. If it was a stereotyped villain who looked evil and laughed wickedly like in many Hindi movies, maybe they would have jumped at the opportunity. What I was offering was a 'negative' male lead, not a Gabbar or Mogambo which they might have preferred.

Finally we found our hero in Bangalore, the south Indian actor Sridhar. It was such a joy to work with accomplished actors like Umashri from Bangalore, Manohar Singh and Sulabha Deshpande whom I admired immensely. Along with Dilip Raj we made up the cast.

Ragini, as the protagonist was called, was the daughter of a music teacher who sang in the temple and all the songs were based on Hindustani classical music. Though Laxmikant and Pyarelal had done over 500 films, they were truly inspired and every song they did was a gem. I had seen Laxmikant in the past give songs to producers and directors at the drop of a hat. And many of those songs became popular too. But for *Bhairavi* (1995) he took great care and was at his creative best. He would not let up until I was fully satisfied. Amit Khanna's lyrics were exceptional and actually came to life in the way they were tuned. Little wonder, then, that he won a National Award for Best Lyrics.

When Pyarebhai took over and did the music with all the orchestration, I think even the gods must have been happy. I consider him a genius and the background score he composed was phenomenal. I had said to him before the background music recording that I was allergic to synthesizers and preferred live musicians playing natural acoustic instruments as against electronic sounds. Given that our budget was limited I was keen to have one real violin as against many coming out of a box. He agreed with me but told me that he would still need to use the synthesizer for support and promised me that I would not hear any electronic sound in the music. I had also asked for human voices to be used, though not in the stereotypical fashion of those days, and he did a great job with that too. There was a freshness and emotion that came through. He was a real master at his art and very few films have background scores like that of *Bhairavi* and it made a huge difference to the film.

While we were working on the songs, I visited some schools for the blind to see how the visually impaired lived their daily life. It was an eye-opener for me. They were so well trained that when they would go shopping, they would give the right amount of money to the shopkeeper and ensure they got the right amount of change back. I saw them cutting vegetables, lighting the gas and even cooking food. Of course I knew that they read and write in Braille, but everything else they did amazed me.

I then took Ashvini to the blind school so that she could study their movements and expressions. We also had Satyadev Dubey come in and do a special session with Ashvini for her to express herself as a blind person in a natural way. Barun was the cinematograper and I discussed at length with him the kind of lighting we would need and he took it well beyond even what I had imagined. He was known for his lighting and *Bhairavi* was a great example of what could be called 'painting with light'.

The locations of *Bhairavi* were simply breathtaking. We shot in the coracles on the Kaveri and a old house we found in Srirangapatnam. We got to the bottom of the Gaganchukki Falls, crane and all, at sunrise, and were very lucky to get a real rainbow in the film, given that every so often people add that on. We also shot at Talekadu, a sandy and desert-like patch in the middle of the green belt with a buried temple, which attracted a lot of tourists as it is supposed to be an oddity. The picturization of the song, '*Om namah shivaya*', was very challenging, given the limited time and a huge crowd in the Nanjangud temple.

Despite a mishap on the sets, when a lightboy fell from the top of a tree and broke his bones and had to be hospitalized, we returned in forty-five days after completing the film's shooting.

I edited the film at my own studio on a Steenbeck. When we began dubbing, we tested some voices for the south Indian actors because the film was after all in Hindi, though it had a strong regional flavour. We found all the voices except for the character of Umashri.

Raghuvir Date, with whom I had worked since my first film, was a senior recordist who had started his career in Rajkamal Studios. His specialized in experimenting and creating stuff 'out-of-the-box' never saying 'no' to anything the director asked for. I remember, during dubbing, sometimes people from the fraternity would visit and wonder what he was doing – sometimes the mike would be upside down, other times it would be on the side – breaking the rules as he fiddled with his knobs on the console and did all kinds of things to create not just the quality of sound but a certain distinctive character to match the person on the screen.

In *Rihaee*, I remember, we were working on a very low budget and for the characters of a single scene, it would have cost us quite a bit to get different voices. Nobody would come for an hour for just one scene – you had to pay by the shift, for six to eight hours. We found a solution; Raghuvir changed my voice and I ended up doing thirteen-odd characters in *Rihaee*. In *Bhairavi* too, when we could not find the right voice for Umashri, I ended up doing her dubbing at his suggestion.

Given that the film was about a blind girl for whom sound was the access to the world outside, I wanted the audience to experience it too in some measure. So I devised my title sequence accordingly. The titles came on a black background but the sound accompanying was not a music track, as is most often the case.

The soundtrack started with the cry of a peacock followed by thunder. Thunder rumbled, followed by the sound of the rain. First it was raindrops, and then the pitter-patter that increased in tempo, was followed by heavy rain. This further led to flowing streams and eventually gushing water. My experience was that I could actually feel wet with just the sounds. The association of the sounds created such a powerful sensation that I would even feel cold and shiver sometimes, just listening to it. A lot of people had the same experience, and felt they had been made aware of a world of sound and its impact. It made me realize how often we all take it for granted and ignore its power and potential.

The person who put this collage of sounds together was Padmanabhan, Paddy, as we called him, a brilliant recordist, an alumnus of the film institute. He worked painstakingly, collecting effect by effect and gradually mixing and blending the sound effects to create a whole – a sound narrative to depict the advent of rain.

When *Bhairavi* was released it created a minor controversy. Ragini, the protagonist, is the only daughter of her parents who die one after another, leaving her alone in the world. Her support is the domestic help who cares and treats her like her own. Ragini's father has left her the house, jewellery and some savings in the bank to secure her future, given her handicap.

A young man comes into her life, woos her and marries her. She is very happy in the beginning but is left heartbroken when, one day, he runs away with her money and jewellery. She does not believe when people tell her that he was a swindler who came into her life just to cheat her. It is discovered that he has committed other frauds too and is arrested. She goes to the jail to meet him, to get him out on bail somehow as she still loves him. In the police station, she overhears a conversation that makes her realize that he does not love her but intends to use her to get out of jail. She confronts him and refuses to bail him out. She gives his clothes away and getting into one of the coracles, goes midstream and immerses her mangalsutra in the river, as is the common practice in India to immerse the ashes of the dead in the river after cremation.

Though some people thought that the symbolism was great, some others had a problem with the immersion of the mangalsutra. As far as I was concerned, Ragini's marriage was over, so what was the point of holding on to the mangalsutra? Given the poetic nature of Ragini's character, the traditional surroundings she had grown up in and the simplicity with which she dealt with situations in her life, it had seemed the most appropriate way to depict it on screen.

Another project I did a lot of work on was *Khajuraho – A Journey*. The film was launched with much fanfare but was shelved because I left the film owing to some issues with the producer. Thankfully, shooting hadn't begun, so it was easy to call it off. Another producer tried to revive it but it did not take off due to budgetary constraints.

However, the research and thinking I did for the project gave me new insights and an understanding of sex and maybe that was all there was to be accomplished, in the larger scheme of things.

Human beings are basically very judgemental and it happens all the time without us even being aware of it. Where there is judgement there is invariably 'right/wrong' or 'good/bad'. Nature has no such issues.

All life on this planet breathes when it has to breathe, procreates when it has to procreate and so on – it's only human beings who consider themselves highly evolved and intelligent and lay down the law to decide what is right and wrong.

What can be right or wrong about love or intimacy or sex? It is what it is – just nature. It is man's arrogance that questions and attempts to have control over this. It is literally like asking the sun not to shine, the wind not to blow and the water not to flow. The sun will shine when it shines, you can't decree that wrong! You can't judge the wind wrong for blowing either nor the water for flowing! I think our predecessors understood that, as is evident in Khajuraho, but we seem to have regressed.

I first went to Khajuraho in 1970 and again a few years later. Each time, the place left a lasting impression on me. It was like being in a time warp. What were the depictions on the temple walls trying to convey? How is it that there has been such a huge shift in the way people think and in their behaviour since those times? What was the role of sex then? What is it now? Why is sex a bad word today? Why don't we have the freedom to even discuss it openly?

Sex education has been done away with in schools. As a result, adolescents are led astray and bungle their way into adulthood. Marriage as an institution that demands fidelity has crumbled in the face of rampant adultery. People indulge in all kinds of sexual behaviour, crossing the barriers of 'so-called' decent social norms in their craving for excitement and meaning in their lives.

My research and what I had read years ago, led me to understand how we had created what appears to be a mess of mammoth proportions. The so-called representatives of God and country, evolved moral and ethical codes in their thirst for power and created sin where there was none. They called something 'bad' and made it 'wrong'. Religion was used by middlemen to keep people ignorant and chronically sinning so that they were always under the control of the priests and the clergy, in whichever part of the world, including India. If there was no crime there would be no policing! So crime was created, right and wrong were established and people continued to be judged and punished for being themselves.

Sometimes I envy animals; my son's cat, for instance. He has no issue of right or wrong, good or bad. He's chilled out while we humans are so overwhelmed by moral and ethical dilemmas negotiating life. As a society, we have complicated our lives instead of simplifying them over time.

History has shown that rulers, political leaders and priests mastered the art of manipulation. Thoughts, words and deeds that don't fit into the approved public norms, even though they are natural, are disowned as aberrant and people who have had the courage to express themselves are condemned, punished and ostracized by society, in spite of us having a Constitution that promises us freedom as a fundamental right.

Sex became sin – it became dirty. It became the weakness of the flesh. Religion and moral diktats made sure that our own body was something we should be ashamed of. They drilled it in, especially with women, that their sensuality was depraved and the sooner they disowned it, the more healthy it was for them.

Sex went into the closet, to be indulged in clandestinely; passively by the woman in the darkness of the night and actively by the man, even in broad daylight. The hangover of morality is so strong that for a woman 'not enjoying sex' is considered morally superior to having sex with pleasure.

Strangely this did not apply to men! Women were branded as cheap whores if they enjoyed the sexual experience. They were considered temptresses, who needed to be hidden away, to be covered. What could the poor men do if these wicked women were at large? Virginity and chastity became measures of a woman's character, the lack of it leading to further oppression of women.

Today, I am ashamed to hear some political leaders talk. What can the poor men do if women cut their hair, wear jeans and short dresses, use mobile phones, don't cover their bodies completely and use make-up? They justify eve teasing, molestation and rape, which is commonplace today, using phrases like 'boys will be boys'.

When there is judgement and morality, freedom and self expression go for a toss. Suppression of sex and lack of healthy conversation around it, a misconstrued image of manhood and the resultant frustration has led to rapes where neither a six-month-old infant nor a ninety-five-year-old woman is spared.

Earlier, in single-screen theatres, there were the front benches with very cheap ticketing. Men could watch the night show and enjoy whatever entertainment, song, dance and drama that was available. Then there were dance bars and men could go and get drunk, throw money and spend their time watching women dance. The red-light areas were spaces that absorbed the 'floating population' all through the night until the early hours of the morning. All these spaces kept men off the streets and away from attacking women arbitrarily anywhere and everywhere.

Even early civilizations had spaces like these so that the men could be kept engaged and their energies channelized, so that they did not have to go hunting for suitable prey to have sex with.

Whenever I go into the low-income busy crowded areas of Bombay, in the evenings or nights, sometimes even just passing by those commercial areas, I see large numbers of men just loitering, hanging around with no purpose, having no place to go to and nothing to do. Many of them are what is called the 'floating population' who are visiting on work, and the rest are day labour with no homes. Many of them end up sleeping on the pavements and that too for a price.

Multiplexes have taken away the cheap film viewing facilities, the dance bars in Bombay have been closed down and so has Kamathipura, a major hub for commercial sex. Kamathipura, considered a prime property of south Bombay, has been undergoing major redevelopment. Thus the brothel business had no option but to move away. After the dance bars in Bombay had closed down thanks to the overenthusiastic efforts of a Maharashtra minister, one had heard that the dancing girls had no recourse but to go into prostitution and operate from Mira Road. The Kamathipura sex business made Mira Road its new home but whether or not any old-fashioned brothels are still run is a question.

To top it all porn is available on the mobile phone, just a click away! The availability of a camera on the phone has given people their own tools to create porn and share. Rapes and intimate liaisons are being shot and MMS and videos circulated, simultaneously also creating situations for blackmail and further oppression of women.

But things have begun to change. Women have started speaking up. Having met thousands of women and interacted with them, I don't know if there is anyone who can say that they have not experienced some kind of sexual harassment in their life.

I remember as a little girl, walking with my mother, young men whistling at her and calling her 'Bina Rai', who was a well-known film actress. Her response had then been to ignore them and walk away briskly. Later, I heard stories of her receiving unwanted attention from my father's colleagues.

It was unheard of to report such happenings until maybe in the last couple of years. At sixty I have been called a 'sex-kitten' by someone I was working with, and even propositioned at sixty-eight years. I still get such kind of messages on WhatsApp or Facebook which I ignore.

I remember there was a time when I used to get phone calls from someone using obscene language. I used to be so terrified to pick up the phone (this was before mobile phones came on the scene). Eventually I did go to the Commissioner of Police and Mahanagar Telephone Nigam Ltd. to complain.

Another time I got a letter saying that there was some obscene stuff written about me in the men's toilet at Nehru Centre. That put me in a fix because I could not go and check it out myself. And I found it hard to share with a male friend or colleague. The experience was of utter humiliation and shame. Finally when I did muster the courage to ask someone to go and check it out, I was told that there was no such message. It had been just a ploy to harass me.

Yet another time I got an inland letter with the male genitals drawn on it. One learnt to ignore such things and move on but thankfully girls and women are not taking it lying down anymore. Whether they are from urban or rural areas, they are voicing their grievances and taking matters to court to have the perpetrators punished. Rather than change the mindset of men with sex education and create a new freedom to talk about it, accept it and cultivate new values, political leaders have taken the path of blaming women. They seek to stifle the women who are perceived to be the source of temptation, putting them out of public sight, dominating them, hounding them, punishing them, humiliating them, brow beating them, raping them and, if nothing works, killing them.

A lot of work to empower women is being done and this has been yielding results. But hardly anything has been done to change the mindset of men. One of the problems seems to be the perception of women as sex objects. The depiction of women in movies and advertising has been that of exploitation of the female body.

A first-ever UN-sponsored global study of women characters in popular films across the world has shown that India tops the charts in showing attractive women in its movies and as much as 35 per cent of these women characters are shown with some nudity. The study finds that Indian films have a significantly higher prevalence of sexualization of women characters and the movies score low in depicting women in significant or 'speaking' roles. While women represent nearly half of the world's population, less than one third of all characters with dialogues in films are women and the UK-US collaborations and Indian films are at the bottom of the pack.

It is not surprising because the trend in Bollywood in the last few years has been an almost mandatory 'item' – a dance number with minimum clothing, maximum gyrations with double entendre or risqué lyrics performed by the leading lady. The Geena Davis Institute of Gender in Media has been doing detailed studies of women's participation in films. The data examining gender prevalence behind the camera revealed a ratio of 6.2 males to every one female in the film industry in India.

In Hollywood too, the 'glass ceiling' continues to exist. According to the *Hollywood Reporter*, women made up only 6 per cent of all directors working on the top-grossing films of 2013, a decrease of 3 per cent since 2012. Women comprised 10 per cent of writers, 15 per cent of executive producers, 25 per cent of producers, 17 per cent of editors and 3 per cent of cinematographers. In India, the numbers are even less, adding perhaps overall to about 15–20 per cent across all departments.

Male domination and chauvinism are rampant. There are stories on the net shared by women; stories of sexism, gender bias, misogyny and sexual harassment. A story I read on the net goes thus: A woman director in Hollywood was sent to meet a studio head. After the interview was over the studio head is supposed to have raged, 'Never send anyone again, who I wouldn't want to fuck.' It has been reported also that though many women directors in Hollywood have given extraordinary hits – films which have made a lot of money at the box office, they still have a hard time getting funding for their new films.

I have also encountered a strange phenomenon in India. Here people mix up my gender; people who have not met me think I am male until they meet me or hear my voice. Can't there be a woman speaker, leader or film director? There are so many women at top positions in all walks of life now, but apparently the number has not reached a critical mass. So often, I am addressed as Mr Patil. Earlier it used to bug me no end but now I am more tolerant. There was even a famous film journalist in his early days who came to interview me thinking I was male. I gave him a piece of my mind and, sure, the next time around, I got a very bad review for my film. Another renowned journalist remarked that I was too glamorous to be a film director.

We turned a blind eye to what was being expressed quite openly in the *Kamasutra* or at Khajuraho, even though they have stood the test of time in more ways than one!

The erotica on the temple walls seem to be paying homage to not only the physical form of human beings but also to love, intimacy and the final culmination in the sexual act in all its various forms.

The female form has never been acknowledged so thoroughly in its so many moods. Why were the outer walls of the inner sanctum adorned with erotic sculptures? A possible explanation is sex education.

People could come freely and partake of the knowledge. In one of the panels, in fact, there seems to be a practical demonstration class in progress with some figures performing, others watching in the presence of a guru, with what seems to be his manual kept in front of him.

It is said that when you are satiated and fully expressed in the area of sex, you actually go beyond into the inner sanctum, to God. So sex too has a larger function in the scheme of things in the universe, besides procreation; it could possibly be the pathway to God. The architects and sculptors of Khajuraho may have designed it to accomplish exactly this.

Those were the times when life was well balanced between Dharma, Artha, Kama and Moksha and people were very clear that all four aspects had to be completely fulfilled. The last of the four, moksha, was possible only if man was happy with the first three, including his raging hormones.

Today we have forgotten our knowledge, our culture and are struggling to be happy. I am almost afraid to use the word 'culture' as it has been bandied about extensively by those claiming that culture demands the complete subjugation of women. And yet history tells us that men and women were actually equal in the Vedic Age. Who knows?

If we can be what nature intended us to be, more than half the battle will be won. Instead, we have created for ourselves a nation of over one billion people born out of a supposedly 'shameful act' and joyless negativity; most of the one billion sods born with bitterness, born out of duty, rape and sexual violence permitted by society and sanctified by the institution of marriage.

I also think that perhaps Khajuraho was advocating the one man-one woman theory as ideal, a more solid foundation for the institution of marriage. It is a fact that in marriage, a variety in love/lovemaking is necessary. It is vital to keep generating excitement, enthusiasm and romance too every once in a while to keep the marriage/relationship alive.

If you had to work your way through all the complex love-making positions depicted in the *Kamasutra* and Khajuraho, it would have been necessary to work with the same partner. Just like two partners who dance together and are in sync with each other no matter what the dance movements are, so also, it would work for the two partners who know each other and can be in sync with each other during the act of sex. The idea propagated is perhaps having variety in sex not through different partners but through multiple and challenging approaches, expressions, positions, etc. Since the art of making love and being in union with another human being was put in public domain on the walls of a temple, it could be understood that it was meant for all.

In any case it would have been impractical and difficult for the common man to have different partners and explore the innumerable possibilities of sexual expression, as it is today too. Only the privileged had it then and have it now.

Maybe what is depicted in Khajuraho meant to keep couples together and ended up keeping families together too, because when couples are sexually satiated and happy, the good cheer spreads to the rest of the family too. In the Indian context, sex is called 'Sambhog'; 'sam' meaning equal and 'bhog' meaning pleasure; 'sambhog' in the real sense meaning equal pleasure for both partners. In today's reality by and large, it is mostly neither 'sam' nor 'bhog'. For those who have no share in the pleasure, it most definitely is a pain.

Each person has to discover for themselves what love and sex mean to them. For myself, I discovered that when the person, place and time is right and there is love, the experience of sex transcends the grounds of physical reality to another plane – a spiritual one. When the union between man and woman is perfect, both end up losing their identity and in that state of 'I'lessness become one with God or the universe.

This is what everyone seems to be craving for. But as the masters have said for thousands of years, it is not possible unless you surrender, give up your identity and be nothing, no one, a cipher, not even a dot – just being love. And love for me means embracing all of humanity, warts and all, accepting people exactly as who they are or who they are not.

11
TAKING NEW RISKS

I have always loved to perform, be it singing, dancing or acting in a play. Initially, it was at home with my siblings, my brothers Satya and Sheel and my younger sister, Uma. In school too, I was part of the plays, though I never did a major role. In college all that changed. I played the principal characters and even won inter-collegiate awards for my performances. At FTII, I was lucky to be in a play done by the direction department. Vikas acted in the play that was directed by Samiran Dutta, assistant professor of direction.

After that, for years together, there was no talk of plays, let alone acting in or directing one. I was passionate about movies so that is what I did but in some corner of my heart I always wanted to do a play. I fulfilled a part of it while working with actors, improvising in auditions and rehearsals, while casting for my films or television serials. I was quite an avid theatre-goer too and one day the unexpected happened.

It was in 2002, when two actors Arvind Panday and Vishwajeet Pradhan walked into my home with a proposal to do a play. They gave me Athol Fugard's *The Island* to read. I was bowled over by it. My mind took off on all the possibilities of interpreting the play because it was so layered. The characters were phenomenal and quite a challenge for the actors.

I did not have to think twice to jump in. Arvind and Vishwajeet were overjoyed. The play, inspired by a true story, was set in a prison on the notorious Robben Island, the same location where Nelson Mandela was held for twenty-seven years. It is considered to be one of the most significant plays of the twentieth century. We felt we would need to do it in Hindi. We set about adapting it. All three of us sat for several days with it until we were satisfied with the script.

That's how *Kothri No. 42* was born. It tells the story of two prisoners, Safdar and Arjun, shackled together for most of the time, caught in the drudgery of futile labour all day under an inhuman authority which is generous with whiplashes. At night they begin to recover from their work, squabbling, fighting, laughing like any couple and find new innovative ways to remain sane. After a hard day's work, we find them rehearsing for a prison concert too. The play brings to the surface the bonds and tensions between them – they, who having been Naxalites fighting for a cause, are rotting in their cells and coping with the inhuman treatment being meted out to them. In the climax of the play, they enact a scene from Sophocles's *Antigone* as a loaded tribute to 'a fellow seeker of justice who deliberately defies an unjust law', as a theatrical gesture of defiance. *Antigone* represents for them the continuing struggle against an oppressive system under the garb of democracy.

I found the play quite extraordinary with its universal theme, its sense of timelessness and the variety of shades and emotions it offered us as a team to explore and express. It was both complex and challenging and with each rehearsal I found newer depths and levels of interpretation. Arvind and Vishwajeet went beyond themselves and it was more than an exhilarating experience for all of us.

Writing was simple but putting the play together was not easy at all and I am known to be a tough taskmaster. The characters in the play are chained and made to dig all day in the sun and simultaneously fill the pits they have dug – mindless hard labour designed to break the spirit.

My actors lived comfortable lives and to get them into such a mode, when they experienced the futility of their back-breaking activity and could be so tired that they were left even incapable of thinking, was a tall order. I was clear that this play did not need acting. It needed being, and I had to do whatever to get them to be, rather than try to take on a persona and act it out.

When the rehearsals began, they might have regretted coming to me with this play. To begin with they had to drive to the other end of town, to south Bombay, for over an hour to be at my place at 7 a.m. The first thirty minutes of the rehearsal involved walking around on the carpet in my large drawing room with some exercise weights tied to their legs. This was followed by the ritual of digging, filling the pans, carrying the dug sand and dumping it and repeating the same over and over again until I would ask them to stop. Almost an hour of that physical exercise and they would be dead tired. The only redeeming factor during those rehearsals was the pohe we had for breakfast, which they liked and looked forward to.

I must say they were quite extraordinary in that they were open and willing to do whatever I asked them. Gradually they began to get the world of their characters. The readings and enactment began to gain more depth as time progressed. Bits and pieces began to fall into place and after three or four months, perhaps six, the play began to take on a life of its own. Slowly the layers began to emerge both in the characterization and the commentary on society and human life.

The two inmates living for years together in that cell develop an intimate relationship. They are part of the play *Antigone* that they are performing for the prison officers and cell mates. Arjun takes on a woman's persona that comes naturally to him, while Safdar plays King Creon. They get the news that Safdar will be released soon and Arjun visualizes it – his companion and lover going back to a normal life to be with his wife and family. He finds it hard to digest this and is upset. They enact the play but it becomes about them and their right to freedom and a life of their choice.

Our attention turned to costumes and it was interesting to put together all that was required. Their convict uniforms were easy enough to get but there were other items that needed a different kind of thought process and execution. Arvind was an alumnus from the National School of Drama and with the help of a colleague of his we managed to create the special props/costume. For the play within the play which the prisoners enact, we needed a wig and a woman's costume for Arjun as Antigone. Since the setting was a prison and we had to make do with simple available materials to make it authentic, we fashioned a wig made of coir rope and a bikini top with coconut shells. A gamchha or cotton towel served as his skirt while we got a bedsheet to serve as King Creon's cape.

The play was ready and the question of how and where to show it loomed large before us. We thought of showing it to Naseer, in whose theatre group the actors had worked in the past. Naseer had already done two films with me, *Situm* and *Rihaee*, and had played the lead in *Masoom*, which I had edited.

We requested him to help and guide us and he came over one day, saw the play and gave us some feedback. By and large he seemed happy with it and we knew we were on the right track. We asked him for some support in logistics, how things were done in getting theatres, etc. He put us on to his art director and his secretary Jairaj who helped us.

The set of the play was just the jail cell. The prison bars were at the back, with a little door in them opening into a dimly lit corridor where a naked bulb hung from the ceiling. The audience made up the fourth wall. This allowed us, through the lighting, to create shadows of the bars so they looked like they were trapped in a cage. There were other props which were minimal, like an aluminium plate, mug, bucket and blankets.

The play opened with a scene in which they keep digging and filling the pits mindlessly. When Arjun stumbles and falls he is beaten up. A while later Safdar is flogged too and they come back to their cell, shackled, bleeding and injured.

Safdar then goes to the corner, towards the back of the stage, and with his back to the audience, pees in a mug. He returns with the mug and tries to wash Arjun's bleeding wound, using his urine as an antiseptic. We had recorded the sound effect of the pee hitting the aluminium mug. It was so real and shocking that it made the dehumanizing condition of the two prisoners very vivid. We had recorded the sound of the whiplashes and the abuses too, which gave a cutting edge to the performers.

Kothri No. 42 premiered at the National School of Drama in Delhi in 2003. It was also shown at the National Centre for Performing Arts, Karnataka Sangha theatre and Prithvi theatre in Bombay, and at the film institute in Pune. It was revived as a part of Naseeruddin Shah's Motley Group festival a few years ago. So many years after its first public performance, the play has remained deeply etched in the memories of the people who put it together and the people who saw it. Simply, because it is no ordinary play – everything in it is so relevant, perhaps even more so today because it is about freedom.

Through the course of civilization and so much development in the world of knowledge and technology, is a human being really free – free to be? Is our search for happiness and the aspiration for the ultimate life of satisfaction trapping us in unbreakable cages of our own making? Recognized as a basic human fundamental right, does freedom really exist? We may not find answers but to take a leaf out of Socrates's book, we must at least inquire, at least ask the questions relevant to our life.

I had been teaching film-making, writing, editing or directing and at times even producing films. At some point of time there was an opportunity to go to Pune to my alma mater, as the director of FTII but I turned it down. I wanted to continue making films and explore other things that caught my fancy and I was afraid of being stuck. However, I contributed in whatever way I could as the vice president and vice chairman of the FTII society and governing Council respectively, under Vinod Khanna and Dr U.R. Ananthamurthy. And when there were strikes at the institute, I was always ready to help out as a mediator and peace-maker and would rush off to Pune in response to a call at any hour of the day or night.

But there was something more for me to contribute in the field of film education in a major way and I could not escape that. Film-maker Subhash Ghai, an alumnus of the FTII, was planning to start a film school in Bombay and he asked me to join his team in making his dream come true. I thought it was great because there were so few of us who came out trained from FTII. I genuinely felt more film schools were needed. Though the film industry has a lot of talented people, it takes years for the talent to be honed. Also, beyond a point, it becomes difficult, sometimes even impossible, to work with untrained people, no matter how sincere they are.

Initially I began as a consultant, designing the syllabus and curriculum, working with Olivia Augustine, who was a part of Subhash's company. I got a lot of people on board from different disciplines to work on the syllabus with me and once we had the basic programme in eight different disciplines in place we went to the Australian Film, Television and Radio School to have the syllabus vetted, as was the arrangement with them.

Olivia and I spent three weeks in Sydney. It was a great experience discussing not only academics but also finding out what running a film school entailed, with regard to infrastructure and administration, all of which was going to be useful when we returned. We worked all day through the week. On the weekends we did whatever we wanted to and it was mostly meeting people off the campus and faculty.

I remember Olivia went trekking one weekend and I decided to go to a riding farm as I loved riding. I hadn't ridden a horse in years because of my chronic back problem and I thought it might be a good idea to give it a shot. I asked for a docile horse that would not be much trouble handling. They nodded and what was brought before me was a huge black stallion. He looked like the devil himself, like in the movies, so perfect for the part. I gingerly reached out to pat him. I was helped to get on. I was quite scared. I kept thinking, what if I fall and hurt myself. How irresponsible would that be, given that I had a job to do? What if the injury would need operation or long hospitalization? How would I deal with it?

The horse was called Sinbad and he did not like the slow gait that I was subjecting him to. He must have lost patience and, after a while, he took off merrily, racing across the undulating land while I clung to him for dear life. My talking to him to slow down and my lack of expertise with the reins did not help at all. After a while, when he was done, we returned to the stables. I was thankful to get off in one piece.

When I returned, the film project *Tum?* (2004) was waiting for me. Ratan Jain of Venus Films had approved the story for a film I had in mind and was keen to go ahead with the project. I started working on the script and we began to look for the cast. The protagonists were a middle-aged couple in their late thirties or early forties with teenage kids. There was another couple too – a photographer and a model – and we planned to take newcomers for that.

Most Bollywood male stars don't like to play their age – that is why we have many in their forties and even fifties still playing college boys and courting new young girls. The female stars did not like to play mothers even of young children, so the casting was a challenge. As a director, I focused a little more on the acting ability as we went through the names that we could approach.

I suggested Manisha Koirala's name, because I thought if anyone could do justice to the role it would be her. Mr Jain had doubts whether she would agree but I, who believes in 'giving anything a shot', asked him to fix an appointment for a narration. I did not know her but I believe there is always a first time for everything. And I have no issues with people saying 'no' to me. If something doesn't work for someone, it doesn't work. It is as simple as that. I went over to her place and narrated my script.

She listened very attentively and immediately said that she would do it. I mumbled my thanks. When I got back to my car, I informed Mr Jain and he found it hard to believe. But she was on. We got Rajat Kapoor – also from FTII and someone whose work I admire, whether he is directing or acting – to play the corporate husband. For the young photographer we had Karan Nath, Rakesh Nath's son, and a new girl Netanya Singh. A performer I grew fond of was Bobby Darling for her commitment and sincerity. I think she has a huge untapped potential, waiting to be explored.

A very important segment of the film was to be shot in Mauritius. The story was about an affluent couple celebrating their eighteenth wedding anniversary at a resort in Mauritius. The husband is a busy corporate honcho scheduled to arrive from London on the eve of their anniversary. The wife reaches before him from Bombay, and while she waits for him, a young photographer befriends her. The husband's flight gets cancelled and he does not arrive. The photographer, in an attempt to cheer up the disappointed wife, plies her with too much wine. Finding her drunk and unsteady on her feet, he takes her up to her room and, succumbing to temptation, makes love to her.

When she wakes up the next morning, she is horrified to realize that she has slept with the photographer. She regrets the incident and avoids him. When her husband arrives, she goes out of her way to express her love for him. They return to Bombay but the photographer, having fallen in love with her, pursues her. He meets her family and charms her young daughter who is aspiring to be a model. His relationship with his girlfriend deteriorates. The peace of the family is shattered because of his intrusion. As tension mounts, all the family members get involved in some way or the other and he is murdered. Everyone suspects everyone else of the murder.

In the film we had a sega performance to be given by the local performers at the resort and we wanted the original song as sung by a Mauritian band in Creole. So when we went on a recce, we got in touch with a group, found a studio and came back with a recording of an authentic sega. Himesh Reshammiya did the music and had some soulful numbers sung by Adnan Sami and Alka Yagnik. Mr Jain was keen to take new people in some departments and we did that too. Sandip Soparkarr was one of them. He choreographed a song enacted by Netanya and Karan.

The film was completed soon enough but did not turn out as expected. I had realized at some point of time that what would come out was not the film I had envisaged, but I had a commitment to see it through until the end. I had to give it my fullest. This was probably the most Bollywood-ish film of my career, including a sexy dance number, with Netanya in an itsy-bitsy costume as well. It also made me realize something I used to say – that the journey is as important as the destination. You compromise on the journey, you compromise on the destination as well! And film-making is a journey very few privileged people get to undertake.

The commercial considerations diluted what the film was originally meant to be and, of course, most of the reviews were not good, though some people liked the film. A lot of people as well as I were disappointed but as they say we can't win every match we play. Like in every other profession, a creative person in films too has his highs and lows. Anyway, you learn as you go along!

When the film was being released there was a huge hue and cry, thanks to a court case and a blow-up in the media between Manisha and Shashilal Nair over the film she had done earlier called *Ek Chhotisi Love Story* (2002). It was unfortunate that Manisha had to deal with what she did, given the sensitive human being she is, not to mention an extraordinary performer. It is admirable today how she is committed to make a difference in the world after her bout with cancer.

As soon as the film project got over I went back to working on the film school project. Construction was in full swing at Film City and even before it was ready, we moved in with our computers and basic infrastructure and staff. Subhash insisted that I join Whistling Woods as a full-timer and in 2006 I did that. It was the first time ever that I was working in a job so to say, having been a freelancer all my life. But given the enormity of what we had set out to accomplish, I joined as vice president (Academics) and later became the head of direction department as well. The dean appointed was an American and he ensured that the building and infrastructure were ready when the school opened.

When Olivia and I were preparing the syllabus we had tried to get a software to schedule courses with the units of time, personnel, available rooms and equipment over the semesters. Unfortunately a lot of time and money was wasted but we could not get a software for that. It meant doing it manually. Olivia had quit the company by then and I was left with the eight courses to be scheduled.

I got to work, literally not taking my eyes off my laptop, working long hours and falling asleep on the laptop too, which was a major irritant for my son. He felt I was overdoing it, not having my meals on time and not sleeping enough. But we were racing against time and there was no formula or model to emulate. The dean wanted the entire timetable and break-up for the first year on his wall before the school opened.

It was like a huge puzzle. But all my life I had done jigsaw puzzles, crosswords, sudoku, played Scrabble and solved logic problems and mensa puzzles. Bit by bit it started falling into place. I became an expert at working on the excel sheet. I colour coded the disciplines and worked through timings and facilities and people and infrastructure. I actually had every single day on the dean's wall for all of the first year. He was surprised that I had worked with so many coordinates at a time and so impeccably. He called me a whizkid and asked where I had learnt to do that. I laughed and told him that I had trained my entire life just for that job.

I brought in most of the faculty, people I had known over so many years. Many were excellent technicians and alumni of FTII. The dean believed in interactive teaching and as I had been leading programmes doing exactly that in Landmark Education, on a voluntary basis, he was delighted with me.

Landmark Education was a company that conducted transformational programmes and I had had major breakthroughs in my life after participating in them. Given my ability to speak and stand for people, I got trained to lead some of their courses like Self Expression & Leadership Program, and the Introduction Leaders Program.

The dean called me the 'Queen of Interaction' and between him and me we trained the faculty, who were experts in their own fields, in the interactive teaching methodology. This kind of teaching is critical because you engage the students and allow them to discover things for themselves. It also creates the freedom to make mistakes or fail and learn from that.

It was an exciting time when Whistling Woods opened its doors to so many aspiring young people wanting to make a name for themselves in films. Meghna, Subhash's daughter, took over the reins with Subhash watching over her proudly. I had too much to handle but what I loved most was being with students and I am happy that many of them are doing very well.

Whistling Woods was well set on its course and I wanted to move on. I was restless, wanting to make another film. Meanwhile, in-house problems had started between the dean and the faculty. It came to a head when a majority of the faculty wanted to resign en masse. I was forced to take the matter up with Subhash. Of course, the dean was upset.

Around that time, I was invited to San Francisco as a keynote speaker on global transformation by the Landmark Education Wisdom Course group. I had to prepare a paper and an audio-visual that included clips from some of my films and deliver that to an audience of over 450 people. It was an awesome experience to share my life and my work and create huge new possibilities for people worldwide.

When I returned from San Francisco, things had changed. New equations between people had been struck, and some cosmetic changes made. Though I had given my letter of resignation, on Subhash's insistence, I stayed on a little longer.

At that time my chronic back problem returned to plague me. When I was in the studio one day, I found that I could not stand; my legs could not support me and I kept crumbling to the floor. Since I did not want to cancel the exercise with the students, I got myself an office chair with castors and moved around on it, guiding the students. By afternoon, things got worse.

An ambulance was called and I was taken to Nanavati Hospital. A back/spine specialist attended to me and said I would have to get admitted right away. He would not even let me go home to pick up my things. Some tests were conducted and my legs were put on traction. I was told that the problem had been severe and I needed to be on complete bed rest. After a week, I was allowed to go home under the condition that I would continue with the bed rest and have my legs in traction. Luckily, Maa had a traction kit, which was fitted to my bed.

Some weeks passed and finally my resignation was accepted.

I did some writing for a corporate film and a documentary when Ananth Mahadevan approached me to write a script for him on the Naxalite problem. All I knew were basic things about the Naxals that were common knowledge and information I had gathered from some documentaries I had seen. Ananth had a basic concept and over the next few months I got busy in research and was able to create a compelling narrative on Naxal life. I worked on the characters in detail with back stories so that it would be easy for Ananth and his actors. I even had a lot of pictures for reference which I thought would be useful for the team to create the authentic look. The film was called *Red Alert* (2009) and opened to all-round good reviews. Suniel Shetty, who played the protagonist, broke through the normal Bollywood mould and gave a stellar performance.

12

DOCUMENTARIES, MY OTHER PASSION

A major part of my life and work in recent years has been documentaries. I like to engage not just myself but others too in matters that concern us as a society. I may miss my cup of tea in the morning but would not like to miss the newspaper. Nowadays it's the paper in the morning and the news channels at night.

Documentaries are like mirrors. They reflect a true-to-life picture of the world around us. But mirrors can be coloured. Yet, they certainly represent a truth about life, about society and about people. Strangely enough, truths also vary and we know how the same incident appears different to different people and, as a result, opinions are formed and actions taken, followed by a variety of consequences.

Today documentaries have a role to play more than they have ever done, because there is so much information, misinformation, views and opinions floating around in social and electronic media that it is hard to get to the facts. Fifty years ago, anything in print had a fact-like quality to it and it seemed like the truth until one realized that everything in print is neither factual nor the truth. So it is with electronic media too.

Life has become so complex and the tortuous nature of it, though we may not think so, affects each one of us no matter how remote a corner of the world we are living in. Technology has become intrusive. You cannot live a simple life untouched by what the world wants, what the world thinks and what the world is doing.

Initially, documentaries were thought to be an objective representation of society, people and incidents but that's not really the case. Anywhere you put your camera, it becomes a point of view to observe things from. Your statement arises from that almost automatically. Every shot, thus, is subjective and it is that choice the documentary maker exercises to showcase to people his view of the subject in question. Yet there could be a distortion of facts too, a different interpretation of what is occurring.

There may be a point of view, but if it is a documentary, at least you can be assured it is dealing with incidents, issues of a non-fictional nature. However, the intention of the maker comes through as well as his/her belief.

Why I feel documentaries are critical is because we need to reflect as a species with thinking power, what we have become as human beings and as a society. Documentaries provide the stimuli for introspection not just at a personal level but at many levels of community and country and can help bring about social change. They help us to evaluate civilization and our place in it, give direction to our power to create and realize the immense potential that exists within each one of us.

In the consumerist age of today, when there is so much corrosion of values, big-time corruption, exploitation of the poor and needy, we really need to see objectively where we are headed – where we are going as a people – as a society, and it is only documentaries that can give us some idea, as both the record of facts and the makers' perception of truth. And that may inform, educate or goad us into action.

They wake you up to a real world as against most television programming that numbs your brain and leaves you incapable of any thought. That's why television at one time was called the 'idiot box' and most governments like people to watch television so that they don't question them.

Unfortunately, in this country, documentaries have been the poor country cousins of feature narratives and films made by the booming film industry, mostly for financial gain. So documentary makers would end up using the lower end of what was available to tell their stories with reality and depth. There were the 8mm and 16mm films. The latter was the primary gauge used for documentaries all over the world but in India the lack of infrastructure in 16mm not just limited but retarded the growth of the documentary movement.

The 35mm film was almost prohibitive since it was far too expensive. Corporate and advertising films having big budgets could afford it. But documentaries suffered because they had to be made on shoestring budgets, there were no takers, no possibility of release and, hence, no way to recover costs. As a result there was no money for research and a lot of struggle was associated with documentary makers. Even sponsored documentaries suffered for lack of research.

Documentary makers have adjusted to the changing technology with much more ease than the makers of narrative features, going digital without celluloid or videotape. Today people shoot on mobile phones and even make films on them. But the tragedy is that documentaries are still unable to reach people as much as they should/could. YouTube has been a boon but it still has limited outreach, given the large numbers of people in India who do not have internet access.

To share a little history of the documentary in India, B.D. Garga, eminent historian and film-maker, in his book, *From Raj to Swaraj:*

The Non-fiction Film in India, published in 2007, has described the Indian documentary film as being 'a war baby', conceived by the British and nurtured by the Indians. At the beginning of the Second World War, the British Ministry of Information set up the production of documentaries to promote war propaganda and create a positive image of British rule in India.

In 1943, as the political situation intensified, the ministry created a new organization: Information Films of India (IFI). They then brought in compulsory exhibition under the Defence of India Act, the same year, making it mandatory for the exhibitors/theatre owners to show a minimum of twenty minutes of the government film for every show they had. They felt that as the majority of the population was illiterate, it was necessary to educate them through films and created their own newsreel called Indian News Parade.

But as the Indian freedom movement escalated, the IFI, for lack of funds, was closed down in 1946. Even Nehru's famous speech, 'Tryst with Destiny', delivered to the Indian Constituent Assembly in Parliament on the eve of India's independence on 14 August 1947, was not recorded on film and exists only on audio.

After India got independence, the Films Division was created in place of the IFI, in 1948, almost in the same mould, to record the country's history and update the masses through regular newsreels.

These films were made to cater to a mass audience from both rural and urban areas as well as the literate and illiterate population. The result was a large number of clichéd, unwatchable, boring films that lacked creativity. It was expected, for they seemingly aimed for the lowest common denominator.

As against that, many foreign film-makers like Jean Renoir, Roberto Rossellini, Roman Karmen and Arne Sucksdorff came to India to shoot their documentaries. The Shell Company too produced some excellent short films, having brought in James Beveridge from the National Film Board of Canada to supervise.

Cinema was continuing to evolve both in its narrative as well as documentary aspects. People were experimenting with the medium too to tell interesting stories of real people. Though some exemplary films did come out of Films Division from time to time, particularly in the '60s and the '70s, it was in one sense a betrayal of the public trust, for the funds and the wherewithal to reach the public lay with Films Division but were not used to their potential.

Whatever was churned out by the Films Division was compulsorily exhibited in the theatres and shown before every movie three or four times a day. To keep their licence, the theatre owners/exhibitors had to pay 1 per cent of the net collection to Films Division. Newsreels were part of this fare but the problem was that they became the government's mouthpiece and propaganda machine and there was no place for independent or thought-provoking, or even anti-establishment, documentaries. There was no space for questioning what was going on and what could be, and people had to take what was dished out. In response, a lot of the movie-going public retaliated by taking loo, cigarette and coffee breaks when the documentaries were being shown, coming back to their seats only for the main feature film.

Given that the Films Division had the monopoly, the independent documentary makers continued to survive only through sheer grit and determination and passion for what they believed in. A handful of pioneering independent documentary makers started the Indian Documentary Producers Association (IDPA) in 1956 for the promotion of documentary films and to support and develop the voice for independent documentary.

Initially all raw stock, i.e., film negative, was imported and the Film Federation of India (FFI), the apex body of the film industry, was in charge of monitoring what the film industry wanted after discussing the bona fide need of each constituent within it. The FFI had under its umbrella, different bodies – associations of producers, directors, distributors, exhibitors, writers, cinematographers, editors and sound recordists. It distributed the raw stock to its constituents, one of which was IDPA, which had as its members, not only documentary makers but also makers of shorts, advertisement and animation films. All producers of these films needed to get a permit from IDPA, which certified their bona fide needs.

I was very active in IDPA, working for the cause of documentaries, and was the president of the association twice. We worked to fix minimum rates to avoid exploitation, get due recognition from the state, inform members of forthcoming documentary festivals all over the world and promote the art and craft of documentary. We also took our issues to the government and contributed to policy making when required.

Apathy and lethargy had set in and Films Division continued to make films as a matter of routine, with no research or involvement on the part of the director. The films were stereotyped and predictable. When Doordarshan made its presence felt in the early '70s, Films Division found itself redundant. Doordarshan expanded its reach and soon became the favoured propaganda device of the government. With the advent of colour TVs nationwide in 1982, Films Division further lost its theatre audiences.

There was a strong opposition to the compulsory exhibition of documentaries in the theatres and payment of 1 per cent for the films no one wanted to see. It was perceived to be a waste of the taxpayers' money and a burden for the industry. Films Division operated as a typical government department and did not do much to salvage the situation. There was a complete lack of vision, imagination and intention to turn things around.

Films Division and the exhibitors fought it out in court, winning some and losing some, finally going all the way to the Supreme Court. Meanwhile, the documentary makers waited with bated breath to see the outcome.

I still remember the celebration of the documentary makers when the Supreme Court delivered a landmark judgement in favour of documentaries on 15 July 1999. It stipulated that, 'When a substantially significant population body is illiterate or does not have easy access to ideas or information, it is important that all available means of communication, particularly the audio-visual communication, are utilized, not just for entertainment, but also for education, information, propagation of scientific ideas and the like.'

The Supreme Court upheld not only the compulsory screening of documentaries in theatres but also the payment of 1 per cent of the net collection there.

We had more than 14,000 theatres and the Supreme Court verdict making screening of documentaries in cinema theatres compulsory had given new hope to the committed but struggling documentary makers. The court ruling had clearly stated that the documentaries shown could also be from any other source, not just Films Division. But Films Division monopolized the circuit and did not open the doors to independent documentary makers. They compromised with the theatre owners, showing films of five to ten minutes' duration and some of even two minutes. These were not documentaries; no subject can be dealt with in such a short span of time. The compromise by Films Division cost the documentary movement and the promise of the court ruling died a premature death.

Doordarshan, whose original mandate was to inform and educate the teeming illiterate masses, was not proactive either in the matter of documentaries, since documentaries were considered to be lacking in commercial value. Doordarshan also churned out news stories and superficial documentaries that lacked depth and enquiry, again going with the government's view of things. To make things worse, it got into unhealthy competition with private news and entertainment channels, whose primary intention was revenue.

Many of my colleagues and I, as part of the IDPA, had innumerable meetings with the Ministry of Information and Broadcasting and with Doordarshan but all we got were empty promises. We made a strong recommendation at the Broadcast Bill Workshop held by IDPA, Radio and TV Advertising Practitioners Association of India (RAPA) and others that 10 per cent of playing time be mandatorily put aside by private broadcasters for public service documentaries. But as usual the politicians and people in power nodded their heads and went away with no real intention of making any difference.

One breakthrough, however, that happened a few years ago, when I was heading the IDPA body as president, was getting a slot on Doordarshan for showing independent documentaries and having Doordarshan pay the documentary makers for the screening. We were given a Sunday slot of 10 p.m. and we grabbed it, believing that half a loaf was better than no bread. Those days the BBC had started showing documentaries on television and it had somehow whetted the appetite for Indian fare and people were asking for Indian documentaries to be shown.

The Sunday night IDPA slot became quite popular and we began receiving hundreds of letters every week with feedback from the public. In a few weeks the 10 p.m. slot began to be considered a primetime slot and a year later Doordarshan took it back to telecast their own programmes. Around that time, Public Service Broadcasting Trust (PSBT), headed by Rajiv Mehrotra, came into being. It tied up with Doordarshan and, in partnership, was able to make the documentaries and also show them.

Most of the private channels were not interested in showing documentaries and their sympathy for the documentary movement only extended to showing some of them in the afternoon for free, as mere fillers between programmes.

What made a big difference was finally the government agreeing to have a separate international film festival for documentaries, short films and animation films. Initially called the Bombay International Film Festival, it was launched in 1990. Later on, it became the Mumbai International Film Festival (MIFF). Since the government had a strong base and infrastructure in Bombay, in Films Division, it was easy to make it happen with the existing infrastructure of staff and facilities. The unfortunate part was that MIFF happens once in two years and that is too long a gap in a festival calendar.

Many documentary makers over the last fifteen to twenty years perforce have had to develop entrepreneurial skills. As a result, some found success in getting the funding and also exhibition on foreign television networks. The question raised by some other documentary makers is, 'What kind of documentary is it if it is tailored to suit the requirements of a foreign channel or agency?' It then becomes a commercial enterprise made to suit the market, like the rest of the films that are made for commercial consumption with an eye on profits. Even so, the documentaries did their job of bringing hidden issues in the world out in the open or exploring unknown aspects of societies or governments. In this age of commercialization, I think the real fear documentary makers might have is, 'Is the documentary losing its context as a documentary and selling out?'

I have made a lot of documentaries and short films in the last forty-nine years. Initially many were corporate documentaries where one honed one's skill in the way one took the shots and edited them. But I was always more interested in the human stories.

One thing documentaries offered me was an opportunity to travel across the length and breadth of the country, interact with different people, learn a smattering of languages, eat authentic local cuisine and discover their lives. The travels enriched my life.

A documentary that I was happy making was called *Blossom in the Desert.* In the face of a high degree of female foeticide and infanticide in Rajasthan, there is an educational institution called Banasthali Vidyapeeth for girls near Jaipur. The kind and quality of education that it imparts is absolutely stellar. Seeing girls from middle-class homes flying an aircraft and riding horses as well as taking German and Japanese lessons was awe-inspiring.

Another film I was proud of making was a biography on Mallika Sarabhai. Mrinalini Sarabhai, who played a major role in the documentary, is a legend. There are very few people like her. What I admired about both of them was their focus, their forthrightness and commitment to what mattered to them.

What was challenging in the film was weaving the three strands of Mrinalini, Mallika as a dancer/performer and her activism and personal life. I made it for Films Division on invitation and that was the only film I did for them. They must have been delighted because we won the National Award that year, adding a feather to their cap as producer while I got awarded as director.

It is strange that in the last fifteen years, I have made documentaries only with and for the differently abled. I got associated with S.P.J. Sadhana School and have had the opportunity of working closely not only with the special educators and teachers but also with the special children with various disabilities/disorders.

The first film I made for them was in 2000. It was called *A New Paradigm*. It showed what the parents have to deal with bringing up special children and how creating a partnership with the school and special educators made the biggest difference. Sister Gaitonde, who was the principal, and Radhike Khanna, the vice principal, were two very inspired people ready to take on challenges and break new ground. They were able to get jobs for many of their students and have them be accepted in mainstream society.

This film too got a National Award. Sister Gaitonde counselled a lot and her voice still rings in my ear, telling a parent, 'Always look at what these children can do, not at what they cannot do.' I think this applies to all parents – even those with normal children. Often parents have high expectations and push their children too much, criticizing, even punishing them for their inability to perform, which makes it totally counterproductive in the end.

A few years later I did another documentary with them called *Every Cloud Has a Silver Lining* (2009). We recorded a song for them, '*Born to be a winner*', by Rahul Bhatt and they learnt to sing it with gusto. The film showcased the extraordinary skills of the special children as they worked on the clothes for a fashion show, painting, embroidering and creating beautiful designs. They even made the jewellery out of terracotta. The show, a collaboration between S.P.J. Sadhana School and Hemant Trivedi, was a stupendous success. How well it was appreciated was evident from the thundering applause from the audience in the large theatre at the National Centre for the Performing Arts (NCPA), when the students walked the ramp.

The strange thing about these children is that they are called special children. According to the dictionary, special means unusual, superior, distinct, exceptional, extraordinary, unique! But human beings are hypocrites. They call them special but they don't mean special. They mean just the opposite. In the world there is a high premium for the ordinary and mediocre and these children can never be that. So being special, they don't fit in the so-called ordinary, normal society. And for that they have to suffer along with their families!

The hypocrisy extends to a point where people will use politically correct language but do nothing for the ones with the new politically correct names. The same thing happened with the Dalits. The name Harijan, popularized by Gandhi, referring to them as God's people – 'hari-jans' – was considered inappropriate and insulting. They took on the name Dalit, popularized by Dr B.R. Ambedkar. The point is not really what you call them but how you relate to them and what you are doing to them. Can you embrace a Dalit and include him in your life and have him be a part of your family? That's the real question. It's the same with special or differently abled children.

There was a parent who shared that when her daughter was born, she was told by the doctor that the child is abnormal and does not deserve to live. The parents were literally asked what they wanted to do about it. They chose to keep the child and for years, it was utter misery. What kept them going was the fact that it was *their* child!

As she grew, the girl could not take instructions, could not manage her daily activities like going to the toilet, brushing her teeth, maintaining personal hygiene, bathing or eating. She needed someone round the clock and, even though under constant supervision, threw things around and broke anything that she could lay her hands on. The television sets had to be placed high up on the wall and nothing could be kept within her reach. She would also push, pull, hit or bite her mother or tear at her mother's hair.

These kids are special in the truest sense. Some of them are highly gifted, but cannot be normal like other children. I sometimes think that they are on this planet to transform lives – lives of parents, teachers and the environment in which they exist. We may not realize it but they come as 'gurus' to teach humility, patience, love, fortitude, courage, perseverance, gratitude for what people have, to make them think outside the box, to challenge them, to even break them apart maybe, so that the parents and teachers discover themselves, their own humanity and maybe even their purpose on this planet.

I also got familiar with two of the trusts associated with them, Om Creations and Shraddha Charitable Trust, that run sheltered workshops for the more severely disabled. The 'kids' of Om Creations are not kids anymore; they make the most delicious chocolates one can buy and also eco-friendly Ganeshas and are such a joy to be around – full of energy and love.

The special adults in both of the trusts work all day to create all kinds of artefacts and get a stipend at the end of every month. Being an earning member of their families in spite of their disability, it gives them a life of respect and dignity, not to mention acceptance in society. The advantage of this is that their caretakers get a break for the working part of the day, doing what they need to do.

One of the biggest issues that I noticed was the lack of awareness in society about the disabilities, particularly autism. This led to people avoiding autistic children, being scared of them, calling them names and humiliating them. The parents have enough on their hands and this cruel and callous, unsympathetic behaviour breaks their hearts.

My research led me to a huge number of parents, lots of material on the net and books. I realized that if there is no awareness about autism and no early intervention, ideally by the age of two to three years, it becomes a very steep climb for the teachers to train them and even more traumatic for the parents to manage them as they grow older.

I felt a sense of urgency to bring this film out to people – to parents and also to the society which alienates them and shuns them. The film was an attempt to explore the world of the autistic – to become aware of their inability to socialize and communicate with the world, followed by their own frustration and that of the people living with them – and looks at what is really possible for them.

I was very shocked when I was told that many doctors get away with the excuse that autism is not part of their MBBS curriculum – they advise sedation to reduce hyperactivity. A mother said to me, 'My son had become like a sack of potatoes and I could not stand it.' It doesn't really help to render them lifeless. Sometimes they even give them shock treatment, which doesn't make the real issue go away at all.

Even when the children are in a special school and undergoing therapy, it takes months and years before any results are visible. A simple activity that a normal person can learn in five minutes, may take the autistic two to three years, even more. The children are often not cooperative – they inhabit their own world and strongly resist change, so the trainer works through their tears, tantrums and even physical violence inflicted on themselves or others.

I heard innumerable stories of highly educated people going on pilgrimages, visiting holy men in far-off places and even doing all kinds of pujas to have a life that works for their children.

Some people believe that the autistic should be left alone – and there are groups advocating that. Many of the children who are left alone do not even have toilet training or know how to eat properly without dropping food. They are not taught how to deal with their sexuality and may be seen playing with their genitals in public or stripping. When they are disturbed – it could be any kind of provocation – they can get violent. What is worse is they are prone to self-injurious behaviour. They need constant attention and the question is who is going to be able to provide that kind of attention and quality care?

And yet, to my pleasant surprise we found in the small town of Wai in Maharashtra, not only a special school but a teachers' training college as well. However, the curriculum is government-designed and needs much more than it is currently providing to serve the autistic. But given that there is such a dire need, any support is welcome.

S.P.J. Sadhana has a very systematic approach with a methodology it has developed over many years and produces 93 per cent–99 per cent results in integrating the mentally challenged students into mainstream society through some vocation they are trained in.

I found these children working at the Taj Hotels doing a variety of jobs – in the kitchen with Chef Solomon, in the patisserie, in housekeeping and so on. There are many others working in Indigo Deli and Orchid hotels.

A recent success story of these kids is that four of them are working in a multinational, no less than Deloitte. They do data feeding, manage a lot of correspondence and are pretty efficient office assistants.

A parent who lived in Bombay shifted to Pune, thinking that he would have to scale down the lifestyle of the family on his retirement. His son who trained in Sadhana loved to make chocolates. He began to sell his chocolates which sold like hot cakes and instead of the father supporting the son, the son has become the major earning member of the family. There are many such stories about these children that make your heart sing with joy!

Many of the employers told me that these kids do a perfect job, whatever job it may be, exactly as it is meant to be done. They do not shirk work, do not take tea-coffee-cigarette breaks and are honest to a fault.

According to statistics, there are literally millions of autistic children and adults in India. And they are waiting to be included, to be accepted, to be allowed to live a life of dignity like everyone else. Their parents and families have no life of their own and are struggling, living one day at a time, with no hope of a better future. I realized that it is not just the problem of those who are afflicted. It is everyone's problem, our problem. How can one be happy when such a large number are suffering all around us?

After I completed this film, which was eighty minutes long and called *Behind the Glass Wall* (2014) (incidentally it won a National Award for Best Educational Film in 2015), I had three more films to do. One of them was a case study of a severely autistic girl who had just become an adult.

Nicole was a very bright child. I shot with her the first time when she was five years old. She was quiet and loved to hum and sing to herself. Though she understood the language, she hardly had any communication. She liked to be alone and still prefers her own company as against being with people, her peers, teachers or even family.

With the influence of Bollywood films in her life, watching too many at a young age, she fashioned herself like a diva, like a Bollywood actress. She never hesitated to dismiss anyone or tell them off if they suggested something contrary to what she wanted or liked at the moment. Nicole loved to take centre stage and would do anything to sing, dance and perform.

As an adolescent, Nicole became impossible to manage. She not only threw tantrums and brought the house down with her running and screaming through the corridors of the school but became extremely violent. When she attained puberty, there was no controlling the havoc her hormones played and she was found hitting, biting, clawing, scratching, pushing both students and teachers. She pulled their hair, banged their heads and even tore their clothes. She broke glass panes, threw things about and damaged a lot of school property. She had put on a lot of weight during this period and weighed 84 kgs. She was literally a heavyweight and it was next to impossible to hold her or restrain her when she went on a rampage.

Nicole loved to dance in the rain and nobody could stop her from doing so once it started to rain. One day, on a school trip to a mall, as it began to rain, Nicole rushed out and started dancing. Not content with that, she began to strip off her clothes and when her teachers tried to stop her, she manhandled them. It caused a public disturbance and had the mall guards questioning, 'Why do you bring such children out?' It blew up into a major issue as Nicole found it hard to deal with her sexuality. There was no focus in class, the other children were scared of her and the situation was unworkable.

The bruised and battered teachers gave an ultimatum to the school that either Nicole stays or they do. Radhike Khanna, the vice-principal of Sadhana, the school for special children, spoke to the parents and asked them to keep Nicole home until she arrived at a decision. She promised that she would try and put Nicole back in school on the condition that they followed her instructions and cooperated with them instead of pampering and spoiling her.

The film called *The Spirit Shall Fly* showcases the various strategies employed by the school to rehabilitate Nicole with the application of the FACE programme which they have developed. Nicole has now lost around 20 kg and has learnt to control her aggression. She has found focus in her life and paints to express herself. She continues to sing and dance, however, and is currently employed in Om Creations.

In all the films I did with these kids over the years, I had to give them a lot of space. Like with dogs and toddlers, it is counterproductive to go after them – you have to wait for them to come to you. I would be around as a quiet presence and allow them to connect with me.

During the shoot, I also had to be 100 per cent alert. Every so often I would tell my cameraman to just shoot, regardless of whether his lighting was ready or not. There were so many surprises, so many unplanned shots in all these films because the kids were not performing – they were being the way they were in reality and we had to tune in and capture that. So a lot of times I wasn't calling the shots; they just happened. Either we had to grab the moment or miss it altogether.

Such films are not easy to make. They drain you emotionally because you can't make them superficially or make them in cold blood. You have to dig in, get your hands dirty, be vulnerable. Almost all my unit members said to me that their lives had been transformed through the making of these films. Then, suddenly, at some point, they realized that they did not have any real issues in life and were grateful for the lives they had.

As a documentary maker, you could get attached to your subject or you could take a stand for something or someone or you could become an activist if you are passionate about doing something about the issue you are showcasing. I was driven to do the same with the special people. It has become another commitment in my life.

13
TRANSFORMATION

Mahatma Gandhi once said, 'You must be the change that you wish to see in the world.' Changing oneself was initially for the purpose of survival and acceptance and, later, as I grew up it was a way to connect with the world and make a difference. The critical thing was shift of context, from the focus on myself to others, though working on oneself. As a student of ontology, a branch of metaphysics dealing with the being, later in my life, I got the opportunity to make that philosophy an intrinsic part of myself.

As a child, I wanted to change, to be a good kid, to be accepted and also appreciated. So I stayed out of trouble unlike my brothers Satya and Sheel. I did my homework, followed the rules and came first in my class. As a result, I was left to myself to do what I wanted, how I wanted. I played cricket with my brothers, listened to cricket commentary on the radio all day long, discussing my obsession with my brother-in-law Mohan and celebrating India's win from time to time.

I had two passions then as mentioned earlier – reading and listening to music. I was known to be a 'bookworm' as I literally devoured books, reading endlessly, perched so often on a tree with my transistor for company. There were two books always at my bedside, a pocket dictionary and a pocket atlas. I had this habit of keeping them at hand almost all my life until I had a laptop and the internet became available. I loved looking at countries, finding out information and transporting myself to faraway lands and daydreaming. Years later I could actually do it, giving flight to my fantasies.

I realized over time, however, that there was no place to reach – you could not arrive. You had to keep developing constantly and deal with situations anew. No amount of being 'good' in the past or striving to be so in the future was of any use if you could not be 'good' in that present moment.

I remember, in the early days, being knowledgeable gave me an edge over people. I was a perfectionist and being 'right' had become a habit. I knew things and was so sure in my knowledge that I became argumentative too, not resting until I had proved my point.

I remember friends and siblings, sometimes even grown-ups, asking me for the spelling of some words or even about grammar. I would tell them and sometimes they would challenge me and even insist that my spelling or grammar was not the correct one. My last resort then would be to take the large family dictionary and hold it in front of their face, with my finger on the word in question. I always backed up my claims with proof so they could not prove me wrong. Of course, I realized soon enough that it alienated me from people and I was losing out on relationships.

I knew I had to give that up if I wanted anyone around me. In trying to prove I was right, I was actually proving people 'wrong'. I realized later that I was actually invalidating them because somewhere I myself experienced being 'not good enough'.

But life is not as simple as spelling or grammar or some fact in a science or geography book, the rightness of which can be proved. Life taught me that there can be many rights, depending on which angle you were looking at it from. So many viewpoints and all could be right.

Further to this, I realized that there was really no one truth. Every person had their own truth and it was as real and as justified as another person's. So people disagreed and unfortunately did not agree to disagree. And that is a malaise in our society too because everyone thinks they are right and refuse to even acknowledge another's opinion.

I have been a learner all my life but the biggest 'learning' came when I hit rock-bottom in my life. I had been happily married to Vikas. We worked together and brought up the children together. In short, we had an enviable life. People saw us as the 'made for each other couple'. Then came a time I had to deal with what many married women deal with at some point or another – husbands betraying their trust and straying. Our marriage survived the first time it happened but the second time around it knocked me down completely.

However, my own suffering allowed me to make space for other people in my life and see their suffering. I developed a new sensitivity, a new awareness and a new 'listening'. Soon unwittingly, unknowingly, I became a confidant of people who opened up their hearts to me. I realized that most of them did not need any help or advice – they just needed someone to listen to them.

In today's times I think the situation has become much worse – nobody has time for anybody, especially when it comes to listening to another's sob stories. People, by and large, have become narcissistic. It is a struggle to connect one-on-one. There just isn't the time anymore. Social networking sites are an example of this – people need people, to share with, to be heard, to be understood, to be appreciated. So you connect instantly, but unfortunately not in a deep, intimate or meaningful way.

After my marriage ended, when I had a lot of time that I spent connecting with people, filling up my empty life, it had become a joke amongst my friends that I would end up being 'Maa Aruna' with followers and disciples. All I needed was an ashram.

I learnt compassion and developed an attitude of gratitude. So much so, that every day I would look at the sky, the flowers outside my house, the little sparrows sitting on my window grille and thank God and the universe for their benevolence. Sometimes I would wonder if it was normal to do that or if I was losing my mind. Later I felt reassured when I learnt Reiki and found that it was one of the principles I had stumbled upon.

Even today, I look at the mangroves and the sea outside my window and thank the universe. Just being connected to nature in some way not only enriches your life but teaches you acceptance and humility. And certainly makes you feel peaceful and happy.

One of the blessings that came into my life was the Manley family. We met Maya and Edward in New York at the Memorial Sloan Kettering Hospital where Gaagi had been admitted. Their daughter Cynthia, who had a brain tumour, shared the same room as Gaagi and we soon became friends with the family.

At the end of one month, Gaagi was in a plaster cast, covering an entire leg, from waist down. She could not sit up and transporting her was not easy. We had to find a way to be mobile – even to take her back to the Lexington hotel, where we were staying. Being film-makers and having done production, Vikas and I both knew that if a scene demanded something, it had to be made available somehow. So we went looking for a stretcher. But hand stretchers were just not available, there were only mechanized ones in New York.

We had seen *M*A*S*H*, the American television serial, which had hand stretchers. We decided to tap the source. We contacted Bill Greaves, a documentary maker living in New York, for some leads. Following them we ended up buying a 6.5 ft army stretcher from one of the army shops. It was very big but the hospital administration was helpful in getting their carpentry section cut the stretcher for us to make it 5 ft long. It was a big breakthrough because we could fit it into the back of a yellow taxicab. We took Gaagi back to the hotel riding in a yellow taxicab.

When we had gone to the United States for Gaagi's treatment, Vikas and I had thought that after the treatment we would take Gaagi to Disneyland. But her condition did not allow that. Realizing that we had to go straight back to India, the Manleys invited us to their home in Chappaqua in upstate New York. We were happy to accept and Gaagi was once again taken in the stretcher in their huge station wagon.

Those were such happy days – we were all so pampered. Maya was from Switzerland and she made Swiss fondue for Gaagi and all of us. We met their other children – Audrey and Cathy – apart from Cynthia whom we knew from the hospital. Each one was such a gem. We left for India after three days at their beautiful home, stretcher and all, which remained with Gaagi till the very end.

My friendship with the Manleys has lasted for more than thirty-three years and Chappaqua has been a second home for me. After Gaagi died, I took Hith on a whirlwind trip visiting twelve cities in the US and London. Since we had not been able to take Gaagi to Disneyland, I thought at least I should take her ashes and scatter them there. In fact, I ended up scattering her ashes in the Atlantic Ocean, in the Pacific Ocean, in the Thames, in the Hudson and, later in the Seine, actually, everywhere I went. And I made sure we put some ashes in Disneyland and Disney World too.

So on the trip with Hith, when I visited the Manleys in Chappaqua, I was really happy when Maya asked if she could have some of Gaagi's ashes in her garden. I scattered some because it was a place Gaagi had loved. It was a place I too got attached to over my numerous trips. When their daughter Audrey came to India, she visited us. Recently, Catherine (Cathy) also came over to visit us. I was invited to Cynthia's wedding and had the honour of reading a verse from the Bible. It was a grand wedding, straight out of a Hollywood movie, and until then I had no idea that the Manleys were so well off because they lived a very simple life.

On that first trip out with Hith, I sent him back to Bombay and went on to Paris. I have had a strong attachment with Paris since my childhood. Just walking by the Seine or sitting by a roadside cafe and having a glass of wine with cheese or a piece of a baguette made me feel like I had come home. Going to the Notre Dame Church and lighting a candle became a ritual for me. Every time I stepped out of the country for a film festival or a conference, I made sure that I routed myself through Paris. The city had a healing effect on me.

My divorce affected Hith badly. Vikas had remarried and adopted his wife's daughters and Hith felt alienated. He hated being shunted between my house and his grandparents'. Helpless as I was, I did not make it any easier for him, dealing with my own depression and talking of jumping into the sea when things got too difficult. Living with a depressed mother must not have been easy and he became angry with his parents because the situation got worse.

I did everything to deal with my depression. Apart from taking support from my psychiatrist friend, Dr Sheth, I read a lot of motivational and spiritual books. Ranga, who is more like a younger brother – he calls me Didi – suggested that my son Hith do Reiki. He did it and I followed suit on Hith's recommendation. We were both looking for some peace in our lives and it brought us some healing.

Our Reiki master, Ila Ghosh, was an amazing person. Though she had lost both her legs in an accident in her youth while crossing the railway tracks, she had made a life for herself. She had married and was a mother of two wonderful children. She conducted Reiki classes, travelling all over the world with prosthetic legs. She was so full of life, empowering people around her all the time.

My determination to evolve and find meaning and purpose in my life, and my suffering, led me to try all kinds of meditation techniques but I was never faithful to any one method. I even attended vipassana classes at Igatpuri, near Nashik, for ten days. It was quite demanding and rigorous but I stuck through it.

At that time what showed up on my radar was past life. I had read a lot of books by Dr Brian Weiss and Dr Goldberg and was curious to know about my own life, trying to find some answers.

Ranga used to conduct past-life-regression sessions for people to access their past lives which helped them deal with their present-life traumas and bring closure to issues that were incomplete in their lives. He suggested that I attend one. We arranged a session in a small hotel in Nagothane that he owned with some friends.

There were many things that I had an affinity towards, many things I abhorred and I had no idea where it all came from since there were no direct associations in the present life. My attachment to Paris or my extreme anger at men who molested, raped or ill-treated women had no reference in the present life. The past-life session untangled all that.

Initially, there were fleeting images of me in France, maybe in Paris, dancing at a ball and being wooed by admirers. Then there was another bit in which I was a soldier in a trench fighting a war somewhere in Europe. Then I came upon something which was like a film I was watching.

After almost twenty-five years or more, it is still so clear. Ranga attributed my capacity for strong visualization to the fact that I was a film-maker. The setting was again somewhere in France, on a farm. I was a chubby child of five and a woman who looked like a maid was bathing me in a round wooden tub. The water was very hot and steam was coming off my chubby pink body. She got me out of the tub and wrapped me in a towel, patting me dry. She then put me on the bed so she could dress me.

At that time my stepfather walked in. He was a heavy, burly man, rough and unshaven, and he came and sat on the bed next to me. He sent the woman out on an errand and started to touch me. He touched my face and lips and all the way down my body to my private parts. I started squirming because I hated his touch. I kept pushing his hand away. The woman came back and the spell was broken. Ranga asked me what was happening and I replied that I hated the unwanted, unwelcome touch of that man.

In the next scene, I found myself in a barn where there were animals. I don't know how I got there. The monstrous stepfather was on top of me in a pile of hay, groping me and trying to pull my panties down. He smelt foul and I wanted to throw up. During the session, I even raised myself from the bed where I was lying, as waves of nausea swept over me. Ranga again asked me what was happening and I kept describing things as we went along.

Somehow I managed to push my stepfather away and ran out of the barn. I kept running, not knowing where I was going, just to escape from him. I went up a steep slope on the top of a hillock. I was out of breath and before I knew what was happening, he had caught up with me. He dropped me to the ground, pulled my panties down and raped me from the back as I had fallen on my face. My screams did not have any effect on the monster. I was completely knocked out and felt like a dead rag, limp and lifeless. But more was to come as he finished his job and pushed me over the cliff.

I realized that I was falling. I was terrified and there was nothing to grab at. I flailed my arms and legs in vain. Finally, after what seemed forever, I hit ground. All was still. I wondered if I was dead and opened my eyes. All around was just white snow. I tried to move and realized I was actually dead. My back was broken and that was it. I once again described to my guide what had happened. I was shivering by now and had to be covered with a shawl. My guide slowly brought me back to the present.

I felt so horrible having been a part of such a dastardly thing. I wished I had not done the past-life regression. My friend asked me to just be and sleep it off, which I did involuntarily since I was so exhausted.

The next morning I felt no better. By afternoon, my guide said it would be a good idea to take me back and complete whatever was incomplete. I had no choice but to go back, given what I was feeling.

What I saw now were bits and pieces of scenes and not a continuous narrative unfolding like before.

Apparently my stepfather had abused and raped other little girls in the village too and he was now being tried in some court of law. One day, when the maid brought the news that the man had been punished, I asked, 'Did they hang him?' She replied in the affirmative and added that she and my past-life brother had attended the hanging as it was a public one. I felt better now that the perpetrator had been punished for what he had done.

When we sat down to analyse and look at what I had gleaned from the past-life regression, some things were very clear. My attachment to Paris and France was the most obvious one. The second thing was my anger and almost militant stand against abusers and rapists. It made complete sense to me because in my present life I had not allowed myself to be molested or abused or even taken advantage of. And I had never seen such incidents at my mother's home or even in the marital home. The third thing was my chronic back problem for years – it was no wonder that I had carried it into my present life.

Given what is happening in the country today with regard to abuse of women, I want the highest form of punishment for the perpetrators. I feel incarceration or death is a very easy way. The culprits should be allowed to live without the use of that very tool they used to violate women. It would perhaps be a more stringent punishment for them to live as castrated males. Of course, if they have killed the victim, I guess a death sentence or a life sentence could be in order, though personally I don't like the death penalty. A lot of people might think that I am too harsh but anyone, male or female, who has dealt with rape in any life (past or present) would know why I feel so strongly about it.

My tryst with my past life did not end here. A few months down the line I got another opportunity to go into the past. This time it was with Debu Ghosh, Ila's husband, who had also been a Forum Leader involved in bringing about transformation in people for many years. I was attending a Dowsing workshop with him and he took us back into our past lives.

This time I was in the French army, wearing a red coat with gold braids. I had been called to report for battle and my mother was not letting me go to war. As a young soldier, it was my job to fight on the battlefield and I was angry with my mother for trying to stop me. I walked out on her and rode off on a white horse.

On the battlefield, I unsheathed my beautiful shiny sword that glinted in the sun and went on a relentless attack – cutting, chopping, thrusting, stabbing, slashing, slicing – sparing no one. I don't know how many people I killed on that fateful day.

Then one of the enemy fired an old-fashioned musket which hit me in my lower back. I fell from my horse in excruciating pain. I was crying and asking God to forgive me, making the sign of the cross continuously. Debu asked me to tell him what was happening with me. When I told him, he tried to reason with me, explaining to me that I had done no wrong and I had just been doing my duty as a soldier vanquishing the enemy. He asked me to forgive myself for the killings, which I did.

Once again, the cause of my chronic lower back pain was revealed as coming from my past – a carryover into the present. And funnily enough, after all those past-life killings, maybe to compensate for that in this life, I am such a harmless creature, afraid to hurt anyone even with words.

The surprise element in this situation, however, was that the mother I saw in this past-life regression was my Swiss American friend Maya. Every time I went to the United States and visited Maya and Edward at Chappaqua, Maya thoroughly spoilt me. She bought things for me, even gave me money as gifts, sometimes cheques, hidden in my baggage because I would not accept them. Though

I appreciated both her and Edward's love and generosity for some Indian woman from across the world, I found it unusual and always wondered whether there was something more. In fact, I used to joke that we have a past-life connection.

It made complete sense to me now. As her child, I had walked out on her against her wish and got myself killed in battle and perhaps Maya was left incomplete. Maybe, she had found me again in the form of this Indian woman and was drawn to shower love and affection on me. I shared this with Maya and, of course, she laughed it off.

There is so much we don't know about how the universe operates and whether reincarnation exists. Is baggage from a past life carried to a new life until there is completion or closure? I don't know whether any scientific truth exists regarding past life or all the stuff that I experienced. There may be other explanations for this phenomena but what is important for me are the insights I got from the exercise.

Hith had been away for three years at Les Roches and at the end of his stint in Switzerland, he had a hit-and-run accident. I moved heaven and earth, got myself a ticket, a visa, and rushed to Zurich. I checked myself into a hotel near the university hospital where he was admitted. Having quickly showered, I was getting ready to go to the hospital when my chronic lower back problem chose to play up and I just couldn't move. I was on all fours and could not straighten up no matter how hard I tried. Also there was no support to pull myself up with. I tried raising myself with the cupboard handle and almost brought it down as it was so light. I just wailed and wailed, then calmed myself down and kept trying and trying till I succeeded.

Summoning up all my strength, I managed to stand, though I was bent over. I walked half a step at a time, dragging myself like a crippled imbecile and somehow reached the hospital, taking about half an hour for a five-minute distance. When I got into the hospital, the people at the reception knew that something was horribly wrong with me and provided me with a wheelchair. I got to Hith's room immediately and until I saw him with my own eyes, I was not satisfied. As I looked at him with my emotions brimming over, he looked up and said, 'Why did you come?'

The floodgates burst and I could not stop my tears as I moved away, experiencing total rejection. However, tears and all, I consulted the doctors at the hospital for I had to get my back functioning normally. The doctors were amazing. They sat me down calmly, examined my back and gave me some medication right then and there and got me on my feet.

A friend of a friend, who had helped me get information while in India, met me at the time and was kind enough to invite me to stay at his place – a bachelor pad he shared with a German guy. Once again, the universe had come to my aid. I stayed for a whole month in Zurich with them, until my visa expired, using my time off from the hospital to cook Indian meals for the two people I was staying with. Meanwhile, Hith had to have five operations on his leg and a steel rod had to be inserted. By the time I left Zurich, Hith had begun to walk with a crutch.

All of Hith's roommates in the ward and the large number of friends that visited him from all over Europe loved having me around, except, it seemed, Hith. Even though I went beyond myself and did everything to make him happy, it didn't seem to work and all my efforts at reaching out were futile. I could not understand why he was so unhappy with me.

I returned satisfied that he was well but sad that our relationship left a lot to be desired. Ranga had been telling me about the amazing results the programme called the Landmark Forum produced in people's lives and had been asking me to do it for almost three years. Hitting a dead end in trying to improve my relationship with my son, I decided to consider doing the programme. It was the same programme that Vikas and I had wanted to do twenty years earlier in the '70s – a programme called Erhard Seminars Training (EST). I was told it had undergone some changes but the basics were the same.

Three and a half days – that's all it took for me to have a new view of life and shed the baggage that I had been carrying for years. In the programme, I heard the Forum leader say that suffering was a choice. It was as if a bullet had hit me. 'How could that be? I never chose it, I never wanted to suffer, it was thrust upon me...' I even felt indignant that somehow I was supposed to take the rap for the suffering somebody imposed on me. But as the programme proceeded it began to dawn on me that I and only I was responsible for my life. People said what they said, people did what they did but it was just me and me alone who had a say in the matter of my life.

Oh, that was so liberating! I saw how we as human beings attach meanings to words and deeds and it is our interpretation of the situation that gives us the life we have and consequently the happiness or sadness that follows.

I realized during the programme that I had held my husband and my friend responsible for messing up my life. In my heart, I blamed them for my predicament. Indirectly, I had transferred the power to them, as if they called the shots – they held the key to my happiness or well-being. The programme aimed at giving me closure so that I could offload the baggage and experience being whole and complete.

I still remember calling both of them individually, my hands trembling, my voice quivering and telling them that I did not blame them for what had happened. I said that I had taken full responsibility of my life and everything that came with it. I wished them well and left them with a simple 'Be happy'. Later, I also thanked Vikas for his immense contribution in my life, without which I would not have become the person I became.

This was one of the hardest things I had done, but it had been the most liberating! Suddenly, almost magically, the lid was off! My life was mine again, only I could call the shots. Nobody was responsible for my happiness or unhappiness. I was so empowered,

I laughed from my heart for the first time in years and declared that the sky is not the limit. And since then, I have been able to live life on my own terms, exercising my right and my choice of a free life, unencumbered by the past.

I called up Hith who was working in London at that time. I apologized to him for all my mistakes of omission and commission while bringing him up and expressed my love for him. I went to London and shared with him my self-discovery, my completion with past issues and the future I was creating. He was so moved by what I had accomplished and my commitment for us to have a great relationship that he enrolled himself for the Landmark Forum in London.

This created a new space for us to share and I realized that he blamed both Vikas and me for breaking up and disrupting his life. He had hated the way life had changed for him after Gaagi's death, and his helplessness and anger did not allow him to communicate or express any love.

Landmark Education, as it was called then, had an entire curriculum for empowering human beings to live a great life and realize their full potential. I participated in all their programmes and also trained myself to lead some of their programmes as I have mentioned earlier. I loved people and this allowed me to contribute to their lives and make a huge difference.

Another thing I accessed was the discovery of who I thought myself to be. Most of the time we think we are 'x' or 'y' and when it comes to a crunch, say, 'This is who I am or I am like this only.' But we are not that. When we are born, we are not this way or that. We are, in reality, nothing. But as we grow up, we begin to develop certain traits. Some people become shy, others aggressive, some manipulating, some clever. Then it becomes so much a part of us that we believe we are that way only. In the Landmark Forum, I discovered ways of being for survival and success that I had developed to compensate for who I thought I could not be.

One of the issues I seemed to have been dealing with was being dark complexioned. Of the five children, I was the darkest, and was called Blackie in Kannada by my mother. As far as I was concerned, it had nothing to do with colour. It was an endearment and my mother had so many variations of it. It's only later I learnt that it had something to do with the colour of my skin.

I was very young, maybe around five years old, when I heard someone say, 'She is so dark, what will become of her?' That's when I realized that being dark was a problem and somehow it was not a good thing to be. I realized as I grew up that it was not limited to me but the problem of about more than half the subcontinent. Of course, my mom had retorted then, 'So what, she is OK, she'll make us proud.'

But the five-year-old did not know that. I tried to compensate for my colour with my intelligence showing everyone I mattered and was not handicapped by my colour in any way. Of course, this was not planned or deliberate – it's just the way I developed in order to be accepted, showing the world my worth by topping the class and winning the prizes.

Later, when I went to Paris and had the most handsome of men falling for me, actually calling me beautiful, I realized I could be beautiful. Not only did the colour of my skin not matter, but it actually attracted suitors! When I went to the United States on another trip, I found people raving about my complexion and I realized that I was no better or no worse than another person. It seemed suddenly that the ugly duckling had turned into a swan. I could only laugh about it.

Another time when I was left in the jungle, the story of which I have shared earlier, no one seemed to have missed me. Obviously I was not important enough! If I mattered they would have checked and ensured that I was not left behind. A child's logic is pretty simple. So I had to excel, to be so extraordinary, to be known so that I could not be ignored. It's not surprising then that I chose to be a film director in a male-dominated profession and be the first trained woman editor and female technician to come out of the film institute.

At sixteen, when I joined Sophia College in Bombay, and my mother left me at the hostel and went away, my experience was of being forsaken. I was not equipped to deal with the outside world, having led such a sheltered life. But I had to be independent and self-reliant to survive and I became just that. There were so many such incidents that allowed me to find new ways to survive.

Once, I was doing a seminar in Landmark Education and I had taken time out to go on a shoot for a couple of weeks. When I came back I was in bad shape – I had hurt my back and was advised bed rest at least for six weeks, by which time my seminar would be over. I called up the seminar leader and told him what I was dealing with. He told me to be 'unreasonable', which meant to 'go beyond reason'. He said, 'There are always good reasons to not do something – that's what we always do. Look at where else you are stopped from doing something in your life.' What he meant was we as human beings always find excuses to get away from some commitment or responsibility and usually have a good reason or justification for that. Where else in my life was I avoiding some responsibility or commitment and getting stopped?

I was coachable but this was different. My doctor had categorically told me not to sit or walk but have complete bed rest or the consequences could well be fatal. He had said,'You won't die, but you'll end up an invalid.'

I told the seminar leader what the doctor has said. He said, 'Still, how can you be unreasonable?' I shot back – 'I can be unreasonable but how unreasonable can you be?' Now it was his turn to be taken aback. I told him, 'The only way I can be in the seminar is if you can provide a bed with a hardboard.' He took it on – it seemed like both of us were crazy. How awkward would it be – I almost wished I had not challenged him but I had to see it through. I had given my word.

I arrived at the auditorium which, thankfully, was only ten minutes from my house. I was on crutches but someone helped me inside. Right in the middle, in the centre aisle, was this bed with a hardboard on it and a sheet. I had never felt so embarrassed before as I did while lying on it. There was a general awkwardness as I could see people skirting around the bed sheepishly. For the next session I asked them to put the bed on the side so I didn't have to make a spectacle of myself. The experience taught me the meaning of being totally 'unreasonable', to go beyond normal reasons and inconveniences and be unstoppable in my life.

Three years before I did the Landmark Forum programme, I had taken a bank loan of Rs 21.5 lakh for my video studio. In the first two to three years, I had been paying my instalments regularly. After that when the business had not been doing well I had requested the bank to give me permission to sell the equipment and return the money I owed them. But they wouldn't and didn't. All my efforts to convince them somehow failed.

It was after the Landmark Forum that I got a communication from the bank. The liability had mounted with compound interest, etc., and after having already paid Rs 16.5 lakh of the loan amount, I was told I still owed the bank Rs 19 lakh. And I didn't have the money. What I was also worried about was that my office property documents were with the bank and I could lose the property.

I went to the bank, negotiated with them with a newfound confidence, unwilling to let it ride any longer. I told them to settle for something reasonable and if they didn't they would have a non-performing account to their credit. They saw I meant business. They agreed for a settlement of Rs 15 lakh with the terms: 6 lakh on signing the document the following week and 9 lakh in the nine months to follow. I agreed.

I didn't have the money and had no clue where I would get it from. But I was going to play full out and make it happen. I didn't have permission to sell the equipment but I sold it knowing the deal was on. The equipment was outdated and I got peanuts, only 3 lakh. In that same week I got an advance of 2 lakh for a documentary I had bid for. Now one day was left and I needed one more lakh. Miraculously, a stranger made his way to my house looking for me. He wanted a small plot of land that we had bought in my son's name in a village near Nasik long ago for Rs 5000. When I asked him why he wanted that very piece he said he owned the surrounding land and wanted this as well. He gave me a generous amount of 1 lakh in cash right there and then that he was carrying. Of course, there was no question of refusing him.

The next day I went to the bank and gave the money in style. In the next nine months, I could only collect 5 lakh but I went boldly to the bank, gave them 5 lakh and post-dated cheques for 4 lakh over the next two months asking them to charge interest. Of course, I collected my office property documents but I didn't lose any sleep over it. The repaying of that bank loan happened with so much ease and grace it was unbelievable. I got a lot of practical hands-on tools for living a powerful life and overcoming problems. I learnt to live from the future where anything is possible.

A critical piece of wisdom I took away from the Landmark Forum was that there is no inherent meaning in anything. Things are the way things are and they don't mean anything. We human beings give meaning to anything and everything and suffer the consequences of having made up those meanings.

What has allowed me to be happy and fulfilled is simply being one with the universe, not resisting but going with the flow. Whatever I want for myself, for my evolution, the universe has a bigger and better plan to achieve that. I trust the universe and the supreme knowledge that what is mine is mine and no one can take it away from me and nobody can give me what is not mine. It has rendered me free of all envy, greed, competition and even want. Being human, these things do show up but vanish in a moment when I realize the futility of harbouring such feelings.

The discovery that at the core of my being I was nothing opened up immense possibilities of being anything. It allowed me to connect to other nothings, other people and I decided to spend the rest of my life in the service of people.

At the age of sixty-three, I chose to give up my life and be a Landmark Forum leader. My mentor, Laurel Scheaf, a very senior Forum leader, saw the possibility and nurtured me to be one. I was the only woman Landmark Forum leader in India, amongst the fifty-four that were in the world at that time. I trained in the United States, Australia and India. It was a very rigorous life, living in transformation 24×7, creating value for people and I am happy to say that it was worth it.

The people I could impact in the programme hailed from all walks of life, were of all ages and from different backgrounds – CEOs, IAS officers, businessmen, professionals like doctors, lawyers, chartered accountants, teachers, religious leaders, students and housewives. The one question that came up in Delhi almost every time from some of the men, was, 'Is this woman going to teach us how to live our life?' It was so hard initially for them to get past the fact that I was a woman and look at their own life. Many of them confronted me too but with the training I had I could alter the conversation they had about me and other women too.

One of them, when I was coaching him about a long-standing issue with his brother, threatened me upfront on the mike. He said he was from Haryana and added, 'You don't know who we are. We can have you picked up and you will not be found again.' I just smiled and continued to coach him. The next day he was the first one wanting to share. For a minute I was concerned that he would shout, threaten, dominate, etc. But I got past my own barrier and invited him to speak, ready to deal with whatever came up. It was amazing. He had had a huge breakthrough with his brother whom he had hated for over twenty years and was actually grateful for the coaching that I had given him. He could express his love for his brother, forgive and be forgiven and that had brought peace to both the families.

The programme was a place for miracles. It could bring warring siblings together, have couples on the brink of divorce discover love again, or move on whole and complete without baggage, inspire students to study out of a new future they created and so many amazing transformations happening in a room of 200–300 people each week. It was exhilarating for me to leave people with a world of unlimited possibilities so that they could create a life they wanted.

There were also people in my programme who would stammer and had tried all kinds of remedies. But in a five-minute conversation they were able to actually stop stammering, even sing normally. There were also women and sometimes men too who had been sexually abused and were leading unfulfilled lives. In a conversation we could have them get past their trauma, obtain closure and create a new future. There was nothing in life that the Landmark Forum could not address. It was all in conversation, introspection and choosing the new way of being with new possibilities.

After about three years as a Landmark Forum leader, another tragedy struck and I had to make my way back to life as it were. My niece, Rajeshwari, a brilliant doctor who had been in the US, had returned to set up home in Pune along with her husband and her child. Her parents Chitra and Mohan had moved in with her to help her. By sheer chance, a blood test revealed that she had blood cancer. Further investigations revealed that she had Acute Myeloid Leukemia (AML). Her family did everything to get her the best medical treatment.

I used to be on the road those days, travelling every week to a different city, leading the Landmark Forum. It was the most hectic period in my life as I had to travel to cities like Delhi, Bangalore,

Ahmedabad, Chennai, Shimoga, Jaipur, Ludhiana, Aurangabad and Akola. The days were long – the programme started at 9 a.m. and ended at 11 p.m. There was a lot to be managed, teams to be organized, trained and coached.

But on my break, one week in four, I would rush to Pune to be with my sister's family. My younger sister, Uma, who was very attached to my niece, went to live with them in Pune.

Rajeshwari's response to chemotherapy initially seemed positive, but there was a dip one day and a bone marrow transplant became essential. After a long search, a donor was found in the family, the same younger sister, who had gone to live with them. They travelled to Israel and the transplant was successful. I visited them in Israel too, unable to stay away. When they returned from Israel there was bad news waiting for them.

My elder sister, Chitra, Rajeshwari's mother had also been struck by cancer. It was oral cancer – something associated with cigarettes, smoking, gutkha. She was a God-fearing religious woman, the perfect wife and mother. Let alone any of the above-mentioned substances, there was no paan supari even to be found in their house.

In the Landmark Forum, I would bring people and families together and it seemed to be an integrity issue for me that when my family needed me the most I was not there for them. There were two patients to be looked after. I could not stay away any longer and subconsciously created a situation for myself to leave Landmark and be there to take care of them.

Being with Rajeshwari and her mother took a lot out of each one of the family as we struggled to keep a straight face and deal with the fact that they were suffering and that their departure from this world was imminent. I kept reminding myself in everything I did that it was God's work and just kept at it.

Each one of us had become an island. My brother-in-law, Mohan, for whom the word in-law is a misnomer, was bent and broken. His daughter meant everything to him and to see her in pain, suffering, was too much for him to bear. Married for fifty-four years, he was a family man who had worked hard to build his beautiful family and to lose his life partner as well as the child he loved dearly was unbearable.

What was of concern to everybody was the eight-year-old Shivey having to deal with the loss of her mother and grandmother, all at one go. Rajeshwari's husband, Ravi, had tried valiantly to save his dear wife but had to give up in the face of destiny.

But human beings are resilient. Uma and I had both survived divorce and also the loss of our precious daughters and here we were watching another drama of life and death unfold before us.

I had no idea what life had in store for me after my stint in Pune. But I went with the flow. I was called to Delhi when I was still with them in Pune to head the National Award jury for non-feature films. Seeing about 134 films over ten or twelve days was indeed therapeutic. What came up after that was an invitation from the KASHISH Queer Film Festival, to be on the jury for LGBT films. I watched over a hundred films. Later I saw about 234 films while heading the Selection Committee for the Mumbai International Film Festival for Documentary, Shorts and Animation Films (2014).

This was a masterplan and I could not have designed it. The universe conspired to put me back where I was needed. It was clear that I had completed my karmic commitments over three years while leading the Landmark Forum. There were other assignments waiting for me. I returned to my basic passion of making films and made some on the specially abled and the autistic.

In all these years of living, I have realized that I am not like an object, fixed and unchangeable. Objects have limitations, they are finite and they can't really be changed because if you change them they become something else. I found myself evolving all the time as I went through the highs and lows, from agony to ecstasy and vice versa. I haven't changed into anything because I was not something to begin with, like a fixed entity. Like water I can flow into anything and take a new shape and then be something else and yet again be something else and so on. I experience being infinite and limitless!

Every day is a new day and I am alive and as I look at the sea outside my window, I literally thank the universe for everything I have and the opportunity to express myself and make a difference.

INDEX

ACKNOWLEDGEMENTS

I want to acknowledge the people who have contributed to my life and accomplish whatever I did. My mother, Putamma Patil, known as Mummy Patil, my father, K.F. Patil, Pitaji to us, my siblings, my other family members, including Vikas and his extended family, my teachers, the people I worked with and last but not the least my friends who not only helped me survive but were there when I was down. My nine-year-old daughter Gaagi taught me in that last one year of her life what I couldn't have learnt in a lifetime ... And my son Hith, who continues to open my mind to a world and perspectives that I know so little about.

All my actors and technicians who gave me the space to express myself, many of whom have remained friends for life, for over fifty years. Also my critics, coaches and teachers and my students too without whom I would not have evolved and grown to be the person I am today. And the people who formed the infrastructure to support me in all my endeavours, whether at home or at work.

I want to thank my consulting editor Sathya Saran who approached me to do the book and held my hand, Debasri Rakshit,

Shantanu Ray Chaudhuri and Bidisha Srivastava who gave me timely and relevant feedback and walked me through every sentence and punctuation mark, Saurabh Garge, the designer of the book and the various photographers who took the stills over fifty years, and the publishers, HarperCollins.

I thank Shyam Benegal, someone I have known for almost fifty years, for taking out the time and writing the foreword.

Thank you all!

25 HarperCollins India Ltd

Celebrating 25 Years of Great Publishing

HarperCollins India celebrates its twenty-fifth anniversary in 2017. Twenty-five years of publishing India's finest writers and some of its most memorable books – those you cannot put down; ones you want to finish reading yet don't want to end; works you can read over and over again only to fall deeper in love with.

Through the years, we have published writers from the Indian subcontinent, and across the globe, including Aravind Adiga, Kiran Nagarkar, Amitav Ghosh, Jhumpa Lahiri, Manu Joseph, Anuja Chauhan, Upamanyu Chatterjee, A.P.J. Abdul Kalam, Shekhar Gupta, M.J. Akbar, Satyajit Ray, Gulzar, Surender Mohan Pathak and Anita Nair, amongst others, with approximately 200 new books every year and an active print and digital catalogue of more than 1,000 titles, across ten imprints. Publishing works of various genres including literary fiction, poetry, mind body spirit, commercial fiction, journalism, business, self-help, cinema, biographies – all with attention to quality, of the manuscript and the finished product – it comes as no surprise that we have won every major literary award including the Man Booker Prize, the Sahitya Akademi Award, the DSC Prize, the Hindu Literary Prize, the MAMI Award for Best Writing on Cinema, the National Award for Best Book on Cinema, the Crossword Book Award, and the Publisher of the Year, twice, at Publishing Next in Goa and, in 2016, at Tata Literature Live, Mumbai.

We credit our success to the people who make us who we are, and will be celebrating this anniversary with: our authors, retailers, partners, readers and colleagues at HarperCollins India. Over the years, a firm belief in our promise and our passion to deliver only the very best of the printed word has helped us become one of India's finest in publishing. Every day we endeavour to deliver bigger and better – for you.

Thank you for your continued support and patronage.